❧

Big Business, Strong State

❧

SUNY series in Korean Studies
Sung Bae Park, editor

Big Business, Strong State
Collusion and Conflict in South Korean Development, 1960–1990

Manuot. Guillén
Philly, 1997

Eun Mee Kim

State University of New York Press

1197

Cover photo credit:
Top photo:
Namdaemun (South Gate) in Seoul.
Photo taken by Homer Williams in 1970.
Bottom photo:
Same area in 1994.
Photo taken by author.

Published by
State University of New York Press, Albany

For information, address State University of New York Press,
State University Plaza, Albany, NY 12246

Production by Cynthia Tenace Lassonde
Marketing by Bernadette LaManna

Library of Congress Cataloging-in-Publication Data

Kim, Eun Mee, 1958–
    Big business, strong state : collusion and conflict in South
Korean development, 1960–1990 / Eun Mee Kim.
        p.   cm. — (SUNY series in Korean studies)
    Includes bibliographical references and index.
    ISBN 0-7914-3209-2 (hc : alk. paper). — ISBN 0-7914-3210-6 (pb :
alk. paper)
    1. Industrial policy—Korea (South).   2. Big business—Korea
(South)   3. Conglomerate corporations—Korea (South)   4. Labor
policy—Korea (South)   5. Labor movement—Korea (South)   I. Title.
II. Series.
HD3616.K852K56   1997
338.95195′009′045—dc20
                                                        96-30390
                                                        CIP

10 9 8 7 6 5 4 3 2 1

For My Father, Dr. Hogwon Kim,
and My Mother, Kyung Ae Kang

Contents

PART II HISTORY OF DEVELOPMENT

Tables

Figure

Acknowledgments

When I returned to the United States to begin my graduate studies in 1981, I had an ambitious goal of trying to work without the network and support of family and friends. Coming from a tightly knit society of South Korea, I wanted to see if I could do it on my own. I even selected Brown University because no one I knew lived in the radius of 100 miles. I was younger then and thought I had to prove myself. After a month of graduate studies, I quickly realized that my goal was a futile one. During the years of graduate work and afterwards, I am reminded constantly of the love, friendship, and support I received from many people with whom I came into contact. This book is another indication of their support.

The research for this book was conducted over a number of years during the 1980s and 1990s, with research grants from an International Doctoral Research Fellowship by the Social Science Research Council (1986–87) and a Faculty Research and Innovation Fund by the University of Southern California (1988–89). During the nine months I spent in South Korea between 1986 and 1989, and many shorter visits to Seoul between 1991 and 1994, South Korea itself was going through tumultuous social changes. A project germinated in the early 1980s as an effort to understand why South Korea's economic

xi

development was so miraculous yet its democratization was so dismal; it grew to encompass a broader range of questions about how the two processes were interrelated. Visiting South Korea during the late 1980s and early 1990s put me in the center of a flurry of political and economic changes, which kept forcing me to rethink the formula for South Korea's economic success and to question whether a monolithic South Korean model even existed.

My thinking on these broad questions and my research have been guided by fellow students of economic and political development. Peter B. Evans, my advisor and mentor at Brown University, who encouraged me from the very beginning that trying to understand South Korea's phenomenal economic development was a worthwhile project, has been a source of inspiration and perseverance over the years. Dietrich Rueschemeyer, another mentor from Brown, helped me think through the ideas of the relationship among the state, capital, and labor, and the relations between capitalist development and democracy. Alice Amsden, whose research I am indebted to, was also an encouraging friend and helped me explore the inner workings of the *chaebol*.

My colleagues at the University of Southern California, in particular, Jon Miller and Linda Fuller (who is now at the University of Oregon), have read various versions of the manuscript and provided a great deal of constructive advice. Jon and Marcia, Linda and Greg, and Carol Warren (now at the University of Kansas) were also my dear friends who let me from time to time forget about my work and accompany them to the desert or the mountains. Nora Hamilton, Gary Dymski (now at the University of California, Riverside), John Odell, Tom Biersteker (now at Brown University), Mike Mochizuki (now with the Brookings Institution), Nazli Kibria (now at Boston University), and Michael Robinson (now at Indiana University) have also helped me think through the comparative aspects of the South Korean case. During my year at Temple University in 1990–91, colleagues in the Sociology Department were generous with their time. In particular, Howie Winant and I spent many lunches discussing mutual interests we had about Third World development. Discussions with him helped me to think through the inherent limits of the developmental state. Annette Lareau and Kevin Delaney read earlier versions of the manuscript and gave me feedback from a non-Koreanist perspective. Their advice helped me position the South Korean case in a broader theoretical and comparative perspective. Carter Eckert of Harvard University was a good friend and supporter during my sabbatical leave at the Korea Institute at Harvard in fall 1994. Our common interest in the genesis and growth of the *chaebol* and in the South Korean society in general allowed us to have many interesting and fruitful discussions. Alice Amsden, who had just joined the Massachusetts Institute of Technology as the Ellen Swallow Richards Professor of Political Economy, was also a kind and generous friend during my leave at Harvard.

Many people who have conducted research in Asia understand the significance of having generous people who can connect you to the right people and right organizations for your research. I benefited enormously from my teachers and friends in Seoul who introduced me to their colleagues and provided referrals. Professor Hyoung Cho of Ewha Womans University helped me with several interviews for the book and over the years provided a great deal of moral support. Professor Kwang Woong Kim of Seoul National University introduced me to many of his former students and colleagues who worked at various government ministries. He spent many hours with me helping me navigate and understand the maze of the South Korean government bureaucracy. I owe a special debt of gratitude to Mr. Soo Man Chang at the Economic Planning Board. He introduced me to his colleagues at the EPB and the Ministry of Finance. His candid opinions and insider's knowledge of the South Korean government was vital for the research of this book. Mr. Sung Jong Cho at the Bank of Korea was also very helpful with research on the South Korean economy. Many others, including Dr. Lee-Jay Cho, who was then the director of population studies at the East-West Center in Hawaii, also introduced me to various individuals in South Korean business and government. Professor Syn Duk Choi of Ewha Womans University and others at Ewha provided access to libraries and research facilities during my numerous visits to Seoul. And most of all, I would like to thank the government officials, business people, scholars, and journalists who spent time with me for interviews. Their willingness and openness to discuss various issues regarding the South Korean political economy were critical for this book.

Over the years, many colleagues have read and provided helpful comments for the book, and many more have engaged in discussions about this research. I would like to thank the following for their insights and suggestions: Jang Jip Choi, Tun-jen Cheng, Hee-Yeon Cho, Julle Cho, Bruce Cumings, Frederic Deyo, Gary Gereffi, Stephan Haggard, Gary Hamilton, Sang Jin Han, Sang In Jun, Laurel Kendall, Young Whan Kihl, Hagen Koo, Chae Jin Lee, Hong Yung Lee, John Lie, Chung-in Moon, Carol Warren, and Homer Williams.

My friends in Seoul provided me with insights about the inner workings of the South Korean society, as well as friend-ship over the years. They include Mee Hae Lee, Youngju Ahn, Sook Jin Sohn, Young Hyun Kim, Suni Lee, Yeonwook Kang, Hwayŏl Lee, Manje Kim, Mili Kim, Miok Park, and Jeong Weon Kim. Yeanjae Woo in Germany and I had many conversations about the difficulties and joys of studying and working in a society not your own. With my friends in Los Angeles, Providence, and elsewhere, I have discussed our mutual research projects and went to restaurants, movies, concerts, plays, and museums. They include Ruth Milkman, Nathan Laks and Jonathan, Laurel Kendall, Homer Williams and Henry, Nazli Kibria and Allen (Jim) Littlefield, Nora Hamilton, Barry Glassner and Betsy Amster, Michael Messner and Pierrette Hondagneu-Sotelo, Elaine Kim, Magali Larson, Jaesoon Rhee, Judy McDonnell, Lindy Williams, Philip Guest, Chris Ryan, and Yeonhee and Changseob Kim and their two boys.

A special thanks goes to Mary Nadler, an editor, with whom I worked for many years, and who helped me with an earlier draft of the book. And I would like to thank my editors at SUNY Press, Christine Worden and Cindy Lassonde, who have been very supportive of the book project from the beginning to the end.

I would like to thank the Centre of Asian Studies at the University of Hong Kong for permission to reprint and excerpt from my article, "The Industrial Organization and Growth of the Korean Chaebol: Integrating Development and Organizational Theories" in *Business Networks and Economic Development in East and Southeast Asia,* edited by Gary Hamilton (1991); *Social Problems* for permission to use my article, "Contradictions and Limits of a Developmental State: With Illustrations from the South Korean Case," Vol. 40, No. 2 (1993); *In Depth* for permission to use my article, "Socioeconomic Development in South Korea," Vol. 4, No. 2 (1994); and Korea University Press for permission to reprint a table from Jang Jip Choi's *Labor and the Authoritarian State: Labor Unions in South Korean Manufacturing Industries, 1961–1980* (1989). A special thanks go to Homer Williams who allowed me to use a photograph he took of the Namdaemun (South Gate) area of Seoul in 1970 for the cover (top photo). I took the 1994 photo of the same general area in Seoul to highlight the dramatic changes that took place in just over twenty years (bottom photo).

Lastly, I wish to thank my family for providing me with their love and support. My father, Dr. Hogwon Kim, showed me what hard work and discipline meant. My mother, Kyung Ae Kang, inspired me that even a woman could achieve whatever she wanted if she worked hard. My brother, Chung Hwan, and his wife, Kassy, were always there for me, for the times of work as well as relaxation. My grandmother and my aunts— Kyung Eun Kang, Kyung Shin Kang, and Kyung Hye Kang— and their families reminded me of the kindness and love of my extended family. I cannot thank enough my uncle and my aunt, Dr. Jaegwon Kim and Sylvia Kim, who invited me to their home during my graduate studies and ever since, introducing me to wonderful music, art, traveling, and cooking. Their love and caring sustained me through many difficult times during the writing of this book.

I am grateful to all those who provided friendship and support for this book. This book is for them all.

Abbreviations

AFKN	American Forces Korean Network
EOI	Export-Oriented Industrialization
EPB	Economic Planning Board
FDI	Foreign Direct Investment
FKI	Federation of Korean Industries
GTC	General Trading Company
HCI	Heavy and Chemical Industrialization
IAEA	International Atomic Inspection Agency
ISI	Import Substitution Industrialization
KMT	Kuo-Min-Tang (Chinese Nationalist Government)
MNCs	Multinational Corporations
NICs	Newly Industrializing Countries
POSCO	Pohang Iron and Steel Company

1
The Paradox of South Korean Development

South Korea's rapid economic development since the 1960s, based on export-oriented industrialization, has been hailed as one of the Third World's most successful such cases. Its development has been one of the fastest in the world, with an average annual growth rate of gross national product (GNP) per capita of 7.1 percent between 1965 and 1990 (World Bank 1992).

Before 1961, South Korea was a poor, agrarian society. Sixty-six percent of the labor force worked in the agricultural sector and only 9 percent in the industrial sector. The GNP per capita in 1961 was $82 (Bank of Korea 1984). South Korea was barely recovering from the ruins of the Korean War, which had left 45 percent of the factories substantially damaged (Jones & Sakong 1980). Every spring, there was a famine in the countryside in the period after the rice harvested the previous fall had run out and before the barley could be harvested. Families were often further impoverished when, in order to send an oldest son to school in Seoul, they would sell their only oxen or farmland in March (the start of the new school year). Politicians and rich *chaebol* owners did not seem to care, since they were enjoying a luxurious life, not dissimilar to the lifestyle of the elites in the

1

First World. The cycle of poverty appeared to be unbreakable, since the poor farmers did not have resources and those who had power to change things seemed uninterested in doing so.

May 16, 1961, marked a turning point in South Korea's modern history. On that day, General Park Chung Hee [Pak Chŏng Hŭi][1] led a military coup to bring an end to a corrupt and inept government and to achieve economic development. "The Road Toward Economic Self-Sufficiency and Prosperity" became the stated national theme of this military regime (Ministry of Public Information 1965). What followed the coup were a series of changes in the state, in the relationship between the state and the private sector, and in the private sector. These changes, and the favorable international economy of the 1960s and 1970s, helped produce one of the most successful economic development stories of the twentieth century.

Documentaries about South Korea's economic development often refer to it as "The Miracle on the Han River," evoking images of "The Miracle on the Rhine." In these documentaries, the colorful images of the ultramodern city of Seoul are often juxtaposed with the black-and-white film footage of the Korean War (1950–53), which shows masses of people fleeing Seoul on foot, crying babies still wrapped in their blankets. The messages are clear: South Korea has come a long way in a very short time. And, its economic development has been a tremendous success.

There are, however, images that remind me of another side of South Korea's miracle economy. On August 20–23, 1969, President Park Chung Hee visited the United States upon an invitation from President Richard Nixon. They discussed South Korean security, settlement of the Vietnam War, and a proposal for a gradual withdrawal of U.S. troops from South Korea (C. H. Park 1971:144–46). The South Korean media reported endless stories of how President Park was being greeted with open arms in the United States. However, in a stark contrast, the American Forces Korean Network (AFKN) television news showed how President Park was being booed at and pelted with stones. As a young child who both admired her president and still had fond memories of living in Chicago just a year before, these images left a lasting impression.

The implications of the two different portrayals of President Park's visit to the United States are not as rosy as the more widely claimed view of South Korea's economic success. First, behind South Korea's glittering economic miracle lies censorship, a feature common to authoritarian regimes. Censorship represents a more widespread phenomenon of political repression and a failure to promote democracy during the early years of South Korean development. It seems odd to pair curtailment of civil liberties with rapid economic development. The questions loom large: Why did the South Korean government engage in a cover-up when its economy was boasting remarkable growth? What was the government trying to conceal, and who was it trying to control? Second, these images remind us that international actors and international geopolitical context are important for South Korea. Domestic state-society relations are inexorably tied to the changing international conditions and, in particular, South Korea's relations with its powerful neighbors—i.e., the United States and Japan.

Together these issues point to the tension and strain embedded in the South Korean miracle. Understanding that South Korea's economic growth is closely linked to its lack of political democratization, and that South Korea's fate is closely tied to the international geopolitical and economic contexts, is important in the analysis of South Korean development.

With these issues in mind, this book focuses on the two main institutions of South Korea's economic development: the state, and the *chaebol*. These two domestic institutions shaped South Korea's industrialization and economic development, especially during the 1960s and 1970s. During the early 1960s, the Park regime's Economic Planning Board (EPB) played a central role by charting out the pace and method of industrialization and by coercing and courting the *chaebol* (the large, family-owned and family-managed business groups) in order to enlist their support. Big business groups played an increasingly greater role over time as not only the implementers of the EPB's industrial policies but as entrepreneurs who took advantage of both political and market incentives.

The state and businesses worked together, in large part, at the exclusion of labor. This does not mean that labor and labor movement were nonexistent or unimportant in South Korea's economic development. It means that economic policies were made without any input from labor. Labor was severely repressed by the Park regime, and the labor movement was not as well organized as the state or businesses. In spite of repression toward labor from both the state and businesses, labor unions grew and the labor movement expanded during the 1970s and 1980s (both underground and legally). Labor became a formidable voice for democratization and social change by the 1980s. In this book, partly as a result of labor's changing and ascending role in South Korean economic development, labor is dealt with prominently in chapter 6 (the 1980s) and less so in earlier chapters (chapter 4 on the 1960s and chapter 5 on the 1970s).

A central assumption in the analysis of the state and the *chaebol* in the book is that these institutions changed in their internal structure and in the relations between the two institutions as economic development proceeded. The latter point regarding relations refers to the balance of power between the state and the *chaebol*, which shapes the content of economic policies and the ways in which economic policies are constructed and implemented.

The changes in the state and the *chaebol*, and the relations between them, are analyzed in the context of the world economy and geopolitics of the cold war. As a latecomer, South Korea's ability to enter, and to profit from, the international economy is circumscribed by the condition of the international economy and the receptivity of foreign capitalists as providers of needed capital and technology. However, it is important to note that Third World actors and institutions are not completely helpless.

I offer four arguments in this book, which depart from either market- or state-centered studies by examining critically both the state and capitalists. First, South Korea's rapid economic development was attained initially by a tight alliance formed between a strong, developmental state and big businesses. This alliance repressed labor and excluded it from enjoying the fruits of economic growth. The coexistence of a strong state and big businesses goes against arguments made in earlier state-centered studies (Johnson 1987; Koo 1987; Migdal 1988). These studies assume that a strong state exists on the basis of a weak society, which includes businesses. In other words, state and society are depicted in a zero-sum relationship with one group's interests at odds with the other's. However, the South Korean case demonstrates that a strong state is not necessarily antithetical to big businesses. Post–World War II Japan is another example of the coexistence and alliance between a strong state and big businesses (Johnson 1982).

Second, the relations between the state and capitalists changed in the course of successful economic development. The relationship is a dynamic one as suggested by Rueschemeyer and Evans (1985: 69–70). This argument opposes earlier studies, which assume that the relationship is constant over time. In South Korea, the power balance between the two institutions shifted from state dominance to symbiosis and later to competition. Conflict and tension, which are embedded in the relationship between the two institutions, intensified over time.

Third, the developmental state underwent significant transformations in the course of successful economic development, from a "comprehensive" to a "limited" developmental state. The concepts of "comprehensive" and "limited" developmental state are created to clearly distinguish the qualitatively different types of developmental states. The comprehensive developmental state is plan rational rather than market rational; its orientation is developmental rather than regulatory; and industrial policy takes priority over foreign policy (Johnson 1982: 17–20). A limited developmental state also focuses on development and economic development plans, but to a lesser degree, and it works to accommodate policy goals other than development: certain segments of the economy remain plan rational, while the rest become market rational; the orientation is developmental in certain segments, but in reduced degrees, while the regulatory function increases in sectors that have become market rational; and the primary policy objectives include development and other goals, such as foreign policy and welfare.

A comprehensive developmental state is a transitory form of state. Inherent limits within a comprehensive developmental state make it inevitable that it reduce interventionist tendencies and become a limited developmental state. It will face pressures to transform, regardless of its success or failure in attaining its goal, that is, economic development. If it fails to deliver its goal, there will be pressures from within the state and from the public to change the state in order to bring about economic development. On the other hand, even if it is successful in attaining economic development, there will be pressures to transform. This is the paradox of the comprehensive developmental state, which is forced to abandon and change its very formula for success. The contradictions and limits inherent in this state type, I argue, compel the state to change its structure and goals. (See chapter 2 for definition and discussion of the contradictions.) In South Korea, this process was further hastened by the industrial policies of the state, which favored big businesses over small- and medium-sized enterprises and fostered heavy and chemical industrialization.

Fourth, the *chaebol* were not complacent rent-seekers in spite of generous state subsidies provided to them. The largest and most successful *chaebol* did not solely rely on state subsidies and protection. The successful business groups sought and cultivated new markets abroad, acquired technology and investments from multinational corporations (MNCs), and took advantage of the state's shifting economic policies.

The analysis of the *chaebol* in this book examines how foreign institutions have affected the organizational structure and interaction patterns of domestic institutions. In particular, I investigate how the South Korean *chaebol* borrowed from and modified the Japanese prototype, *zaibatsu*, which were present in Korea during Japanese colonial rule (1910–45). In chapter 3, I examine the broader historical and structural context of the *chaebol* to explain their birth and growth. I also provide a critical comparison among South Korea's *chaebol*, Japanese *zaibatsu*, and Taiwanese enterprises, in order to shed light on the debate about their similarities and differences. In addition, this comparison is presented as a way to challenge the claim made by Cumings (1987) and others that Japanese colonial rule played a decisive role in the East Asian newly industrializing countries' (NICs) growth. In the last chapter, I offer some comparisons between

South Korea and Japan in the context of the changing international economy. There are similarities, but the different historical structural context in which nations like South Korea and
Taiwan interjected themselves in the international market,
make it difficult to easily equate the experiences of these
economies.

The interplay of the state and the *chaebol* in South Korea's
economic development is presented inside a broader context of
geopolitics and international economy. The significance of
foreign capital and foreign states in the development of Third
World nations is a controversial topic. Modernization scholars
tend to see foreign influence as positive, and even necessary, for
underdeveloped nations to modernize. Foreign culture and
institutions are important conveyers of modernity (Eisenstadt
1964; Inkeles & Smith 1974). On the other hand, earlier dependency scholars view foreign capital and foreign states as inim-
ical influences on Third World nations (Dos Santos 1970; Frank
1967). Foreign capitalists obstruct long-term economic growth
and create and exacerbate income inequality in the Third
World. In both sets of studies, foreign capital is seen as having
omnipotent power over domestic actors. My argument in this
book is that although the Third World nations cannot effectively influence and alter foreign capital, foreign states, international geopolitical conditions, and international markets, the
Third World nations are not completely at their mercy either.
Third World states and businesses *can take advantage of*, and in
some cases *change*, the international context.[2] As demonstrated
by Mardon (1990), Third World states are capable of controlling
the type, amount, and share of ownership of foreign capital
investments. Mardon (Ibid.:138) also points out that studies on
South Korea should not focus so much on whether foreign
capital is "beneficial" or "detrimental" to the host nation's
economic growth but "on the structures and strategies that can
be developed by the state in order to induce necessary inputs in
a manner that will maximize the benefits to the domestic
economy."

As Haggard (1990) noted, favorable international geopolitical and market conditions were present in many nations
throughout Asia, however, they produced varying degrees of

economic success. While this region contains some of the very prosperous nations in the world—e.g., Japan and the Gang of Four[3] (South Korea, Taiwan, Hong Kong, and Singapore)—, it also includes the Philippines, which has been an economic failure. The implication is that at least when regional geopolitical and economic contexts are similarly presented to developing nations, the domestic actors in the developing nations are important in bringing about different outcomes for the nation's economic development. The *differential ability* to utilize the international context is one important reason why some Third World nations are able to develop while others languish, even when similar international conditions are presented to them. This by no means suggests that powerful international actors—e.g., foreign states as well as foreign capitalists—are at the mercy of Third World states and capitalists. Quite the contrary, the argument here is that *even* Third World nations can utilize the international context to their advantage, albeit with great difficulty and low probability of success. South Korea is one of only a handful of Third World nations that were successful in taking advantage of, and overcoming structural obstacles presented by, international actors and contexts. South Korea's lessons for other Third World nations are presented in the concluding chapter of this book.

Studies on South Korean Development

This study relies on several bodies of work about South Korean development. Most notably, the market-centered studies and state-centered studies are utilized in this study. The analysis of South Korea's *chaebol* also benefits from the organizational sociology literature, in particular from studies about the relations between the organization and its environment.

Market-Centered Studies

The market-centered, neoclassical economics approach produced a wealth of studies on East Asian development. The endorsements of East Asian development as based on market principles came from international economic organizations, including the International Monetary Fund (IMF) and the World Bank. In a 1990 report, the World Bank argued that South Korea's economic growth was due to the provision of incentives for investments and the manipulation of exchange rates, interest rates, and domestic prices (World Bank 1990). The report concluded that South Korea's success was "broadly in line with market based outcomes" (Ibid.:299). The argument is that South Korea did not use a significantly different strategy to attain economic development compared to its counterparts in Western Europe and the United States. The market was primarily responsible for South Korea's remarkable growth, and the state played only a supplementary and complementary role to the market, fine-tuning certain rates to ensure that the market would perform at its optimum.

The IMF and the World Bank have taken this model to other Third World nations and recommended strongly that the recipient nations conduct market reforms as a condition for economic development loans. However, this type of market-centered approach ignores the fact that the state played a greater role in the economies, including South Korea's. In some cases, the state *created* new markets, even when the private sector objected to it. As Amsden (1989) and Wade (1990) argue, the state did not correct the prices but in fact "distorted" and deliberately set the prices "wrong."

A more recent study by the World Bank (1993) departs from its earlier studies' findings and recognizes a significant role played by the state in East Asian miracle economies. However, as pointed out by Amsden (1994b) and others (Kwon 1994; Lall 1994; Perkins 1994; Yanagihara 1994) in a 1994 issue of *World Development*, the World Bank goes only so far as to acknowledge the state's role in East Asian development as getting "the basics" right. Amsden (1994b) criticized the World Bank for not portraying the findings as supportive of a stronger endorsement of the developmental state's role in East Asian nations, due to the Bank's free market ideology and internal politics. The main arguments in *The East Asian Miracle* by the World Bank (1993) with only mild support for the role of the developmental state and stronger endorsement of basic liberal market reforms, are consistent with the Bank's insistence in many

Eastern European nations after 1989 that the latter adopt liberal market reforms without any role provided to a developmental state (Amsden, Kochanowicz & Taylor 1994).

A series of books published jointly by Harvard University and the Korean Development Institute, a government-sponsored research institute in South Korea, took a more conciliatory approach to the role played by the market and the state (Ban, Moon & Perkins 1978; Jones & Sakong 1980; Kim & Roemer 1979; Krueger 1979; Mason et al. 1980). According to these studies, the government led the economy toward rapid development through market augmentation. These books, however, did not analyze the government's role beyond simple market augmentation, and they did not explain state behavior in creating markets and in getting the prices wrong. Many studies from the market-centered approach did not adequately consider the roles played by nonmarket actors, most importantly the state.

Responding to criticisms on earlier market-centered studies that they under-emphasized nonmarket factors, Song (1990) incorporated neoclassical economics with cultural arguments. He provided an eclectic mix of Simon Kuznets's (1973) theory of modern economic growth and Walter W. Rostow's five stages of economic growth with Wei-Ming Tu's (1984) "new Confucian ethic," as a way of explaining South Korean development. He argued that South Korea's economic development based on exports was primarily due to private enterprises and noted that Confucian ethics helped to provide a moral and social foundation for economic growth. However, the state's ability to create markets and distort prices is not dealt with. Furthermore, Song is unable to explain why Confucianism took several hundred years to finally produce economic growth after its introduction to Korea. And like many other studies that focus on Confucianism as a major explanatory variable for economic growth, Song is unable to explain why some Confucian nations have achieved remarkable economic development while other Confucian nations still struggle to eradicate poverty. It is too simplistic to assume that certain religions, values, or culture could bring economic development. The study also underestimates the domestic and external structural obstacles to economic development. In sum, Song's (1990) eclectic mix of different theoretical approaches fell short of providing a logically coherent or persuasive study about South Korea's economic development.

The market-centered, neoclassical economics approach had three shortcomings: (1) it neglected the role of the state as having an independent and leading role in the economy; (2) it assumed the private sector in South Korea to be not very different from the "rational," "free" enterprises found in the West, which tend to work in relatively freer markets; and (3) it ignored structural obstacles that may hinder economic development, such as unreceptive international market and MNCs, and destruction of economy caused by war, and so on.

This study will help overcome the shortcomings of the market-centered approach. In particular, the role of the developmental state, which sometimes creates markets based on political signals and against market signals, will be analyzed. The examination of the *chaebol* in South Korea will reveal how their organizational structure is also, in part, a creative adaptation to the developmental state. Thus, the state plays an important role in creating markets and in influencing the organizational structure of businesses. These are roles that have not been analyzed in market-centered studies.

State-Centered Studies

The state-centered approach challenged the studies by neoclassical economists by focusing on the active role played by the state in leading the process of economic development among latecomer developing nations. Amsden (1989) and Wade (1990) provided detailed critiques of the market-centered approach to South Korea's and Taiwan's success, respectively. Koo (1987) summarizes what many state-centered studies have argued as the main cause of South Korea's economic development:

> The South Korean economy is one of the capitalist world's most tightly supervised economies, with the government initiating almost every major investment by the private sector. South Korean development is thus often defined as state-led industrialization (Koo 1987:173).

Within the state-centered approach, there are two different schools of thought. One group has been influenced by the Weberian notion of the state, which emphasizes the institution(s) of the state. Johnson's (1982) seminal work on the role played by Japan's Ministry of International Trade and Industry in that country's economic development is an example. Other studies in this tradition include Okimoto's (1989) and Samuels's (1987) studies of Japanese bureaucracy that provided revisions to the earlier work by Johnson (1982) and B. K. Kim's comparative study of the economic ministries in South Korea and Mexico (1987). These studies provided important insights into the inner workings of the developmental state. However, they showed the following weaknesses: they viewed the state as a homogeneous institution lacking internal conflict and tension; they equated the existence of a developmental state with economic growth without clearly demonstrating causality; and they highlighted harmony between the state and society (Lie 1990a).

Another group of state-centered studies comes from the neo-Marxist perspective. Although most studies in this group are not economic determinist, they have nonetheless focused on the relationship between classes—in particular between the state and society—as a way of understanding how capitalist development is attained. Many studies in this tradition were influenced by the dependent development perspective, originally devised to explain the rapidly growing NICs in Latin America. Despite some critical differences between the two regions, this approach has helped to shape the basic thinking on East Asian development. Grounds for applying the lessons of Latin American NICs to the East Asian situation are three-fold: first, the East Asian nations were also trying to break into the international economy, which was already dominated by advanced industrialized nations in Western Europe, the United States, and Japan; second, they had to rely on foreign capital and technology for development; and third, each nation had a relatively strong state apparatus.

However, studies that used the dependent development perspective to explain the growth of East Asian NICs proved to be only partially right. While they did show that East Asian NICs were dependent on the advanced industrialized nations, especially the United States and Japan, they failed to note that these nations did not endure the costs of dependence—that is, the lack of sustained long-term development and the extremely unequal distribution of income. Barrett and Whyte (1982) cited these critical differences to argue that the dependency perspective cannot adequately explain the East Asian cases of development.

More recent studies on East Asian development have focused on the strong developmental state (as a key difference compared to Latin America) to explain why economic growth was achieved at unprecedented speed without serious negative side effects (Amsden 1989; Evans 1987; Gold 1986; Johnson 1987; Koo 1987; Lim 1987; Mardon 1990; Woo 1990). The questions asked in these studies were shaped by the experiences of the Latin American NICs, and those conducting the studies often approached the developmental state with the awe of one approaching a "rain man" or other such miracle maker.

Among the state-centered studies based on South Korea, Amsden's (1989) and Woo's (1990) books provided solid contributions. Wade (1990) also provided a fine comparative analysis of Taiwan and South Korea. It is noteworthy that Amsden (1989) and Wade (1990) provided a convincing account of the role of the state in governing and leading the process of economic development, using a wealth of empirical evidence to counter key arguments made by neoclassical economists.

Amsden's (1989) book on South Korean industrialization stands out as an important contribution on its development, providing a rich theoretical analysis based on detailed empirical evidence. Amsden (Ibid.) provides a critical analysis of the mechanisms of the state—e.g., discipline and punishment—that enable effective execution of economic development plans without corruption, as well as an analysis of how large business groups work under the guidance and control of a strong developmental state. She hints that the balance of power between the state and businesses began to change in the 1980s. However, because the book focuses on the state's achievements and takes us only to the mid-1980s, Amsden's book does not deal adequately with the declining state and with the *chaebol* as an emerging social class. Furthermore, she underplays the problems and abuses of the state and businesses.

Woo's (1990) study focuses on the role of financial institutions in shaping South Korea's economic development. She argues that the Japanese colonial period institutions of the state and the banks provided an important foundation from which more recent economic growth has been based. Woo's (1990) study, however, stops before the 1980s, during which time the power balance between the state and capitalist changes significantly. Thus, she gives the impression that the control the state and state-owned financial institutions have over businesses remains constant over time. And similar to the studies by Amsden (1989) and Wade (1990), Woo (1990) does not adequately deal with abuses and problems resulting from state-led development.

Wade (1990) provides a compelling counterargument to the neoclassical economists' assertion that Taiwan's economic development is a prime example of market principles at work. He provides ample evidence that the role of the state in Taiwan's development has been to govern the market, rather than to simulate the free market. However, since his book focuses on the role of the state in attaining economic development, he does not deal with the political challenges facing the Taiwanese state, which have come from the middle class and workers in recent years.

Although state-centered studies have provided us with critical insights into the role of the developmental state in economic development in East Asia, they are nevertheless limited in several ways. First, they tend to promote a static understanding of the state and of development by assuming that if a state becomes strong and developmental, it will necessarily remain that way.[4]

Another related issue is that due to these studies' static appraisal of state power in absolute terms, they do not examine how the balance of power between the state *vis à vis* other actors in society may change as a result of economic development. Furthermore, such an appraisal of state power is based on an assumption that the state and society are locked in a zero-sum relationship. States are depicted in dichotomous terms such as "strong" and "weak," which are often juxtaposed against "weak" and "strong" societies, respectively (Johnson 1987; Koo

1987; Migdal 1988). The South Korean case illustrates that the state's power (both in relative and absolute terms) changes over time and that the state is not necessarily locked in a zero-sum relationship with businesses—e.g., a strong state can coexist with big businesses, and conversely, a weak state and can coexist with weak businesses.

Second, actors other than the state in the developmental drama are treated lightly. The private sector is often seen as a mere follower of the state's initiatives and therefore not much different from public enterprise. It is an irony that many studies on South Korean development written from the state-centered perspective often examine only nonmarket factors, such as the state and the geopolitical context. In these studies, the private sector is seen as merely "puppets" of the state—i.e., taking orders from the state and implementing them. The logic is clear: in order to understand the activities of the puppets (the businesses), one must look at the hands (the state) that are moving the puppets and not the puppets. The puppets cannot make decisions or move on their own. Thus, private businesses are often portrayed as *created, maintained,* and *managed* by the state, which are not very different from public enterprises (Hamilton & Biggart 1988; Koo 1987). Although the state may have a relatively strong hold on the *chaebol,* the latter are ultimately private enterprises that make decisions and take risks. Therefore, it is important that they be studied apart from the state policies. The studies by DiMaggio and Powell (1983), Powell and DiMaggio (1991), and other institutional analyses of organizations are utilized in this book to provide an analysis of the emergence of different types of industrial organizations in response to the external environment, in which the state is a major actor. Evans's new book, *Embedded Autonomy: States & Industrial Transformation* (1995), provides important insights in explicating how an autonomous state is able to intervene in the market effectively, yet able to resist societal pressures. His analysis provides a clear way in which the South Korean state intervened effectively, unlike its counterparts in Brazil and India. His conceptualization and analysis informs this study in important ways.

Third, since the state-centered approach is intended to explain the remarkable achievements of the state, it tends to ignore the social costs and abuses that also result from development.[5] Both the market- and state-centered studies have been fascinated with the remarkable achievements of the South Korean case, and thus neither has provided a critical analysis of the social/political/economic costs of rapid economic development. Finally, while this approach provides a good explanation of how the developmental state is created and gains power, it does not deal adequately with the weakening of the developmental state.

The present study revises and improves upon the one-sided analysis of either the market- or state-centered studies by incorporating both the state and the capitalists into the analysis. The two institutions are examined since they formed an alliance to attain rapid economic development. However, this alliance was neither an egalitarian or a static one. As noted earlier, the power balance shifted from state dominance to symbiosis and later to competition. This argument departs from earlier studies, which tend to assume that the institution in control (whether it is the state or the capitalists) will retain its power over time.

By examining the alliance formed between the state and the *chaebol*, this study illuminates the repression of labor. Relatively low-paid female and male workers provided the competitive edge in terms of prices for South Korean–made products in the international market. Yet, these workers did not enjoy the fruits of their labor, neither in the forms of wage increases, improvement in working conditions, or enhancement of labor rights. This study examines social costs that resulted from economic development based on a tight state-capital alliance.

In sum, this study rejects the one-sided and static understandings of both the market- and state-centered approaches, and offers an integrated analysis of the state and capitalists in economic development. This study begins with an assumption that the alliance formed between the two institutions is a dynamic one, in which the power balance shifts. The study also argues that the relationship between the state and the capitalists is not necessarily a harmonious one and examines the sources of tension and conflict embedded in the relationship.

Finally, this study is more about social change, in which institutions and organizations change in the process of rapid economic development, than about how rapid economic development is attained.

Toward an Analysis of State and Business in a Dialectical Process of Social Change

In this book, development is understood as a dialectic[6] process of social change in which the state and big businesses work together to attain economic development; and in the process, the state and businesses are fundamentally transformed and the relations between the state and businesses are altered.

The analysis in the book covers the period from 1960 to 1990, during which time South Korea experienced dramatic social, economic, and political changes. The collaboration and conflict between the two domestic institutions of the developmental state and the *chaebol* are analyzed during three periods: the state and the remaking of the *chaebol* (1960s); the state-*chaebol* alliance for development (1970s); and the decline of the developmental state, the rise of the *chaebol*, and the growing labor movement (1980s). An in-depth examination of labor is not presented until the chapter on the 1980s, since it was prevented from having a voice to determine South Korea's economic development and industrialization during the earlier decades. The conclusion summarizes the South Korean model, provides lessons for Third World nations, and discusses future prospects for South Korea.

The first part of the book deals with theoretical analyses of the two main institutions. The concept of the developmental state, which was first developed by Johnson (1982), is further refined. First, the concept is modified to include two different phases of the developmental state: comprehensive and limited. Unlike earlier studies, which tend to focus on the state's ability to transform society and to bring about economic growth, attention is paid to how the state changes as a result of societal changes and economic growth. Emphasis is on the fact that the developmental state's internal structure and its relations to the capitalists and labor change as a result of its success in attaining economic development. Thus, the comprehensive developmental state refers to the stage prior to state transformation, while the limited developmental state refers to the stage after the transformation. The underlying assumption is that these two types of the developmental state are qualitatively different and merit a separate analytical treatment.

Second, the comprehensive developmental state is presented as an inherently unstable and transitory form of state structure, since it has limits embedded in its construct. The notion that the state must rely on a certain degree of autonomy from the capitalists at the beginning of economic development is one of the reasons why the state will have difficulty retaining its supremacy over the businesses. This is because capitalist economic development will inevitably result in the growth of the capitalists, who can then threaten the autonomy of the state. Another source of instability stems from the goal of the state—i.e., economic development—and policies and services provided by the state to attain this goal (e.g., long-term economic development plans and forecasting, capital and technology, and marketing know-how). These services are not usually provided by the state in other advanced industrialized nations. In such nations, these services are often provided by the private sector. What this implies is that although the comprehensive developmental state may have an independent domain of services when the private sector is in its infancy, the comprehensive developmental state will increasingly face competition from the private sector as capitalist economic development progresses. These limitations on the state's autonomy and institutions are important factors in explaining why the comprehensive developmental state will be forced to change, despite its built-in inertia against drastic changes.

In addition to providing an analysis of the developmental state, this book examines the historical structural context, industrial organization, and tremendous growth of the *chaebol*. A conservative alliance between a strong state and domestic big businesses is not as easily found among developing nations as we may expect. In many Latin American nations, MNCs were brought in to assist with economic development (Cardoso & Faletto 1979; Evans 1979). In Taiwan, the three largest enterprises are state-owned (Gereffi 1990). Even in pre–World War II Japan, when large family-owned business groups proliferated, the state provided less direct incentives to the business groups than the South Korean government. Thus, an understanding of this group of capitalists, whose growth was supported extensively by the state in the earlier phase of development but that later grew to challenge the state, is important for the analysis of South Korean development.

In order to understand how the *chaebol* were created and became dominant in the domestic economy, we incorporate the broader context in which the industrial organizations exist and then link the broader context to the internal organizational structure. This is because the internal structure is not merely a reflection of the environment, as the state-centered studies tend to assume, nor is it completely neutral, as the neoclassical economic studies argue. As Hamilton and Biggart state, "enterprise structure represents situational adaptations of preexisting organizational forms to specific political and economic conditions" (1988:s87). Studying the broader context is particularly important when we examine industrial organizations in developing nations. The broader context or the environment of the developing nations is not only qualitatively different from that of the advanced industrial nations when they began to industrialize (Kiggundu, Jorgensen & Hafsi 1983), but it also has a much greater impact on its organizations.

In this book, an analysis of the *chaebol* is produced by incorporating the organizational theory offered by DiMaggio and Powell (1983), which can explain how the *chaebol* as an industrial organization flourished in South Korea, and the more macroanalyses provided by development studies and the political economy perspective. The latter will provide historical insights into the process of how certain institutions and organizations gain power and resources to become the origin of isomorphic change (rather than the receptor of such change). The state, colonialism, and internationalization are the three focal points in the analysis of the historical structural context of the *chaebol*.

Here, the *chaebol* is analyzed as both an industrial organization with attributes that help explain its phenomenal growth and as a newly emerging capitalist class of *chaebol* owners, high-ranking managers, and their families, whose relationship with the state changes with development. The *chaebol* is a family-owned and family-managed, extremely diversified business conglomerate. It is based on a unique blend of the Confucian ideology of filial piety and loyalty to family and the West's notion of free enterprise. The industrial organization and growth of the *chaebol* are examined utilizing a data set I have compiled that contains firm-level information on the *chaebol*.

In the course of successful economic development, the developmental state and the *chaebol* have faced challenges to transform themselves. In a way, the demands faced by the state are far more critical than those faced by the businesses. The state faces challenges to alter its *raison d'être* and institutions, since its primary goal—economic development—has been attained; while business faces less drastic challenges, since its goal—profit maximization—is one without a finite end point. The developmental state's transformation has been brought about in part by the inherent contradictions and limits of a comprehensive developmental state, as well as by the state's industrial policies of favoring big businesses and heavy industrialization, which have fostered the growth of the *chaebol* and a militant labor force. Furthermore, the restructuring of the developmental state faced further difficulties as the state became subsumed within the more dramatic breakdown of the authoritarian regime and democratization surrounding the Declaration for Democracy on June 29, 1987.

A cheap, abundant, and well-disciplined labor force has been a mainstay of the success of export-oriented industrialization in the East Asian NICs. In many cases, wages have been suppressed and labor rights have been repressed. Since the voice of organized labor was relatively small during the early phase of development, outsiders tended to assume that labor was content for the reason that jobs, albeit low-paying ones, are better than none at all. However, we know now that the labor force in Asian NICs is not content with its wages and working conditions. The voice of discontent has been loudest in South Korea. In 1989, there were 1,616 strikes and lockouts in South Korea, compared to seven in Hong Kong, 1,458 in Taiwan

(1986 figures), and ten in Thailand (1987 figures) (International Labour Office 1990). Increased labor movements in South Korea developed in spite of one of the most repressive labor regimes among the Asian NICs (Bello & Rosenfeld 1990; Deyo 1987b, 1989; Ogle 1990). Labor, as an important social group that demanded changes in the comprehensive developmental state as well as the authoritarian state, is analyzed in chapter 6.

Data and Sources

This study is based on interviews and secondary data I obtained during a nine-month field study in South Korea between 1986 and 1989, with financial assistance from an International Doctoral Research Fellowship by the Social Science Research Council (1986–87) and a Faculty Research and Innovation Fund by the University of Southern California (1988–89). Many shorter visits to Seoul between 1991 and 1994, which often lasted from two to four weeks, allowed me to conduct more interviews and to collect up-to-date information and publications. In South Korea, I interviewed both past and present government officials from the three economic ministries (the Economic Planning Board, the Ministry of Finance, and the Ministry of Trade and Industry), business executives, bank executives (Bank of Korea and Korea Development Bank), newspaper editors, and academics.[7] Over the years, I interviewed over fifty individuals. Each interview lasted one to two hours. The interviewees were selected with the help of my colleagues in South Korea, and they were chosen because of their first-hand experience and knowledge of the issues I was researching for this book. I spoke with many others, both in the United States and in South Korea, and they provided valuable insights on the inner workings of the state and businesses in South Korea.

The research on the *chaebol* was based in part on a data set I compiled for the ten largest *chaebol*. The ten largest *chaebol* were selected to be included in the data set, because this was one of the two places in which a natural break in terms of total assets and sales occurred. The other was after the four largest. Since financial data on the *chaebol* as a unit of analysis was not

available until the mid-1980s, I created this data set based on
financial statistics of individual firms compiled from business
directories published in South Korea. Two business directories
were used for this purpose: Maeil Kyŏngje Shinmun's *Maekyung:
Annual Corporation Reports* (1971–84) and Korea Productivity
Center's *Korean Company Handbook* (1973–82). These business
directories were not published prior to 1971, and therefore all
information is from 1970 (which the 1971 volume contained).
Information on the firms included the foundation date, total
assets, total debt, capital, sales, major products, export, and
industry from 1970 to 1983. Information was put in the
computer using SPSS-X. The data on individual firms were then
polled for each of the ten largest *chaebol*. The statistical information on the *chaebol* as the unit of analysis has been available
since the mid-1980s from several sources including the
Management Efficiency Research Institute (1988–92) and
Bankers Trust (1989). I relied on these new publications to
complement the data set I compiled for the analysis of the
chaebol. No such longitudinal analysis of the *chaebol* based on
firm-level data has yet been published either in English or in
Korean.

I conducted archival research in the libraries at Ewha
Womans University, Seoul National University, and the Korea
Development Institute. I also obtained important and often
classified documents from government offices: these documents included statistical information on South Korea's
economy, data on foreign and domestic capital, and internal
government reports on policies. I also secured South Korean
bank documents, business directories, newspaper articles,
papers from research institutions, and various other published
articles and books.

Organization of the Book

The book is organized into two parts, in addition to an
introduction (chapter 1) and a conclusion (chapter 7). Part I
(chapters 2 and 3) discusses the state and the *chaebol* as two key
institutions that brought about rapid economic development
through alliance and competition. The discussions in this

section are centered on the theoretical analyses of the two institutions. Part II (chapters 4–6) is an in-depth analysis of the changes of the state and the *chaebol* in the three decades of dynamic economic growth.

Chapter 2 focuses on the state, and the concepts of the authoritarian and developmental states are developed. The contradictions inherent to the comprehensive developmental state are presented. These contradictions help explain how and why the comprehensive developmental state undergoes a transformation to a limited developmental state, even when it is successful in attaining its goal of economic development.

Chapter 3 analyzes the *chaebol*, focusing on their unique industrial organization relative to their Japanese prototype, the *zaibatsu* (the pre–World War II Japanese business conglomerates), and to Western enterprises. The broader historical context of the *chaebol*, which helps explain how they were established and flourished, is analyzed.

Chapters 4 and 5 trace South Korea's industrialization during the 1960s and 1970s. South Korea's journey toward rapid industrialization based on exports is analyzed in terms of the alliance that was formed between the state and big businesses. The changing nature of the state-business relationship was as important as the changes in the institutional makeup of the state that occurred with the 1961 military coup led by Park Chung Hee.

Chapter 6 explores the challenges presented to the comprehensive developmental state by the *chaebol* and labor in the 1980s. The restructuring of the developmental state, which began in 1979, was overshadowed by the more dramatic breakdown of the authoritarian Chun regime. The dramatic economic, social, and political changes that occurred in the 1980s attest to the dynamic nature of the South Korean development model.

In the last chapter, I address three issues. I summarize the key features of the South Korean model and contemplate in what ways the South Korean model is similar and different from the Japanese model. The second question is whether South Korea can serve as a model for other Third World nations, in view of the findings of this book. The discussion includes the decline of the developmental state, the advantages and dangers of a development strategy based on a tight alliance between a strong state and big business, and the social problems of injustice and inequity stemming from such state-business alliance. The last issue is the future challenges facing the South Korean political economy. Future prospects for South Korea's economic development are presented in light of recent events, including heightened expectation for reunification with North Korea, the Kim Young Sam [Kim Yŏng Sam] regime whose presidency represented a first civilian regime in over three decades, and continued efforts for political democratization.

Part I
Institutions of Development

2
The State

Few organizations in the world are as capable of bringing drastic changes to a society as the state. In particular, it has played an integral role in the development of the latecomers (Amsden 1989; Evans 1987; Evans, Rueschemeyer & Skocpol 1985; Gerschenkron 1962; Gold 1986; Haggard 1990; Johnson 1982; Lim 1987). In East Asia, the state has been largely responsible for abolishing the old class system through land reforms (Evans 1987; Koo 1987), for bringing young women to the workplace in unprecedented numbers through export-oriented industrialization based on light manufactured products (Barrett & Chin 1987; Deyo 1989; Koo 1990), and for transforming an agrarian economy into a bustling industrial economy in less than two decades.

The state is a set of organizations, including administrative and legislative bodies, that has the authority to make and implement binding rules over all people and all action in a particular territory, using force if necessary (Migdal 1988:19; Rueschemeyer & Evans 1985:46–47; Weber 1964:156).

In addition to this definition of the state, I use specific names of government offices and state institutions whenever it is possible. The use of specific names underscores the potential

27

for dissension and tension within the state, which is an important argument of this book. The concept of the state assumes that a coherent set of policies are to be developed and implemented by various state organizations and that state offices will act as one homogenous entity. However, in reality, this is not always the case. Discussions in Part II of this book present cases where state organizations were not in consultation with one another and where there were visible signs of conflict. The introduction of conflict and tension in the analysis of the state, even if it is an authoritarian or developmental state, helps us to understand the complex process of how the state works in order to attain economic development.

The ability of the state to enforce its policies rests on two facets of the state: autonomy and capacity. State autonomy refers to the relative autonomy of state officials from dominant economic classes and social groups, which allows for effective implementation of policies (Rueschemeyer & Evans 1985: 46–50, 350–51; Skocpol 1985:9–11). State capacity refers to the existence of a state apparatus that facilitates the implementation of state policies (Rueschemeyer & Evans 1985:50–53, 351).

Many state-centered studies have used the concepts of state autonomy and state capacity to compare the states in East Asia and Latin America. In East Asia the states had high levels of capacity and autonomy, while in Latin America the states had high capacity but a relatively low degree of autonomy. As a result, the East Asian states were able to bring about industrialization under inauspicious circumstances (lack of natural resources and capital, and a relatively small domestic market), while preventing some of the perils associated with rapid economic growth that plagued Latin America (rapidly rising income inequality, structural distortion, and deepening dependence on foreign capital and technology) (Barrett & Whyte 1982; Deyo 1987a; Gereffi & Wyman 1990; Mardon 1990). On the other hand, the Latin American states were relatively weak, and economic development was, thus, obstructed and distorted by large landholders and multinational corporations (Cardoso & Faletto 1979; Evans 1979, 1987).[1]

Although these studies have helped us understand why the East Asian states were more effective in attaining economic development, they have not helped us understand why economic development was chosen as a goal in the first place. A state that has a high degree of autonomy from civil society and a well-developed government bureaucracy could engage in a number of endeavors, only one of which is economic development. Therefore, in this chapter, we focus on the state, which has designated "economic development" as its main policy goal. Johnson has called this a "developmental state" (1982). I further refined the concept to differentiate between a "comprehensive" and a "limited" developmental state (see chapter 1). The emphasis in this chapter is on the main attributes of this state type. An examination of the developmental state will help us understand the specific ways in which the state leads and controls the market in order to attain economic development.

The developmental state in South Korea was also an authoritarian state, which refers to a style of governance antithetical to democracy. The authoritarian state is introduced in the analysis, since the developmental state in South Korea utilized the mechanisms of the authoritarian state to pursue the goal of economic development. An examination of the authoritarian orientation of the state sheds light on how the goals of the state are formulated and negotiated both within the state itself and among the state and businesses. Such an examination also shows how political leverage is utilized by both sides to implement economic policies.

The chapter is organized into two sections. The first section deals with a theoretical debate in development studies about the necessary coexistence of developmental and authoritarian state types. I argue that the two orientations of the state (i.e., developmental and authoritarian) are not necessarily found together and that they be analyzed separately. This debate is followed by a discussion of the key attributes of each state type and an examination of the broader historical and structural factors that contributed to the ascendance of these state types. The second section focuses on how the developmental state changes over time. Particular emphasis is on how successful economic development will put pressure on the developmental state to restructure.

The Developmental State and the Authoritarian State

There is a controversy among development scholars about whether a developmental state is necessarily authoritarian. Gerschenkron (1962) and others (Amsden 1989; Gold 1986; Lim 1987) studying latecomer nations have generally agreed that a strong state is a necessary condition of development for these nations. The concept of the bureaucratic authoritarian state developed by O'Donnell (1973, 1977, 1978) and others also focuses on the authoritarian and repressive nature of governing as an integral component of certain phases in development.[2]

However, I argue that the two orientations of the state should be analyzed separately for the following reasons. First, confusion in the development literature has stemmed from equating the developmental state with its outputs, and this needs to be corrected. To put it differently, a state has been defined as a "developmental state," *post facto*, when it has been successful in bringing about economic development, without a careful examination of whether the main characteristics of the developmental state were present, *ex ante*. As a result, studies that focus on the so-called success cases have erroneously presented us with a list of qualitatively disparate attributes of the state, only some of which can be defined as "developmental." Therefore, it is important to carefully delineate the different attributes of the state without confusing them with the outputs of the state. And, we must leave open the possibility that a developmental state can fail to deliver economic development.

Second, not all developmental states are authoritarian (e.g., Japan), and not all authoritarian states are developmental (e.g., North Korea and Eastern European nations before 1989). This suggests that there exists many different pairings of these state types and that the developmental-authoritarian is only one of the possible pairings. Thus, these two state types need not occur simultaneously.

Third, changes in each state type are not necessarily interrelated. Changes in the developmental state are primarily associated with capitalist development, while changes in the authoritarian state are a part of political democratization. Of course, changes are not necessarily oriented toward a goal of capitalist development or democratization.

Many earlier studies have argued that capitalist development promotes political democracy and that there exists a positive correlation between capitalism and democracy (Cutright 1963; Lipset 1980 [1959]). However, more recent studies indicate that the relationship between capitalism and democracy is not a simple one-to-one relationship (Moore 1966; Rueschemeyer, Stephens & Stephens 1992; Stephens 1989). Rueschemeyer, Stephens, and Stephens (1992) argue that a complex process of class transformation intervenes between capitalist development and democratization and that capitalist development does not necessarily lead to political democratization. They argue that only certain types of class transformation, shifts in power balance between classes, and political movements will bring forth democratization. According to their book based on case studies from Western Europe and Latin and Central America, not all capitalist development resulted in promoting democracy. Similarly, in a comparative study of South Korea and Mexico, Hamilton and I argue that the processes of economic liberalization and political liberalization are triggered by a different combination of domestic and international political and economic factors (Hamilton & Kim 1993).

In sum, the analytical separation of the state's main attributes (especially between the developmental and authoritarian) helps us examine the respective political and economic factors that contribute to the transformation of these different state types. The analytical separation between the processes of capitalist development and political democratization helps us further explore the complex processes in which they affect each other.

The Developmental State

The developmental orientation of the state was critical in South Korea's development. As presented in chapter 1, the developmental state is found in a continuum, from "comprehensive" to "limited," rather than existing in dichotomous, static terms.

A comprehensive developmental state focuses on economic development as the primary goal of the state and invests capital and human resources in pursuit of this goal. This state performs the following three major functions:

1. *Provider of long-term goals for the economy.* The state provides comprehensive economic development plans, long-term goals, and projections for the entire economy (Johnson 1987; Lim 1987; Mason et al. 1980).
2. *Provider of capital and technology.* The state provides capital for investment through domestic and foreign capital loans, capital assistance for research and development, and technology and technical assistance through national and regional research facilities (Jones & Sakong 1980; E. M. Kim 1987; Krueger 1979; Lim 1987; Mardon 1990; Mason et al. 1980).
3. *Provider of indirect assistance.* The state acts as a mediator with multinational corporations for foreign direct investment and technology transfers, establishes trade offices for expertise on exports and imports, provides tax breaks and tariff exemptions, and eases regulations (Jones & Sakong 1980; E. M. Kim 1987; Krueger 1979; Mardon 1990).

These services, in particular the last two, are designed to support the private sector in its infancy, when it cannot provide the services itself due to lack of resources, information, and know-how.

The limited developmental state can perform these three functions but in limited degrees. There will be sectors that will become more market-oriented, while others will remain under the state's close supervision and control. Goals other than economic development are included as priorities of the state. The changes in the government's economic policies from *developmental* to *regulatory* is significant in this transformation, since it indicates not only a shift in policies but, more importantly, a qualitative change in state-business relations.

Under developmental policies, the state provides incentives for businesses to invest in state-designated sectors. The state is able to *lead* businesses into certain sectors, even when businesses are reluctant to do so due to poor market projections, if the state is able to offset the risks with a substantial incentive package. In this case, the state's goals are not dissimilar from the businesses'. The state and businesses both want businesses to flourish and prosper. The relationship that is engendered between the state and businesses tends to be more cooperative. Although "sticks" are involved to force cooperation, the state more often uses "carrots" to entice businesses. Two things are important here: the state and businesses are likely to work in cooperative relations and the state *leads* businesses to invest in certain sectors with generous incentive packages.

On the other hand, regulatory policies are based on qualitatively different principles of state-business relations. Regulatory policies are often key to state-business relations in many advanced industrialized nations. These policies are based on assumptions that are fundamentally different from those of the developmental policies. First, the relations between the state and businesses are prefaced upon a principle of *laissez-faire*. In other words, businesses and the market are best left alone without active state intervention. Moreover, active state intervention is assumed to negatively impact on the efficiency and productivity of the market. Based on these assumptions, regulatory policies are developed to intervene in the market only to control abuses and malfunctions of the market. Regulatory policies often include the following items aimed at regulating and controlling businesses: (1) expansion of businesses (e.g., antitrust legislation); and (2) unfair transaction in the market (e.g., legislation against price-fixing, inside trading, etc.). These policies tend to put the state in an antagonistic relationship with businesses, as the former tries to monitor and control the latter, while the latter are trying to attain their goal of profit maximization. The goals of the state and businesses are different, and this difference becomes a source of conflict and tension in the state-business relations.

In sum, the nature of state-business relations is qualitatively different in developmental versus regulatory policies. Thus, a shift from a comprehensive to a limited developmental state implies a critical transformation in state-business relations.

A comprehensive developmental state was established when Park Chung Hee came into power in May of 1961 through a military coup. Park defined economic development as the penultimate goal of his regime. Other goals, such as national security took second place to economic development. To help implement Park's goal for economic development, the Economic Planning Board (EPB) was founded on July 22, 1961, only two months after the coup. The EPB became an elite government ministry, and the brightest college graduates aspired to have positions within it (see chapter 4 for further details on the EPB and the founding of the comprehensive developmental state).

President Park justified the interventionist comprehensive developmental state on the grounds that the private sector and the market were underdeveloped. He argued the following (1971:113):

> One of our big problems was the shaky foundations of private industry, which was unable to carry its share of the development burden. Furthermore, the market structure was not modernized. Consequently, the government had to play the leading role in the development plan, though we knew well that such a plan must, in the long run, rely on the creativity and initiative of private industry.
>
> In the meantime, the government tried to readjust existing systems to help accumulate private capital, with a view to laying the groundwork of an efficient market competition system. We hoped to encourage businessmen who could play leading roles in planning. On the other hand, rigid restrictions were put on such business activities as run against these efforts.

The establishment of a comprehensive developmental state clearly differentiated the Park regime from its predecessors. The founding of the EPB and other government offices geared toward economic development, the creation of comprehensive Five-Year Economic Development Plans, and the nationalization of banks are evidence of the increased capacity of the state under Park. And as is discussed in the next section, the comprehensive developmental state of the Park regime was authoritarian. This made it easier to implement the Five-Year Economic

Development Plans, since potential societal resistance was repressed by the state.

The Authoritarian State

The authoritarian state, which is the opposite of a democratic state, is defined by several key elements:

1. *Formal institutional characteristics*
   - Power is concentrated in the executive branch (Poulantzas [1978] as quoted in Jessop 1990), a leader, or an elite (Merriam-Webster 1988).
   - There is no free, open contestation of power through which people can change the leader in a just and peaceful manner. Thus, the leader is not constitutionally responsible or accountable to the people (Merriam-Webster 1988).
2. *Content of authoritarian governance*
   - Formal liberties, which include habeas corpus, freedom of expression, and freedom of association, are curtailed (Jessop 1990:66; Hamilton & Kim 1993:111–12).
   - State control is intensive in every aspect of citizens' lives (Jessop 1990).

A comprehensive authoritarian state is defined as having both the formal institutional traits and the content of governance. In theory, the formal institutional traits can exist without the content, but this is seldom found in the real world. It is because lack of legitimacy (i.e., existence of formal institutional traits of an authoritarian state) compels the state to adopt measures that will ensure its survival and minimize the likelihood of a takeover. These measures of survival include curtailment of civil liberties and control of every aspect of the people's lives. I use the term, *limited authoritarian state*, to refer to the state, which has legitimacy and its head of state and/or representatives are elected in an open and contested election but which has the content of authoritarian governance.

According to these definitions, a comprehensive authoritarian state was established in 1961 by Park Chung Hee. However, an authoritarian state had been in existence in South Korea for some time. The Rhee regime, which was the first Republic in South Korea, was not a comprehensive, but a limited, authoritarian state. President Rhee was elected in an open and democratic election. However, the Rhee regime began to exhibit contents of authoritarian governance toward the end of his term, and finally he was ousted by a popular uprising led by high school and college students in April 1960. On the other hand, the Japanese colonial government (1910–45) was a comprehensive authoritarian state, which increasingly controlled Korea with an iron fist as Japan's war efforts in Asia escalated in the 1930s.

With the legacy of an authoritarian state behind him, the Park regime justified the establishment of a comprehensive authoritarian state by arguing that political stability was a precondition for attaining economic development. Two important assumptions were made by Park in making this argument. First, he argued that political instability was a major cause of poverty and rampant corruption of the past (Park 1971). Thus, Park saw the establishment of an authoritarian regime, which could install stability, as an important first step in attaining economic development. His arguments are presented in his book, *To Build a Nation*:

> I was also aware of the fact that economic development in the capitalist manner requires not only an immense investment of money and materials, but also a stable political situation and competent administrators.
>
> To achieve this stability, the military revolutionary government temporarily suspended political activities of students, the press, labor unions and other social and political organizations, which had caused political crises and social unrest during the rule of the Democratic Party regime (Park 1971:105).

Second, Park blamed political instability as an indirect cause of the Korean War. The Park regime argued that freedom of expression and freedom of the press had led to social unrest, creating an opportune moment for North Korea to invade

South Korea. Thus, "democracy" was blamed indirectly for the Korean War, and its suspension was declared justified in the name of national security. This twist of logic that political openness and democracy were the cause of the Korean War meant that a nationalist and patriotic ideology was invoked to justify the suspension of democracy; this made it very difficult for the opponents to mobilize against the suspension of democracy.

Although the suspension of political rights and limitations on civil liberties were announced as being a temporary measure, they in fact continued during the entire tenure of the Park regime. Park called this political system a "Korean-style" of democracy and justified it in the name of national security. However, as earlier discussed, this "Korean-style" democracy did not resemble the formal and substantive democracies found elsewhere.

The authoritarian style of governance continued during the eighteen years of the Park regime. Instead of high levels of economic development leading to democracy as argued by modernization scholars (Lipset 1980 [1959]), political repression intensified over time. In October 1972, Park promulgated the Yushin Reformation, which was a draconian and repressive regime, after a decade of unprecedented rapid economic growth based on exports. (See chapter 5 for details.)

The Developmental-Authoritarian State

In South Korea, the comprehensive developmental state was also a comprehensive authoritarian state during the 1960s and 1970s. The comprehensive developmental state in South Korea implemented economic development plans in an authoritarian manner. In other words, the state forcibly intervened in the market, the state was in control of the market, and the state was omnipresent in the market.

There were two ways in which the South Korean state used its authoritarian muscle to enforce its economic policies. First, it used discipline and punishment in its relations with the *chaebol* (Amsden 1989). In the early 1960s the state was clearly the dominant partner when it formed a loose alliance with the large businesses. The military government forced cooperation from the business leaders, who were indicted on charges of having illicitly accumulated wealth under the Rhee Syngman [I Sŭng Man] and Chang Myŏn regimes.

As development proceeded during the 1960s and early 1970s, the relationship between the state and the *chaebol* became more symbiotic. However, the state continued to control domestic and foreign capital, and it used its power to enforce strict guidelines for domestic and foreign loans (Mardon 1990). The *chaebol* had to compete with one another to receive further credit from the state; those that could not compete could no longer receive the state's low-interest policy loans (Ibid.). Amsden argues that this discipline and punishment prevented the South Korean state and *chaebol* from becoming corrupt, as has been the case in many other developing nations (1989).

The second way in which the state used authoritarian means to achieve its economic goals was repression of labor. The state's policies were intended to keep wages low and to limit and prohibit labor movements (H. Cho 1993a; Choi 1989). The lack of minimum-wage legislation prior to 1988 and the poor enforcement of laws relating to working condition resulted in worker exploitation (Song 1991). The police and the Korean Central Intelligence Agency were ordered to monitor and report labor activities, and extensive force was used to prevent and control labor strikes (Ogle 1990). During the 1960s and 1970s, there were several prominent cases in which underground labor leaders were prosecuted as pro–North Korean communist agitators (Ibid.). Conviction carried a maximum penalty of death.

The Structural and Historical Context of the State's Rise

Several domestic and international political and economic factors help explain why the South Korean state became developmental and authoritarian. International factors important for South Korea's economic development include the geopolitical conditions, the state of the international market and foreign capital, and the Japanese model of economic development (Cumings 1987; Mardon 1990). The geopolitical conditions, in particular, helped sustain the authoritarian state in South Korea during the 1960s and 1970s. The international market was favorable for South Korea's export-oriented industrialization strategy, since export markets were relatively open to South Korean goods and there were a few competitors from other Third World nations. The expanding international market also provided South Korea with much-needed foreign capital in the form of loans rather than direct foreign investments from MNCs. And, the Japanese model provided a tangible guide for the South Korean developmental state. These international factors were favorable conditions that were also present in other developing nations in Asia during the 1960s.

Geopolitics: The geopolitical significance of South Korea to the security of the Pacific as recognized by the United States resulted in the United States's provision of aid to South Korea. U.S. military and economic aid, which amounted to $13 billion between 1945 and the mid-1960s, helped sustain the regimes of Rhee Syngman and Park Chung Hee (Mason et al. 1980). As Cumings (1987) noted, the fact that South Korea was interjected into the world because of geopolitics rather than economic conditions allowed the South Korean state some autonomy to pursue economic development plans that were guided primarily by domestic concerns, rather than by the interests of MNCs (as was the case in many Latin American nations). Later, dwindling military and economic aid was replaced with public and commercial loans from the United States and Japan.

The political implication of U.S. support was significant for the Park regime. The United States's quick acceptance and approval of Park's coup in 1961, in which Park overthrew a democratically elected president, indicated the United States's endorsement of a nondemocratic state in South Korea. Many South Korean opposition leaders and dissidents argue that Park's authoritarian regime would not have lasted as long as it did without continued U.S. support.

The International Market and Foreign Capital: The favorable international economic conditions during the 1960s helped South Korea to sustain its developmental and authoritarian state. During the 1960s, foreign loan capital was more readily available to Third World nations as the international economy was in expansion. The United States (South Korea's major export market) and other advanced industrialized nations in Western Europe had not erected extensive trade barriers against cheap, light-manufactured products from East Asia. As Mardon (1990) points out, South Korea's significance in U.S. security in northeast Asia allowed a lenient treatment of South Korea by the United States. Without much competition from other developing countries, the economies of Japan, South Korea, and Taiwan enjoyed an export boom in the 1960s and 1970s. If the international economy had not been favorable, and the South Korean state and businesses had been unable to deliver prosperity, South Korea's developmental and authoritarian state could have faced a serious political challenge.

The Japanese Model: The Japanese developmental state of post–World War II offered a tangible model for the South Korean developmental state. In 1965, South Korea and Japan signed a Normalization Treaty. Most importantly, this treaty allowed South Korea to import Japanese capital and technology. The geographical proximity of the two nations, and the similarity in their economic-development trajectories (based on limited natural resources and capital, with a relative abundance of well-trained and well-educated labor) in the post–World War II era help explain the Japanese influence on the South Korean state and businesses.

On the other hand, I argue that the impact of the Japanese colonial legacy is more indirect and coincidental rather than direct and consequential. Some scholars (McNamara 1990; Woo 1990) argue that the roots of the post-1961 South Korean state are in the Japanese colonial government's sophisticated bureaucracy and interventionist economic policies. However, this argument should be reexamined in light of the fact that political regimes that immediately followed the colonial period were not developmental, thus leaving a conspicuous gap of some fifteen years before the developmental state surfaces in South Korea in 1961. If Japan were more separated from South Korea geographically or, more importantly, if Japan did not have capital and technology to offer South Korea since the 1960s, the Japanese influence on South Korea's state and businesses would have been limited in spite of the colonial legacy.

Structural Obstacles

Apart from the favorable international factors, South Korea faced serious obstacles to overcome in order to attain economic development. These obstacles included the dual economic structure engendered by the Japanese colonial government that focused heavy manufacturing and electricity in the northern part of the Korean peninsula and agriculture and light manufacturing in the southern part, the near complete destruction of the agrarian and industrial bases of the South Korean economy as a result of the Korean War, a relatively young government bureaucracy that was established in 1948 after thirty-five years of Japanese colonial rule, and a relatively inexperienced private sector in terms of exports and industrial manufacturing. Some of these obstacles were also present, although in different degrees, in other Asian nations.

In spite of these obstacles, the South Korean economy became one of the most successful NICs. Favorable international conditions helped South Korea reach this goal. However, as presented in chapter 1, many of these conditions were similarly presented to other nations in Asia. The emphasis on this book is on the domestic actors' ability to utilize and control the international conditions that were presented to them.

Of particular significance is how the state was able to dominate and control the economy during the first two decades of growth. The relative sophistication and autonomy of the state during the early phase of development set the initial pattern of relations among the state, the *chaebol*, and labor. Three domestic conditions helped the state to dominate the relationship with the *chaebol* and labor. First, the relative organizational sophistication of the military compared to the rest of the society was important in the early stage of development. When Park led the military coup, he justified the role of the military in politics by arguing that it was the only organization capable of ridding the South Korean society of its major problems—

poverty and corruption. The military had developed its organizational structure and hierarchical control during the Korean War. In an attempt to restrict other domestic actors—in particular, the businesses—the military government sent owners of large *chaebol* to prison, charging them with illicit accumulation of wealth. Such a military-style disciplinary act in the early days of the Park regime clearly established who was in control. (See chapter 4 for details.)

Second, the civil society was not well developed. When the military government took control in 1961, few in society were organized enough to voice serious objections to the state or to actively challenge its power. The businesses were relatively young, most of them having been founded since the end of the Japanese colonial period. They had not formed a unified interest group. Labor was not organized at that time, either. Other interest groups were also poorly organized, if at all, especially when compared to a sophisticated organizational structure of the military government. The imbalance between a relatively sophisticated military bureaucracy and an underdeveloped civil society created an ideal condition for state control of the entire society, including the economy.

Third, the state officials of the Park regime were insulated from the class interests of the private sector. The members of the military regime were not members of the capitalist class, and Park himself had been born into an impoverished peasant family. The goals of the military coup thus reflected those of ordinary citizens and peasants, who were disillusioned by the collusion of economic and political elites during the Rhee regime. Moreover, capital resources provided to the state (e.g., military and economic aid from the United States and, later, public loan capital) also helped the state to become autonomous in making decisions about the economy. In sum, the Park regime had high levels of state capacity and state autonomy, and it concentrated on attaining economic development.

Transformation of the Developmental State

How does a developmental state change over time? Will it change even if it is successful in attaining its goal? What is the relationship between the changes in the developmental and authoritarian orientations of the state?

The developmental state is inherently unstable for two reasons. First, it has a goal (i.e., economic development) that has a finite end point, unlike a welfare state or a *laissez-faire* state. The state bureaucratic offices, which were created to develop and implement economic development plans, face pressure to restructure regardless of their success or failure in attaining the goal. If they fail to deliver economic growth, the offices and their occupants are forced to change so that economic growth can be attained. On the other hand, if they are successful, they are no longer needed, since the finite mission has been accomplished. Second, tension also arises from the competition between the state and businesses in the provision of certain services. Many of the developmental state's functions are performed by the private sector in advanced industrialized nations. This implies that the state's role can be supported primarily when the private sector is in its infancy. Thus, the tension between the state and the private sector can be exacerbated with economic development and the growth of the private sector.

The tensions described here point to two contradictions and limits inherent in the developmental state: *contradiction of institution,* and *contradiction of autonomy.* These contribute to the state's weakening of power and decreasing influence in the economy. It is possible to mitigate the effects of the contradictions to keep them from developing into self-limiting tendencies. There can also be variances in the time frames within which these tendencies become materialized. However, the important issue is that the contradictions of institution and of autonomy are common to all developmental states.

The contradictions are paradoxical, since it is success in attaining the goal that becomes the catalyst for the state's decline and transformation. Furthermore, the process involves more than short-term adjustments and includes fundamental changes in the goals and functions of the state. This process thus entails some tension and conflict, as institutions within the state struggle to stay intact.

Figure 2.1 offers a typology to clarify this argument. This figure also presents ideas on the transformation of the state over time, based on the two orientations of the state. The position shown for each nation is not a permanent one, and movement between boxes indicates transformation of the state. (The arrows indicate the direction of change.)

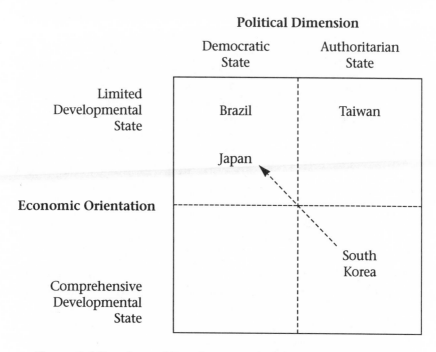

Figure 2.1 Typology of Developmental and Authoritarian States

There are three ways in which the transformation of the state can occur. In the first type, transformation occurs only in a vertical direction (e.g., from a comprehensive to a limited developmental, while retaining the political dimension). In the second type, transformation occurs only in a horizontal direction (e.g., from authoritarian to democratic, while retaining the same economic orientation). These two types represent fewer problems in the transformation of the developmental state. The most problematic one is the third type, when the move is made simultaneously in two different directions, resulting in a diagonal move from one box to another (e.g., from authoritarian/

comprehensive developmental to democratic/limited developmental state). The South Korean case represents this last type of transformation.

Contradictions and Limits of the Developmental State

To understand why a developmental state is challenged to transform itself from being comprehensive to limited, the contradictions[3] and limits inherent in a developmental state must be examined. The first contradiction involves the institution. As discussed earlier, the developmental state performs three types of services: (1) provision of long-term goals for the economy, (2) provision of capital and technology, and (3) provision of indirect assistance. The contradiction lies in the fact that the services provided by the comprehensive developmental state are not inherently against the interests of the private sector. In fact, in many advanced industrialized economies, these services are provided only in a limited scope by the state (e.g., comprehensive and long-term economic projections and development plans) or else they are left to the private sector and the market (e.g., development of new industries, mediating with MNCs for foreign direct investment and technology transfers, and trade).

When development is successfully attained and the private sector gains more resources and know-how, these services provided by the state can become bureaucratic red tape, and hinder the vitality and speed required by the ever-changing modern economy. For its own best interests, the private sector will challenge the state's ability to perform such services and will demand to provide them itself.

The contradiction of the institution of the developmental state is qualitatively different from other state types where there is no *a priori* assumption that a transition of power will take place upon the successful attainment of goals. In a welfare state, for example, various state apparatuses assume vital functions in the development of welfare policies and in the provision of welfare services (Offe 1984). The welfare state comes in to remedy the problems left unresolved by the private sector. Successful provision of welfare services to the public does not change the fundamental picture that the private sector is incapable of and/or unwilling to provide these services and that the state has to provide these services. Similarly, in a *laissez-faire* state, the state assumes from the beginning a relatively confined (regulatory rather than developmental) and augmentative role in relation to the private sector. Even with successful economic growth, no significant transition of power to the market is needed, since the private sector has been in charge from the beginning.

The second contradiction is that of autonomy. The autonomy of the state, which is a vital ingredient and enables the developmental state to devise, implement, and enforce its economic development plans to the private sector, rests on two factors. One is the separation of state elites from the landed or capitalist classes, which insulates state officials from being influenced by their own class interests (Evans 1987). The other factor is the relative underdevelopment of civil society, in particular landed and capitalist classes and labor (Evans 1987; Koo 1990).

The contradiction lies in the fact that the autonomy of the state will face increasing erosion if it is successful. As Rueschemeyer and Evans argue (1985:49), "the state's very success in building its role as a corporate actor may undercut its ability to remain autonomous and that effective intervention may increase the extent to which the state becomes an arena of social conflict." Development will bring wealth and power to new classes and social groups (Koo 1990; Sŏ 1984), who will use their newly acquired status to press for more independence. This will threaten the core of the developmental state, which is its autonomy and its mandate to intervene in the economy. To put it simply, the successful execution of the developmental state will be self-limiting to the state.

Historically, the East Asian cases show that government officials are not drawn from the same class as merchants or industrialists. Instead, officials came from the *Yangban* (aristocracy), which consisted mostly of scholars and government officials during the Chosŏn Dynasty (1392–1910) in Korea, and from the *samurai* (warrior) class during the Tokugawa period (1603–1868) in Japan. Members of South Korea's military junta government in 1961-63 were not part of the small, wealthy capitalist class but were members of poor peasant families.

However, the separation of state elites from landed or capitalist classes is only a short-lived phase in the process of capitalist development. Successful and very rapid development brings drastic changes not only to the economy but to the society as well. As Koo (1990) points out, class composition changed significantly as a result of rapid economic growth in South Korea. The historical class distinction between the state officials and the merchants and industrialists was no longer clearly applicable. Other studies have documented that the upper class in a new social order included merchants and industrialists as well as state officials (Sŏ 1984). Moreover, through intermarriages between the offspring of capitalists and state elites (forbidden during the Chosŏn Dynasty and the Tokugawa period), the class distinction has become even more blurred (Shin & Chin 1989). This process of fusion of state elites and capitalist elites weakens the foundation for state autonomy.

The other factor vital for state autonomy—a relatively underdeveloped capitalist class and social groups—also has a self-limiting effect on the developmental state. The capitalist class grew in size and political influence with development. Other social groups, most notably labor, also grew in the process of development. These newly strengthened classes and groups can significantly challenge the state's power and its mandate in economic relations. Although the state and the capitalist class may have been collaborators for economic development, they are not necessarily allies in power and can become competitors for it.

Challenges of Democratization

Breakdown of an authoritarian regime and democratic consolidation bring challenges to the transition of the developmental state. The former involves a much broader set of sweeping changes and thus makes the latter transition much more difficult.

A developmental state faces at least two challenges in its transformation when democratization occurs simultaneously.

First, economic restructuring will be subsumed under broader, sweeping political reforms. Since political reforms in democratic consolidation involve the creation of new rules and of institutions with uncertain outcomes (Przeworski 1986), there are likely to be added uncertainties in the transformation of the developmental state. Renegotiating the role of the state in the economy becomes very difficult when the rules themselves are being renegotiated by the government, political parties, and the public in the wake of a new democratic order (Cheng & Kim 1994).

Second, democratization signifies openness to, and tolerance of, divergent groups and their demands. Openness to divergent perspectives is a critical component of democratization, and democratic consolidation is a process in which this is institutionalized and formalized. Various groups that emerge in the process of economic growth present different demands to the state. The state is thus challenged to negotiate and bargain with such groups. To do this successfully requires more skills and greater finesse than are found in an authoritarian regime, where the state can simply repress groups and ignore demands.

In South Korea, the transformation of the developmental state from comprehensive to limited was compounded by a more dramatic breakdown of the authoritarian regime in 1987. The democratization movement escalated during the Chun Doo Hwan [Chŏn Tu Hwan] regime (1980–88). The authoritarian Chun regime came to an abrupt end when Roh Tae Woo [No T'ae Wu], the handpicked successor to Chun, finally announced the Declaration for Democracy on June 29, 1987, when he was unable to resist the power of widespread demonstrations in South Korea. The process of democratic consolidation then began.[4] The transformation of the South Korean state as a result of economic development is discussed in chapter 6.

Concluding Remarks

The developmental and authoritarian state in South Korea was important in guiding the nation's economic development, especially during the early stage. The state effectively utilized its two orientations to discipline the private sector, repress labor, and provide incentives for the private sector to conform to the state's economic development plans. The developmental and authoritarian state of the Park regime was established on the bases of a well-organized military, the geopolitics of the cold war, U.S. military and economic aid, and an expanding international market during the 1960s.

The state is not monolithic but is comprised of various ministries, offices, and institutes. In terms of economic development, the Blue House (the president's office and residence), the Economic Planning Board, the Ministry of Finance, the Ministry of Trade and Industry, and the Bank of Korea (the central bank) have played important roles. As is discussed in greater detail in Part II, these offices were not always in agreement with one another nor were they always informed of certain key economic policies in the making.

Tensions arise from different organizational interests as well as from competition between the offices. It is hardly the picture of harmony and order that outsiders may perceive an authoritarian state to be. It is important to note that even within an authoritarian state structure, where hierarchy is rigid, there are tensions, conflict, and divergent interests. The coordination may *appear* to be smoother, since conformity is promoted and dissension is actively discouraged with channels for expressing it severely limited.

The change from a comprehensive to a limited developmental state in South Korea entails that the state reduce the scope and content of its involvement in the economy. However, it is important to recognize that the South Korean state continues to play a greater role in its economy compared to many advanced industrialized states of the United States and Western European nations. After all, its starting point in the 1960s was very high, with exclusive control of domestic capital, near-exclusive control of foreign capital, and dominant power relations with domestic capitalists and labor.

The paradox of South Korean development was that the comprehensive developmental state was forced to reevaluate its *raison d'être* upon tremendous success in attaining its goal. Contradictions inherent in the comprehensive developmental state, as well as the growth of the *chaebol* and labor into a powerful class and social group, respectively, put pressure on the state to reduce its control of the economy. This process of transformation from a comprehensive to a limited developmental state was challenged by a more dramatic breakdown of the authoritarian state. The ensuing democratic consolidation made the developmental state's transformation difficult, since the state was mandated to cater to the disparate demands of the *chaebol* and labor.

3
The Chaebol (Business Conglomerate)

South Korea's economic development and its growing prominence in the international marketplace cannot be understood without a critical examination of the *chaebol*. The *chaebol* are family-owned and family-managed large business groups, such as Hyundai [Hyŏndae], Samsung [Samsŏng], and Lucky–Gold Star. The *chaebol* formed a tight alliance with the South Korean developmental state and spearheaded its rapid economic growth based on exports. During the 1970s, the state provided low-interest-rate loans for heavy and chemical industrialization, from which the large *chaebol* benefited disproportionately. The state's subsidized low-interest-rate loans, and the *chaebol's* shrewd management together generated tremendous growth for the ten largest *chaebol*.[1] On average, the ten largest grew at a rate of 27.7 percent per year during the 1970s.[2] Hyundai, the largest *chaebol* in the late 1970s and 1980s, grew at an average rate of 38 percent every year during the 1970s (E. M. Kim 1991). Daewoo [Taewu], the youngest of the ten, grew at an astonishing rate of 53.7 percent per annum during the same period (Ibid.). The growth rate of the ten largest *chaebol* was 3.5 times faster than the entire South Korean economy. This is remarkable, since the average annual growth rate of real

GNP was 7.9 percent,[3] which was one of the highest rates in the world (EPB 1988).

The *chaebol* have become the most powerful group of domestic capitalists in South Korea. They dominate the South Korean society and market in several ways. First, they employ a large share of the workers. For example, the ten largest *chaebol* employed nearly 12 percent of all workers in manufacturing in 1987 (I and I 1990:28). Second, they dominate the manufacturing sector, especially key heavy and chemical industries. In 1987, the ten largest *chaebol* were responsible for 28.2 percent of total shipment in manufacturing (Ibid.). The largest *chaebol* have a near monopoly or oligopoly in many capital- and technology-intensive sectors. The five largest dominate over 40 percent of all shipment in fabricated metal products, machinery, and equipment (Ibid.:29). The thirty largest *chaebol* are responsible for 28.8 percent of all value-added in manufacturing in 1994 (Shin Sanŏp Kyŏngyŏngwŏn 1996:27). Third, the *chaebol* produce an exhaustive array of manufactured products and services. Finally, the *chaebol's* organizational structure has become a model for South Korean businesses. Partly as a result of the *chaebol's* economic success, their organizational features have been emulated by other small- and medium-sized enterprises in South Korea.

The third point is truly striking if you are a consumer in South Korea. You invariably come into daily contact with the *chaebol's* products and services. You wake up to a tune from a Daewoo clock radio, brush your teeth with Lucky toothpaste, watch a Gold Star television set, eat toast for breakfast that you bought at a Samsung-affiliated bakery, wear a suit made by Samsung or a dress made by a Lucky–Gold Star affiliate, drive a Hyundai car to work, and work on a computer made by Daewoo.[4] And of course, if you are a "Daewoo man,"[5] then your selection of products should reflect your loyalty to Daewoo. So, most of your products would be Daewoo-made products. This is not difficult, since Daewoo is involved in most of the businesses mentioned here. And most importantly, one of the most visible products, your automobile, should be a Daewoo car. If you visit the parking lots of automobile producing *chaebol* in South Korea, they are filled with their own company cars.

The *chaebol* have also become prominent in the world economy. Hyundai, Samsung, and Lucky–Gold Star are familiar names to consumers worldwide. My undergraduate sociology students on both coasts of the United States could easily recall the names of South Korea's major business groups, while they had difficulty remembering the names of three companies from the rest of the Third World. Such company name recognition is an unusual achievement considering that South Korea's GNP per capita was only $7,660 in 1993 (less than one-third of that of the United States), and that its size is a mere quarter of the state of California (World Bank 1995).

In New York City, the gigantic electric signs in Times Square tell the world of the changing international marketplace. In 1991, the *New York Times* reported about a newly erected, multi-million-dollar advertisement for the South Korean conglomerate Samsung (*New York Times* November 15, 1991). The report read that instead of a "Planters sign, with cascading peanuts, urging passers-by to buy 'a bag a day for more pep,'" (Ibid.:c17), New Yorkers and thousands of travelers from the United States and from all over the world were beckoned to buy South Korean electronic products. The cover of the *New York Times Magazine* on December 14, 1986, featured rows and rows of the Hyundai Excel waiting to be exported. The headline was "South Korea: The Next Wave." At the center of these images are the South Korean *chaebol*.

In this chapter, the *chaebol* is analyzed as an industrial organization, which is influenced and affected by the environment—i.e., the historical and structural context—, and at the same time, takes advantage of, and even changes, its environment. The field of organization analysis within sociology will inform our analysis. This approach will help us look beyond "market factors" in explaining the *chaebol*'s success. Accordingly, the *chaebol*'s success or dominance refers not just to success based on profits and growth of assets. Here, the emphasis is on how the *chaebol* became a model industrial organization that other businesses tried to emulate.

The purpose of this chapter is twofold. The first is to discuss the industrial organizational features of the *chaebol* with comparative references made to Japanese and Taiwanese corporations. The second is to uncover domestic and international factors that helped the *chaebol* become the model of emulation for other businesses. Using DiMaggio and Powell's (1983) analysis of how organizations mimic other organizations, I provide some explanations as to why the *chaebol* became so dominant in the South Korean economy.

Industrial Organization

The *chaebol* exhibit the following industrial organizational features: (1) *family ownership and management*, with a centralized and hierarchical system of control based on filial piety and loyalty; (2) *flexibility* in mobilizing and in exchanging capital, technology, and personnel among member companies; and (3) *horizontal diversification* in an unusually wide range of often unrelated business activities. Each of these attributes distinguish the *chaebol* from Western business conglomerates. Despite important similarities, the *chaebol* are also somewhat different from the pre–World War II *zaibatsu* of Japan. Unlike the *zaibatsu*, the *chaebol* do not own banks or engage in the well-known Japanese business practice of life-term employment. The criteria for promotion are also different. Promotion in the *chaebol* is based on a combination of factors, including ability, credentials (advanced academic degrees, licenses, or in-house promotion examination scores), and seniority (C. S. Kim 1992). Chronological age, an important criterion for promotion in Japan, does not operate in the promotion dynamics of large *chaebol* (Ibid.; Lie 1990b). The employees of the *chaebol* also experience more mobility than their Japanese counterparts, although the mobility of *chaebol* employees is still less than that of U.S. workers (Lie 1990b).

Family Ownership and Management

Like the Japanese *zaibatsu* prior to World War II, the *chaebol* are usually owned and managed by one or two families. The large number of the *chaebol's* member companies—e.g., in 1994, Hyundai had forty-eight, Samsung had fifty-five, Daewoo had twenty-two, and Lucky–Gold Star had fifty companies

(Shin Sanŏp Kyŏngyŏngwŏn 1996)—is coordinated by a powerful chair. The chair derives his power through ownership, as well as tight control over his sons and brothers, who are heads of member companies. The relationship between the chair and his sons and brothers is based on filial piety and authoritarian hierarchy. To a Western observer, it must be an irony to visit the state-of-the-art, ultramodern headquarter buildings of Daewoo and Samsung, which appear to happily coexist with traditional Korean values of filial piety and loyalty (see C. S. Kim 1992).

The strong emphasis on family, filial piety, and loyalty are values that date back many centuries in South Korea and reflect the influence of Confucianism and patriarchy. The strong authoritarian control based on filial piety in the *chaebol* can be summarized by the following example. Chŏng Chu Yŏng is famous for his tight reign over his sons, who are CEOs and high-ranking executives of various Hyundai corporations. Even after he relinquished his position as chair at Hyundai, he had regular meetings with his sons. This is how he started his days during his campaign for the presidency in 1992, which is not very different from his days as chair of Hyundai (*Yŏsŏng Chung-Ang* [January] 1993). Chŏng's six sons were expected at his house by 4:50 A.M. every morning. Such an early meeting was partly to avoid Seoul's horrendous traffic jams during morning rush hour and partly to discipline his sons. By 5:00 A.M., the senior Chŏng and his sons sat down for a simple Korean-style breakfast. At 5:10 A.M., they marched with the senior Chŏng in the front of the formation to a nearby health club to work out, and soon afterward they left for the party headquarters. This story is told over and over again in the domestic media as a symbol of family control and filial piety in modern business. This kind of unquestioned filial piety and demonstration of loyalty are trademarks of many *chaebol* and hold the large business groups together beyond effective entrepreneurial skills. Family control is paramount, visible, and effective.

As shown in Table 3.1, many large *chaebol* have been continuously owned and managed by the same families since their founding. For seven of the ten largest *chaebol*, the reigns of ownership have moved from the founder to the second or

Table 3.1

Family Ownership and Management of the Ten Largest *Chaebol*, 1996

Rank[a]	*Chaebol*	A. Founder (Years)	B. Current Chair (Years)	Relationship of B to A
1	Samsung	I Pyŏng Ch'ŏl (1938–87)	I Kŭn Hŭi (1987–present)	Son
2	Hyundai	Chŏng Chu Yŏng (1947–87)	Chŏng Mong Ku (1996–present)	Son
3	Lucky-Gold Star	Ku In Hoe (1931–69)	Ku Pon Mu (1995–present)	Grandson
4	Daewoo	Kim Wu Chung (1967–present)	Kim Wu Chung (1967–present)	Self
5	Sunkyong	Ch'oe Chong Kŭn (1953–73)	Ch'oe Chong Hyŏn (1973–present)	Brother
6	Ssangyong	Kim Sŏng Kon (1939–75)	Kim Sŏk Chun (1995–present)	Son
7	Kia	Kim Ch'ŏl Ho (1944–73)	Kim Sŏn Hong (1990–present)	Professional Manager
8	Hanjin	Cho Chung Hun (1945–present)	Cho Chung Hun (1945–present)	Self

Table 3.1 (continued)

Rank[a]	Chaebol	A. Founder (Years)	B. Current Chair (Years)	Relationship of B to A
9	Lotte	Shin Kyŏk Ho (1967–present)	Shin Kyŏk Ho (1967–present)	Self
10	Korea Explosives	Kim Chong Hŭi (1952–81)	Kim Sŭng Yun (1981–present)	Son

Note: a. Ranking based on total sales in 1994.

Sources: Bankers Trust Securities Research 1989; Hanguk Ilbo 1984; Management Efficiency Research Institute 1992; Pak 1982; Shin Sanŏp Kyŏngyŏngwŏn 1996.

third generations. In six of the seven cases, the son or brother of the founder succeeded the chair. Kia is the only case in which the chair of the *chaebol* was assumed by a professional manager. In other words, the other nine are still owned and managed by the founder's family. Thus, in most large *chaebol*, ownership and management have not been separated, and the founder's family continues to exert strong control over the group and its member companies.

Family ties among top executives are strong, and filial piety among them is the basis of *chaebol* management. The Hyundai *chaebol* illustrates a pattern of family-ownership and management that is typical of the large *chaebol*. First, at the center is the founder, Chŏng Chu Yŏng, who remains active in management even after his retirement in 1987. Hyundai's Chŏng shares similarities with other founders of major *chaebol*, such as I Pyŏng Ch'ŏl of Samsung, Ku In Hoe of Lucky–Gold Star, and Kim Sŏng Kon of Ssangyong. They are charismatic and driven leaders, who often relied more on luck and bold ambition than on calculation and rational thinking. They were powerful centripetal forces.

Second, the boards of directors are dominated by sons, brothers, and sons-in-law. Daughters are rarely given any positions of power. Hyundai's founder and first chair, Chŏng Chu Yŏng, had eight sons, all of whom have been active as upper-level managers in various Hyundai companies. The eldest son, Mong P'il, was president of Inchon Iron and Steel until he died in an automobile accident in West Germany in 1982. The second son, Mong Ku, has become the third chair of the Hyundai *chaebol*, succeeding the post from his uncle, Chŏng Se Yŏng who held the helm since 1987. The fifth son, Mong Hŏn became the vice chair of Hyundai, solidifying the key positions within the founder's family. Before becoming chair, Mong Ku was president of the "MK" group of corporations—i.e., Hyundai Pipe, Hyundai Precision and Industry, Hyundai Motor Services, Inchon [Inch'ŏn] Iron and Steel, Hyundai Housing and Industrial, and Hyundai Construction Equipment. These companies form the nucleus of Hyundai's heavy manufacturing operations. The MK group, widely viewed as the jewel of Hyundai, occupies a formidable position within the *chaebol*, due to the large number as well as the prestige of the companies within it (Seoul Kyŏngje Shinmun 1991). Mong Kŭn, the third son, is president of Keum Kang Development Industrial. The fourth son, Mong Wu, was president of Koryeo [Koryŏ] Industrial Development until his suicide death in 1990. The fifth son, Mong Hŏn is also very active in Hyundai corporations. Before becoming the vice chair of Hyundai he was president of Hyundai Elevator, vice president of Hyundai Merchant Marine, president of Hyundai Electronics Industries, and president of Hyundai Allen Bradley. The sixth son, Mong Jun, headed one of the key Hyundai corporations, Hyundai Heavy Industries, until his election to the National Assembly in 1987 (Ibid. 1991:49). The seventh son, Mong Yun, is president of Hyundai Marine and Fire Insurance. Chŏng's youngest son, Mong Il, is executive director of K-KBC International Ltd., an investment firm that specializes in foreign direct investments.

The Hyundai *chaebol* is typical of other large *chaebol* in several respects. As suggested by the important role of Chŏng Chu Yŏng's sons, the management of the *chaebol* is heavily dominated by the male kin of the founder. The wife and daughters of the founder do not, however, appear to play an active role in management.

Hyundai also resembles other large *chaebol* in its generational succession of ownership. The recent appointment of Chŏng Chu Yŏng's sons to the two top positions at the Hyundai *chaebol*, appears to be an effort by the senior Chŏng to solidify his sons' reign over his brother, Se Yŏng's sons. The senior Chŏng, who still wields considerable power at Hyundai, was able to use his influence, and thereby decrease the possibility of bitter infighting that could occur after his death. Although loyalty to the family business and filial piety are important values, they do not preclude bitter fights to claim "ownership" to the family name and family fortune. Such conflict and power struggle are also important aspects of these families and their businesses.

Samsung, another famous *chaebol* family, is one of the oldest. In 1938, the late I Pyŏng Ch'ŏl founded Samsung, a business that combined exporting with a limited manufacturing of flour and textiles. By the end of the Korean War,

Samsung had become one of the largest business conglomerates in South Korea. I Pyŏng Ch'ŏl had four sons and six daughters. When he died in 1987, his third son, Kŭn Hŭi, succeeded him as the chair of the Samsung *chaebol*. The eldest son, Maeng Hŭi, and the second son, Ch'ang Hŭi, have both left Samsung for various reasons.[6] His fourth son, T'ae Hŭi, was a managing director of Cheil Foods and Chemicals.

Unlike the situation in Hyundai, I's many sons-in-law are active in Samsung. I Chong Ki, who is married to I's fourth daughter, Tŏk Hŭi, is vice president of the *Chung-Ang Daily News*. Chŏng Chaeŭn, who is married to Myŏng Hŭi, the fifth daughter, is the vice president of Samsung Aerospace Industries and is the president of Samsung General Chemicals Co., Ltd.

One of the fairly distinctive characteristics of Samsung is the incorporation of I's daughters and daughters-in-law into upper management. I's daughter-in-law, Son Bok Nam, married to his eldest son, is the largest stockholder (19.6%) in the company and works as a managing director of An-Kuk Fire & Marine Insurance Co., Ltd. She appears to participate in management in a somewhat limited capacity, as she works only two days a week (Seoul Kyŏngje Shinmun 1991). An important reason for her large share of stocks is that her father was the CEO of An-Kuk before his death. Hong Na Hŭi, who is married to I's third son, is a managing director of the *Chung-Ang Daily News*. I's eldest daughter, In Hŭi, was a major stockholder and an advisor to Hotel Shilla. She and her three sons, who were active in various Samsung corporations, left Samsung in 1993 and formed an independent business group, Hansol. Myŏng Hŭi, the fifth daughter, is a major stockholder and a managing director of the Shinsegae Department Store. However, as noted in Son Bok Nam's work pattern, Samsung's women have limited involvement in the daily management of the firms, in spite of their substantial share of ownership. Thus, Samsung's women are more typical of how women are treated in large *chaebol*.

The involvement of family in Samsung, while substantial, is surpassed by Lucky–Gold Star. The third largest *chaebol*, Lucky–Gold Star boasts one of the largest representation of family members in upper management. Almost all male members of the extended Ku family are active in the management of Lucky–Gold Star companies. All three surviving brothers of the late founder, Ku In Hoe, are active: Ku T'ae Hoe is the advisor to the *chaebol*, Ku P'yŏng Hoe is the president of Lucky–Gold Star International, and Ku Tu Hoe is the president of Yŏsu Energy and Honam Oil Refinery. Ku In Hoe, the founder, and his five brothers had twenty-eight sons. With the exception of the second son of Ku In Hoe who died and the fifth son of Ku In Hoe and the third son of Ku Chŏng Hoe (a brother of Ku In Hoe) who started their own businesses, all seventeen of these sons who are over the age of thirty-five are active in upper management. Ku Cha Kyŏng, the eldest son of the founder, was the second chair from 1970 to 1995. The third son, Cha Hak, is president of Gold Star Electron; the fourth son, Cha Tu, is vice president of Lucky–Gold Star Mart Co. (Bando Youth Hostel); and the youngest son, Cha Kŭk is the vice president of the U.S. branch office of Lucky–Gold Star. Also prominent are the Hŏ family members. Ku Cha Kyŏng's mother is from this family, and her brothers and male cousins are active in Lucky–Gold Star. The most prominent of them is Hŏ Chun Ku, who is the president of Gold Star Cable.

The Lucky–Gold Star *chaebol* has exercised "primogeniture" in its selection of chairs. The third chair, Ku Pon Mu, who succeeded this post from his father, Ku Cha Kyŏng, in February 1995, is the eldest son of Cha Kyŏng. And Cha Kyŏng was the eldest son of the founder, Ku In Hoe. Ku Pon Mu is the first of the grandsons of the founders of the ten largest *chaebol* to succeed the highest position within their *chaebol*. Defying the popular belief in Korea that family business cannot remain within the same family for more than three generations due to internal strife as well as external pressure and competition, the Lucky–Gold Star *chaebol* demonstrates solid control by the founding families. In order to make its image more modern, it recently changed its name to "LG Group," which is an acronym for Lucky–Gold Star.

The heavy involvement of family members in the management of Lucky–Gold Star is partly due to the large size of the Ku family. Ku In Hoe, the founder, had five brothers and ten children; of the brothers of Ku In Hoe, T'ae Hoe had six children, and Ch'ŏl Hoe had eight children; and Ku Cha Kyŏng, the

second chair had six children. Nevertheless, the large representation of family members in upper management more importantly reflects active recruitment and professional grooming of
family members for top management positions.

The Ku and Hŏ families are also well-known for their strict
adherence to the traditional values of Confucianism and patriarchy. The hierarchy within the Lucky–Gold Star *chaebol*
follows the rules of Confucianism and patriarchy. For example,
generational order and age matter in the organizational hierarchy and are reflected in the positions held by family
members. Public expression of dissension or betrayal of loyalty
to the family (or, for that matter, to the *chaebol*) is not allowed.
The Ku and Hŏ women, to which both Confucianism and
patriarchy relegate a submissive and minor role, are strictly
prohibited from taking an active role in the *chaebol's* management. None of the Ku or Hŏ wives are allowed to visit the
offices or make unnecessary phone calls to their husbands at
work (Seoul Kyŏngje Shinmun 1991:67).

Daewoo is somewhat different from the three *chaebol* that I
have described. Daewoo's founder and chair, Kim Wu Chung,
has one daughter and three sons (the eldest son was killed in an
automobile accident in 1989 during his study at MIT). Kim's children, who are younger than the offspring of the other *chaebol*
founders, are not in training to succeed him. Neither are Kim's
siblings (four brothers and one sister) currently actively involved
in the management and ownership of Daewoo. The notable
exception is Kim's wife, Chŏng Hŭi Cha, who is president of the
Seoul Hilton Hotel (Dongwoo Development Co., Ltd.).

Kia is truly an exception to the rule of family-ownership
and family-management. Kim Sang Mun, the son of the
founder, relinquished his position as chair in 1982. Kia has
been entirely run by professional managers since then. First by
Min Kyŏng Chŏng from 1982 to 1990, and by Kim Sŏn Hong
from 1990 to present.

The expansion of the *chaebol*, and the growing number of
member companies, made it inevitable to train and recruit
professional managers who are not members of the founder's
family. In an effort to sustain a familistic character, recruitment
based on personal ties has been widely practiced. A study by

Shin and Chin (1989) shows that the board of directors are connected by ties of family, region of birth, and high school affiliation. Of these ties, those of family were the most important. There was a definite hierarchical order: the first tier of managers was dominated by family members, while the second tier was recruited by the first tier from among high school and college alumnae and those from the same hometown.

Such patterns of recruitment and hierarchical circles of management were also evident in Korean businesses during the Japanese colonial period (McNamara 1990). Western-based modernization theorists have viewed such recruitment practices as personalistic and an impediment to modernization. However, these practices may be advantageous in societies where such ties can serve as a means of social control (C. S. Kim 1992).

C. S. Kim's study of a midsized *chaebol*, Poongsan [P'ungsan], revealed that only 7 percent of its managing executives were hired through an open competition (Ibid.:87). In contrast, over 90 percent of upper-level managers were recruited based on "connections." These connections refer to family and kinship networks and school ties (Ibid.). In the case of Poongsan, even in the open competition hiring, one of three qualities sought by the employer was whether the prospective employee was "group-oriented rather than individualistic" (Ibid.:89). This type of screening promotes a more familistic environment in the workplace. In other words, even if the workers are not related by family ties, they are expected to act like members of a family, in which survival of the group as a whole takes precedence over cut-throat competition between members.

Janelli (1993) also reports of a group-oriented environment in one of the four largest *chaebol* in South Korea. In the business group Janelli studied, which he gives a pseudonym of "Taesŏng," after-hour socialization occurred regularly among coworkers, and workers organized a number of high school alumni associations and hobby groups (Ibid.). Janelli notes that these activities and groups fostered emotional ties between the coworkers and promoted a cooperative workplace (Ibid.).

Another important trend found in the large *chaebol* in order to keep the business in the family is the professionalization of family members. Unlike many founders of the *chaebol* who came from nonbusiness backgrounds and had little formal education, the second and third generations have a college education and, in many cases, receive overseas training in business management. Often, they are sent to the United States to earn a master's degree in business administration from prestigious business schools, such as Stanford, MIT, Harvard, Pennsylvania (Wharton), and Columbia. These second- and third-generation managers present a formidable force in the *chaebol* since they not only have the family ties but also the requisite training as professional managers. They are perceived to have significant advantages in terms of hiring and promotion to the top echelon of the *chaebol* management, compared to nonfamily professional managers. Therefore, although the expansion of the *chaebol* has resulted in the growth of nonfamily professional managers, the public's perception has been slow to change. The public still believes that the large *chaebol* are run by a small group of the founder's family members.

Family-based ownership, management, and recruitment are important traits of the *chaebol*. Although there is some variation in the extent of family-ownership and family-management, such as Kia being run by a professional manager, the predominant trend among the largest *chaebol* is strong familial control. Such family-ownership and family-management is a common practice in businesses in developing nations, especially during the early stage of economic growth (Leff 1978).

In a recent survey I conducted in South Korea, 44 percent of upper-level managers who worked in *chaebol* firms responded that inheritance of the family business was the most important reason for hiring family members.[7] Twenty-one percent responded that ease in control and management was the reason. As these findings indicate, a strong desire to keep the business in the family is an important motivator in the South Korean *chaebol*.

Such a desire to keep the business in the family may have been present in businesses in other nations. However, as Leff (1978) points out, the number of family-owned and family-managed businesses tend to decrease with economic development. Market trends and state policies, which make family-owned and family-managed business obsolete, include the following: the state's enactment of antitrust laws in order to curb price-fixing and other violations of fair trade by business groups; losing competitiveness to professionally run businesses due to lack of professional managerial training in family-run businesses; and reluctance of family-run businesses to open themselves to potential stockholders for business expansion. As a result, many family-owned and family-managed businesses had to separate family ownership from management or otherwise be defeated in the competition.

However, in South Korea, the developmental state went against such trends, and instead it actively promoted the ownership and management practices of the *chaebol*. First, the state provided low-interest loans for the *chaebol*'s expansion, so that the founder's family could retain the majority ownership of their businesses. Second, the inheritance law allowed the businesses to be held within the family without excessive tax burdens. And finally, the antitrust law, which was first promulgated in the early 1980s, was probably too late to curb the expansion of the largest *chaebol*, which were already disproportionately larger than other businesses. There is also widespread belief in South Korea that the antitrust law has been ineffective in controlling the expansion of the *chaebol*. This statement was shared by an EPB official I interviewed.

Flexibility in Mobilizing and Exchanging Capital, Technology, and Personnel among Member Companies

A system of strong, centralized control allows a *chaebol* to be very efficient in decision making and information delivery in spite of its huge size. Unlike the Japanese *zaibatsu*, or *keiretsu*, where consensus decision making is advocated (although rarely practiced in a true sense of democratic decision making), there is no mention of such an ideal in the South Korean *chaebol*. The relationship between the chair and the member companies is like that of father and sons in a Confucian society, one in which the father has complete authority over his sons. The flexibility and speed come from the fact that the father makes and executes his decisions without consulting others.

Among the practices that enhances the flexibility of the *chaebol* is the mobilizing and transferring of personnel between member companies. It is common for high-ranking personnel to be transferred, often to head a member company that has a high-growth profile or else is ailing. In addition, the successor to the chair is often trained in many companies within the group in order to broaden his knowledge of operations and to allow him to interact with managers of as many member companies as possible. Such transferring of personnel appears to occur more frequently at the top managerial level.

Member companies of a *chaebol* frequently pool their resources for key services. Research and development are often coordinated between companies, and expenses and even laboratory space may be shared. Although the ownership of companies is maintained separately, the transfer of immediate cash funds can be arranged through financial-service and insurance companies, and companies can provide each other with loans without going through complicated bureaucratic procedures.

An important example of the *chaebol*'s ability to coordinate effectively their business activities is the General Trading Company (GTC). During the State of the Nation message in January 1975, President Park made an announcement that the new goal for the South Korean economy was "$10 billion in exports by the year 1978." This became the core of a massive government campaign during that year, with billboards plastered throughout the nation with that message. Following the president's address, the Ministry of Trade and Industry proposed specific plans to attain this goal, which included the coordination of exports by each business group and the creation of the GTC to support such coordination activities. The GTCs are modeled after Japan's *sogo shosha* (general trading company), but with some differences. For example, the South Korean GTCs coordinated predominantly export activities (88.2% of their work was in exports in 1980), while the Japanese *sogo shosha* coordinated largely domestic sales (46.4% of their work in 1980) with a relatively small role in exports (19.1% in 1980) (T. S. Cho 1988:82).

The law on the General Trading Companies was promulgated in April 1975, and thirteen GTCs were granted licenses by the Ministry of Trade and Industry. Of these, twelve belonged to the large *chaebol*, while only one was established specifically to coordinate export activities for non-*chaebol* affiliated small- and medium-sized enterprises. The *chaebol*-owned GTCs[8] are as follows (the date on the left in parenthesis is the date of establishment; the date on the right is the date when its license was revoked): Samsung Co., Ltd. (May 19, 1975); Ssangyong Corporation (May 27, 1975); Daewoo Corporation (May 27, 1975); Kukje Corporation[9] (November 13, 1975); Hanil Synthetic Textiles (December 30, 1975/1980); Hyosŏng Corporation (August 24, 1976); Bando Corporation[10] (November 22, 1976); Sun Kyong [Sŏn Kyŏng] Corporation (November 23, 1976); Samwha Corporation (December 6, 1976/1980); Kŭmho Corporation (November 15, 1976/ 1984); Hyundai Corporation (February 11, 1978); and Yulsan Corporation (February 11, 1978/1979) (T. S. Cho 1988:49; Maeil Kyŏngje Shinmun 1988). Korea Trading International received a GTC license from the Ministry of Trade and Industry on April 29, 1976, to explicitly help coordinate export activities for the small- and medium-sized enterprises (T. S. Cho 1988:49).

The GTCs played a key role in promoting exports, especially in the largest *chaebol*. The largest *chaebol*, which were already comfortably larger in size than other independent enterprises, received an additional boost with the licensing of GTCs. Partly as a result, the large *chaebol* dominated exports, in spite of the fact that a separate trading company was established for the small- and medium-sized enterprises. This is directly attributable to the fact that there were twelve GTCs allowed to coordinate exports within the *chaebol*, while there was only one GTC devoted to all the small- and medium-sized enterprises. This favorable treatment of the *chaebol* resulted in producing one of the important differences between exports in South Korea versus Japan—namely, in the former, exports are largely the domain of large business groups, while in the latter, exports are largely done by small- and medium-sized enterprises (Amsden 1989; T. S. Cho 1988).

Flexibility in mobilizing and in exchanging capital, technology, and personnel gives the *chaebol* a tremendous advantage over other smaller companies with the varied pool of managers and other resources, greatly increasing efficiency.

Horizontal Diversification: Unusually Wide Range of Business Activities in Unrelated Sectors

Diversification into a large number of unrelated businesses is another trademark of the South Korean *chaebol*. As discussed earlier, the South Korean consumer cannot live even a day without directly interacting with products and services of the *chaebol*. Diversification appears to have grown stronger over time and is the greatest among the five largest *chaebol*. For example, Hyundai, which is known as the "heavy industry *chaebol*," began to invest in light industries in 1980. Samsung, which is famous for its light manufactured products in textiles and food products during the 1950s and 1960s, also shifted its investment emphasis from light manufacturing (66% of total assets in 1970) to heavy manufacturing. By 1983, Samsung's assets in heavy industries (33% of total assets) had exceeded those in light industries (17% of total assets) for the first time in its history (E. M. Kim 1991).

In general, large conglomerates tend to diversify into different businesses as they grow in size (Chandler [1989] and Mueller [1982] as quoted in Amsden 1989).[11] In most conglomerates in the United States and other advanced industrialized nations, diversification tends to occur in related sectors based on technical and technological expertise. What is unusual about South Korean *chaebol* is their diversification into *unrelated sectors*. Table 3.2 shows the diversification and growth of member companies for the four largest *chaebol*. By 1988, the four largest *chaebol* had diversified into all four sectors—light manufacturing, heavy manufacturing, financial services, and other services. For all of them, growth was most pronounced in heavy manufacturing and in financial services.

Three factors explain the growing diversification of the *chaebol*. First, diversification into different industrial sectors was an effective strategy for taking advantage of the state's shifting industrial policies. The state's target industrial sectors have received low-interest policy loans, preferential treatment in receiving foreign loan capital, as well as other protective measures. Such political incentives have pushed the *chaebol* to diversify into target sectors, even when they have perceived the market conditions to be not quite ripe for such industries. For

example, when the state promoted heavy and chemical industrialization in the early 1970s, there was some initial resistance
from the private sector (Koo & Kim 1992). However, when
generous subsidies were announced, large *chaebol* diversified
into heavy industries. By the end of the 1970s, nine out of the
ten largest *chaebol* had investments in these industries.

Second, diversification has been a strategy for gaining independence and autonomy from the state. The *chaebol* diversified
into nonbanking financial services (i.e., insurance, securities,
and short-term finance companies) in order to become less
dependent on the state for capital. This is because, unlike the
pre–WWII *zaibatsu*, the South Korean *chaebol* were prohibited
from owning banks during the 1960s and 1970s. In 1961, the
Park regime nationalized the country's banks in order to
consolidate state control over the economy and the *chaebol*.
The policy remained in effect until 1981, when partial privatization of banks was announced by the Ministry of Finance.
However, even under the liberalized law, the *chaebol* owners
and their families were barred from owning more than 8
percent of any bank stock (Federation of Korean Industries
1987). Thus, the nonbanking financial services of the *chaebol*
have not only been lucrative, but, more importantly, they have
allowed flexibility in cash flow for member companies and
ready access to loans within the group. Recognizing these
advantages, by the mid-1980s, eight of the ten largest *chaebol*
owned at least one nonbanking financial institution (Management Efficiency Research Institute 1988).

Also contributing to the *chaebol*'s autonomy from the state
are its independent research and development centers. Many of
the largest *chaebol* currently have their own research and development facilities. The Federation of Korean Industries (FKI)[12]
also has its own economic research institute, which publishes
periodicals, reports, and books on various aspects of both the
domestic and international economies. The FKI was first organized with the Park regime's blessing. Despite this amicable
relation with the state, which could hamper its autonomy from
the state, FKI has become bolder in voicing its opinions and
objections to state policies. (See chapter 6 for a discussion about
FKI in the 1980s and its growing autonomy from the state.)

Table 3.2

Diversification of the Four Largest *Chaebol*, 1971–94

		HYUNDAI		
Sectors	Light Manufacturing	Heavy Manufacturing	Financial Services	Other Services
1971 (5)[a]		1. Hyundai Motors 2. Hyundai Cement	1. Eastern Marine & Fire Insurance	1. Hyundai Eng. & Construction 2. Keumkang
Share of Assets[b]	0.0%	45.5%	3.6%	50.8%
1994 (33)[a]	1. Hyundai Wood	1. Hyundai Electronics 2. Hyundai Motor 3. Hyundai Heavy Ind. 4. Hyundai Precision 5. Inchon Iron & Steel 6. Hyundai Pipe 7. Hyundai Mipo Dockyard 8. Hyundai Elevator 9. Hyundai Aluminum 10. KEFICO Corp. 11. Hyundai Petrochemical 12. Hyundai Oil Refinery 13. Koryeo Dev.	1. Hyundai Marine & Fire Insurance 2. Hyundai Securities 3. Hyundai Finance Management 4. Kangwon Bank	1. Hyundai Corp 2. Hyundai Eng. & Construction 3. Hyundai Merchant Marine 4. Hyundai Motor Service 5. Keumkang Dev. 6. Hyundai Engineering 7. Suneel Shipping 8. Hyundai Investment Management

Table 3.2 (continued)

HYUNDAI (continued)

Sectors	Light Manufacturing	Heavy Manufacturing	Financial Services	Other Services
				9. Seil Petroleum
				10. Trade Center
				Hyundai: Dept. Store
				11. Youngjin Petroleum
				12. Hyundai Const. Equip. Service
				13. Hyundai Munwha Newspaper
				14. Diamond AD
Share of Assets[b]	1.1%	55.6%	12.9%	30.4%

Table 3.2 (continued)

SAMSUNG

Sectors	Light Manufacturing	Heavy Manufacturing	Financial Services	Other Services
1971 (11)[a]	1. Cheil Sugar 2. Cheil Wool 3. Chonju Paper Ind. 4. Donglip Ind.	1. Samsung Electronics 2. Samsung Electron Devices	1. Samsung Life Insurance 2. Ankuk Fire & Marine Insurance	1. Samsung Co. 2. Joong-ang Dev. 3. Shinsegae Dept. Store
Share of Assets[b]	62.8%	10.8%	20.1%	6.3%
1994 (44)[a]	1. Cheil Sugar 2. Cheil Syn. Textile 3. Cheil Wool 4. Hi Creation 5. Cheil Frozen Foods	1. Samsung Electronics 2. Samsung Electron Devices 3. Samsung Electro-mechanics 4. Shin-Etsu Silicon 5. Samsung Ship & Heavy Industries 6. Samsung Corning 7. Samsung Petrochemical 8. Samsung Aerospace Ind. 9. Samsung Clark 10. Samsung General Chemicals 11. Daehan Specialty Chemicals	1. Samsung Life Insurance 2. Samsung Fire & Marine Insurance 3. Samsung Winners Card 4. Samsung Securities	1. Samsung Co. 2. Samsung Construction 3. Shinsegae Dept. Store 4. Joong-ang Daily Newspaper 5. Hotel Shilla 6. Joong-ang Development 7. Samsung Engineering 8. Korea First Advertising

Table 3.2 (continued)

SAMSUNG (continued)

Sectors	Light Manufacturing	Heavy Manufacturing	Financial Services	Other Services
		12. Cheil Ciba-Geigy 13. Samsung Specialty Chemicals 14. Kwang Ju Electronics 15. Samsung Watch 16. Hanil Electric Wire 17. Samsung Medical Systems 18. Samsung Kloekner		9. Westin Chosun Seoul 10. Samsung Data 11. Korea Info. Computing 12. Samsung Lions 13. Yonpo Leisure Dev. 14. Daekyung Bldg. Mgmt. 15. Sam Tech. 16. Cheil Bozell 17. Samsung Investment Consulting
Share of Assets[b]	6.3%	39.1%	42.1%	12.5%

Table 3.2 (continued)

		DAEWOO		
Sectors	Light Manufacturing	Heavy Manufacturing	Financial Services	Other Services
1971 (3)[a]	1. Koryo Leather		1. Hankook Investment	1. Daewoo Corp.
Share of Assets[b]	7.6%	0.0%	13.3%	79.1%
1994 (19)[a]		1. Daewoo Electronics 2. Daewoo Telecom 3. Orion Electric 4. Daewoo Precision 5. Daewoo Electronic Components 6. Daewoo Motor 7. Daewoo Heavy Ind. 8. Daewoo Automotive Components 9. Daewoo Electric Motor Ind. 10. Koram Plastics 11. Orion Electric Parts 12. Korea A–B	1. Daewoo Securities	1. Daewoo Corp. 2. Kyungnam Enterprises 3. Dongwoo Dev. 4. Daewoo Capital Management 5. Daewoo Info. Systems 6. Dongwoo Management Consulting
Share of Assets[b]	0.0%	60.2%	9.0%	30.8%

Table 3.2 (continued)

LUCKY-GOLD STAR

Sectors	Light Manufacturing	Heavy Manufacturing	Financial Services	Other Services
1971 (9)[a]		1. Lucky, Ltd. 2. Gold Star Co. 3. Gold Star Cable 4. Gold Star Telecommunications 5. Gold Star Electric 6. Honam Oil Refinery 7. Hankuk Mineral Refinery 8. Gold Star-Alps Electronics		1. Lucky-Gold Star Corp.
Share of Assets[b]	0.0%	95.6%	0.0%	4.4%
1994 (53)[a]		1. LG Co. Ltd. 2. LG Cable 3. LG Semiconductor 4. LG Telecommunications 5. LG Instrument & Electric 6. LG Electric Machinery 7. Gold Star Electric	1. LG Securities 2. Lucky Insurance 3. LG Investment & Finance 4. LG Credit Card Co. 5. Boomin Mutual	1. LG International 2. Global Petroleum 3. Hoyu Energy 4. LG Engineering 5. Systems Tech. Management 6. LG Ad. Inc. 7. LG Software 8. LG Sports

Table 3.2 (continued)

LUCKY-GOLD STAR (continued)

Sectors	Light Manufacturing	Heavy Manufacturing	Financial Services	Other Services
		8. Gold Star Electronic Devices		9. LG-Hitachi System
		9. Kukje Electric Wire		10. LG Construction
		10. LG Precision		11. Hoyu Sales
		11. LG-Honeywell		12. LG Distribution
		12. LG Foster		13. Hoyu Marine Shipping
		13. LG Micronics		14. LG Kigong
		14. Sungyo Co.		15. Hammu Development
		15. Honam Oil Refinery		16. LG Leisure
		16. Lucky Metals Corp.		
		17. LG Petrochemical		
		18. LG Chemicals		
		19. LG-Owens Corning		
		20. LG Aligned Signal		
		21. LG MMA		
		22. Siltron Inc.		
Share of Assets[b]	0.0%	64.2%	17.3%	18.5%

Notes: a. Total number of firms.
b. Percentage shares of total assets in each sector.

Sources: E. M. Kim 1987; Bankers Trust Securities Research 1989; Shin Sanŏp Kyŏngyŏngwŏn 1996.

Lastly, diversification into unrelated sectors has been a strategy that has enabled the *chaebol* to take advantage of the lower and middle ranges of the international market and to overcome a lack of technical and technological expertise (Amsden 1989:125–29). Amsden (Ibid.) argues that the South Korean economy in general, and the *chaebol* in particular, pursued a strategy of diversification into unrelated sectors due to their cheap and abundant labor force, which allowed their products to be price-competitive, rather than quality-competitive, in the international marketplace. Diversification, thus, allowed the *chaebol* to diffuse risk and to exploit one of its economic advantages—a vast pool of cheap and low- and semi-skilled labor.

Comparison of the South Korean Chaebol to Japanese and Taiwanese Businesses

The early South Korean *chaebol* shared many features with their model, pre–World War II Japanese *zaibatsu*. The *zaibatsu* influenced the initial make-up of the *chaebol*, as they were an important business presence since the signing of the Kangwha Treaty in 1876 and throughout the Japanese colonial period (1910–45).[13] The pre–World War II *zaibatsu* and the *chaebol* share the following traits.[14] First, the *zaibatsu* and the *chaebol* are both family-owned and family-managed. Second, their businesses diversified into a wide range of unrelated sectors. In Japan, the largest *zaibatsu* were prominent in industrial manufacturing (especially in heavy manufacturing) as well as in banking. Their control of the industrial and financial sectors put them at a tremendous advantage relative to other domestic businesses. In South Korea, the largest *chaebol* have also diversified into unrelated sectors in manufacturing (both in light and heavy manufacturing), and in services except banks, which were nationalized in 1961. Finally, a minor note of interest: the Chinese characters used to write *zaibatsu* and the *chaebol* are identical. Only the pronunciation is different.

On the other hand, there are two qualitatively distinctive features that differentiate the *chaebol* from the *zaibatsu*. First, the *chaebol* do not own banks. Banks were nationalized by President Park in 1961 until the early 1980s, and the *chaebol* were prohib-

ited from owning banks. The privatization of the banks in the
1980s restricted the *chaebol* from buying more than 8 percent of
the bank's stocks, thereby effectively barring the *chaebol* from
owning a bank. This prevented the *chaebol* from exercising the
kind of power and control possessed by the *zaibatsu* in the
domestic market before the end of World War II. The nationalization of banks in South Korea assured more room for state intervention in the market, since the *chaebol* had to rely on the state
for domestic loan capital. Second, in spite of, or in lieu of, the
prohibition of the *chaebol* from owning banks, the South Korean
state actively supported the expansion of the *chaebol*. The state
provided low-interest-rate loans targeted for export firms and for
the heavy- and chemical-manufacturing firms that were dominated by the large *chaebol*. Unlike in Japan or Taiwan, the largest
share of export products are manufactured by large firms that are
members of the *chaebol*. And, as discussed earlier, family-ownership and family-management were actively supported by the
state through lenient inheritance taxes and antitrust laws that
were promulgated after two decades of uninterrupted growth of
the *chaebol*. Such active state support differentiates South Korea
from other nations, where family-run businesses become less
competitive with economic development.

South Korea's rapid economic development based on exports
is often lumped together with Taiwan's, as a new model of Third
World growth. However, there are significant differences in the
way the private sector is organized and in the state-business relations. First, in Taiwan, the state has allowed small- and medium-
sized enterprises to grow, while it has discouraged the growth of
privately owned large business groups (Cheng 1990; Ho 1982).
Restrictions on domestic loans imposed by the financial institutions made it difficult for the Taiwanese firms to grow based on
debt as was the case in South Korea (Cheng 1990). The Taiwanese
state has also been more aggressive in investing in state-owned
enterprises compared to South Korea. In 1987, four of the six
largest corporations in Taiwan were government-owned (Gereffi
1990:94–95). Thus, there are few large privately owned Taiwanese
businesses comparable to the South Korean *chaebol*.

Several reasons are given for this practice by studies from
different theoretical approaches. Culture-centered studies argue

that the traditional Chinese custom of inheritance, in which the wealth is relatively equally divided among the sons, tends to make it easier for family businesses to splinter off after only one generation (DeVos & Sofue 1984). This is accentuated by another traditional custom, in which sons leave the father's household upon marriage, except for the eldest son (Ibid.). This has made it more likely for the family fortune to be dispersed and for a myriad of small- and medium-sized enterprises to thrive.

Politics-centered studies provide a different explanation for the abundance of small- and medium-sized enterprises in Taiwan. These studies argue that the Kuo-Min-Tang (KMT: Chinese Nationalist Government) of Chiang Kai-shek, which was an exile government from mainland China, designed policies to discourage, if not prohibit, the Taiwanese from entering positions of power (e.g., government, parliament, and the military) and of wealth (e.g., large businesses), fearing that the Taiwanese might usurp power (Cheng 1990). The KMT allowed the Taiwanese to operate businesses; however, even in this case, ownership of large businesses was discouraged, and small- and medium-sized enterprises were promoted. The latter was deemed as a more effective way of controlling the private sector and preventing it from becoming a major social force (Ibid.). Therefore, the Chiang regime restricted access to domestic loans for business expansion and invested heavily in state-owned enterprises (Hamilton & Biggart 1988).

The situation in Taiwan has changed quite a bit since the early days of the Chiang regime. The government, parliament, and the military have become more open to the Taiwanese. Several firms have become large business groups due to their tremendous success in the export business since the 1960s. But, this success was achieved *in spite of* the state, unlike in South Korea, where the *chaebol*'s success was in part due to the state's support. And unlike in South Korea, Taiwan is still dominated by a large number of small- and medium-sized enterprises with a relatively small number of large business groups.

In spite of the different composition of the private sector, Taiwanese and South Korean businesses appear to share a cultural trait, which is found in many Asian nations. They rely on personal ties to recruit employees and to conduct businesses. In Taiwan, this is called, *guanxi*, which translates to relationships, connections, or networks (Hamiton 1991; Hamilton & Biggart 1988). *Guanxi* appears to be a more encompassing concept than the personal ties utilized in South Korea. It refers to members of a family or kinship, school alumni, people who are born in the same region, or acquaintances of the just mentioned categories of people. Through *guanxi* one can have an immediate rapport and trust. The argument goes that people seek out others who are related by *guanxi* when looking for business partners, subcontractors, or employees (Hamilton 1991). This practice of hiring and doing business almost exclusively within the *guanxi* network was conducive in the small- and medium-sized enterprises in Taiwan. In comparison, the largest *chaebol* in South Korea cannot rely on hiring and doing business only with acquaintances due to their enormous size. The usage of *guanxi* in Taiwan has resulted in the relatively slow development of formal entrance exams for hiring, official contracts, and legal documents. In contrast, in South Korea due to the early expansion of business groups, formal entrance exams, contracts, and legal documents have been more widely used (Janelli 1993; C. S. Kim 1992).

The Historical and Structural Context of the *Chaebol*

What gave rise to the industrial organization known as the *chaebol*? In order to answer this question, we must look beyond the *chaebol* and to the broader domestic and international political and economic contexts, which are particularly salient for understanding industrial organizations in the Third World at the end of the twentieth century. Three factors in the historical and structural context that have influenced the industrial organizations in developing nations are (1) the state, (2) internationalization, and (3) colonialism.

The institutional approach to organizations offers a way of understanding the development of Third World industrial organizations in relation to the broader historical structural context. In particular, DiMaggio and Powell's (1983) study provides a very useful operationalization of the emergence of different types of industrial organizations as responses to the external environment. Their key thesis is that modern organizations have goals extending beyond internal efficiency, including institutional legitimacy, political power, and social fitness. In the process of attaining such goals, organizations undergo three mechanisms of institutional isomorphic change (Ibid.). The first is the process of *coercive isomorphism*, in which organizations are influenced by direct authority relationships. The expansion of the central state and centralization of capital are examples of institutions of influence. The second mechanism is *mimetic isomorphism*, which results from the organization's attempts to respond to uncertainties in its environment by mimicking existing organizational structures that have weathered the uncertainties. The last mechanism is *normative isomorphism*, which results from the professionalization of managers, either through widespread business and management education in universities or through the growth and elaboration of professional networks.

Taken together, the three factors in the structural historical context and the three mechanisms of isomorphic change can help explain why and how the *chaebol* became the dominant type of industrial organization in South Korea.

The State

The state and its interventionist policies in the market may play an important role in the formation and development of industrial organizations. Increasingly, the states in developing nations are taking leadership roles in their markets. In particular, the East Asian states have often created and changed (distorted) their markets and impacted upon the businesses that operate in them (Amsden 1989; Wade 1990). As Gerschenkron (1962) argued, this extensive and comprehensive state intervention is a distinctive characteristic of latecomer nations. Such heavy state intervention is a sharp departure from the experiences of many advanced industrialized nations in their early phases of development when government played a relatively confined and regulatory role in the market. Furthermore, the states in some developing East Asian nations have also been authoritarian, thus enabling them to effectively intervene in the market with little resistance. This appears to be particularly noticeable during the early stages of industrialization, when the state is considerably stronger than the private sector.

In the 1960s, the South Korean developmental state began to play an important role in shaping the industrial organization of the *chaebol*. The processes of mimetic and coercive isomorphism will help explain how the developmental state was able to influence the *chaebol*.

First, mimetic isomorphism is a process in which organizations mimic one another when there are uncertainties in the environment. The 1960s was a period of great uncertainties. The South Korean economy was still in the process of recovering from the devastating Korean War; the country was under the control of a military government following a coup; and the economic development plans of the new regime called for drastic restructuring of the economy. President Park's First Five-Year Economic Development Plan, which began in January 1962, required fundamental changes in the economy. Before 1961, it had been basically agrarian with relatively few manufacturing firms and a small number of mercantilist businesses (Mason et al. 1980). The development plan called for three major economic transformations: (1) from agriculture to industry; (2) from mercantilist activities to industrial manufacturing; and (3) from production for domestic consumption to exports. These changes were a drastic departure from the past and presented significant risks to the businesses. Therefore, the businesses mimicked each other's organization in the face of heightened risks.

Second, coercive isomorphism occurs when there is a centralization of resources. According to DiMaggio and Powell (1983), isomorphism could occur even when the centralized source of capital does not prescribe a particular type of industrial organization, since the organizations are all responding to the same stimulus in the environment. In the South Korean case, the state not only centralized the resources (domestic and foreign capital) but also promoted the large business group as a model industrial organization.

In 1961, the state nationalized the domestic banks, placing credit under state control. Thus, the *chaebol* and other private firms had no choice but to become dependent on the state for capital. Moreover, due to the military regime's lack of legitimacy and a sense of insecurity, all the economic development plans had to be implemented with swiftness before another coup could force the new regime out of office. In order to attain economic development in the shortest time possible, the *chaebol* and other large businesses were chosen as the state's partner. The Park regime believed that the economies of scale would help attain economic development faster than if it established state-owned enterprises or chose to work with small- and medium-sized enterprises.

The state used the nationalized banks in two ways: the first was to reward companies that conformed to state policies and the other was to attract firms into sectors in which they otherwise saw too little profit and too much risk. An example of the former policy was the low-interest-rate, no-strings-attached export loan given to firms that were successful in exports. This policy was prevalent in the 1960s, while the next decade was dominated by the second policy. For example, in the early 1970s, loans were provided to firms to invest in state-targeted heavy manufacturing industries (i.e., automobile, shipbuilding, chemical, iron and steel, nonferrous metal, and electronics and electrical appliances). And the *chaebol* dominated these industries, since they were the only ones who could invest in such capital- and technology-intensive sectors.

Foreign loan capital and foreign direct investment were also tightly controlled and closely monitored by the state (E. M. Kim 1989; Mardon 1990). The state was the primary recipient and distributor of public loans. Thus, a large share of public loans were invested in state enterprises. Forty-eight percent of public loans in 1959–79 and 63 percent in 1980–84 were invested in state-owned enterprises, which specialized in basic infrastructure and other services including electricity, gas, and water (E. M. Kim 1989:28). The state was also actively involved in the approval and appropriation of commercial loans during the 1960s. The state was able to supervise the appropriation of commercial loans, since it was responsible for repayment of 90 percent of all such loans during that period (Ibid.:31; *Shindonga* December 1968). As a result, between 1959 and 1981, three of six of the state's target industries, which were chemical, steel and metal, and transport-equipment, received over 40 percent of all commercial loans (E. M. Kim 1989:32). And these industries were also heavily dominated by the large *chaebol*.

To summarize, the *chaebol's* prevalence as an industrial organization can be explained by their relationship to the state and the broader environment. The businesses in South Korea responded to uncertainties in the international economy and the state's shifting industrial policies by emulating each other's industrial organization, among which the family-owned and family-managed *chaebol* was a prominent type. Moreover, the state's industry-specific loans during the 1970s, which were predominantly provided to the large *chaebol*, made it more compelling for other businesses to emulate the organization of the *chaebol*. Thus, in South Korea, the state played a very important, proactive role in making the *chaebol* a model for other businesses.

Internationalization

The internationalization that has occurred since the end of the World War II, and more specifically since the 1960s, has reshaped the ways in which business are conducted across national boundaries. Direct interaction between businesses in the advanced industrialized nations and Third World nations has not only increased in volume but has become an inevitable facet of the modern international economy. Advanced industrialized nations' and Third World nations' businesses routinely come into direct contact through trade, foreign direct investment, and technology transfers from MNCs. In sum, internationalization presents challenges to Third World industrial organizations that were not encountered by their counterparts in Western Europe and the United States during their initial stages of economic development.

There are three ways in which the international context helped shape the South Korean industrial organizations. First, the process of normative isomorphism helps explain how the South Korean businesses began to exhibit the free market ideology of U.S. education in economics and business administration.[15] Since the end of the Korean War, many South Koreans went to the United States for college and postgraduate education. In particular, many who went after the war majored in economics in order to help rebuild the war-torn economy. Later, business administration also became a popular major for South Korean students studying in the United States. These students returned to South Korea and worked in three areas: as faculty in the economics and business administration departments in major universities; as technocrats in the government ministries, including the Economic Planning Board, the Ministry of Finance, and the Ministry of Trade and Industry; and as managers of large businesses (Amsden 1994a). Thus, the influence of the "free market" ideology can be found in all three. In particular, this influence can be detected in the fact that South Korean businesses are not an exact clone of Japanese businesses and contain many Western business attributes (C. S. Kim 1992). Thus, the first process, in which the international context affects the South Korean industrial organizations, is through normative isomorphism, whereby organizations resemble each other through education and socialization of professional managers.

Second, direct contacts with MNCs and other foreign corporations can affect the industrial organizations. Coercive isomorphism, in which the centralization of resources results in the emulation of industrial organization, can address the role played by MNCs. MNCs were an important source of foreign capital and technology for South Korean businesses. The influence of the MNCs may not be as great as the state in South Korea, since MNCs are far more heterogeneous than the state, and their activities are restricted by the South Korean state as well as their home nation's policies. Nonetheless, the South Korean businesses were affected by MNCs and developed offices and jobs that were specifically designed to help conduct businesses with them.

Japan-based MNCs had a particularly important effect on South Korean businesses, which were recipients of Japanese direct investments and technology transfers. Between 1981 and 1990, Japanese corporations provided over $2.8 billion in direct investment to South Korean corporations, comprising 45.5 percent of total foreign direct investment (National Statistical

Office 1991:232). This compared favorably to the United States's investment of over \$1.8 billion, which was roughly 30 percent of all direct foreign investment during the same period (Ibid.). Aside from the obvious influence of Japanese corporations through investment and technology transfers, South Korean managers and workers were also aware of the impact of Japanese corporations on their industrial organization. A midlevel manager of Hyundai Motor Company, Mr. I Chong Yŏn, spoke of the influence of Hyundai Motor's Japanese investor, Mitsubishi.[16]

> Mitsubishi does not have a permanent executive director at Hyundai. But, it does have a non-permanent executive director. Mitsubishi does not directly intervene in management. However, they are interested with the results of management.
> We have two established meetings per year with Mitsubishi. One is held in Japan, and the other one is held in Korea. We discuss issues on an equal level. Our discussions include the following issues: cooperation at the foremen level; improvement of the success cases; productivity increase cases; cases in which each party could learn and improve.
> To deal with the executive director from Mitsubishi and the bi-yearly meetings, we [Hyundai Motor Company] have developed counterpart offices.

This interview indicates that even though the foreign investor was not involved in the daily management of the corporation, the subsidiary still had to reorganize to meet the demands of the former. New offices were created or new functions were assigned to existing offices in the subsidiary.

This manager also spoke about the influence of the Japanese corporation at the foremen level. This is revealing of the foreign investor's indirect influence through shared technical manuals and sense of common culture. The following is in response to my question about why Hyundai Motor Company decided to work with a Japanese corporation rather than a U.S. firm, as it did during the 1960s with the Ford Motor Company:

I think Westerners look down upon Asians. They are not sure what we Asians are capable of doing with the technology. Western experts have told us that our level of technology and industrial structure are not adequate for automobile production.

There are several reasons why we chose to work with Japan. First, there is the cultural similarity. Second, they are close by. And lastly, the most important reason is their *after service*. After service by Japanese companies is far superior than that of Western companies. For example, service from U.S. and European companies tends to be bad, and we [Koreans] are supposed to pay for the after service. On the other hand, we don't have to pay much for air transportation for the Japanese, and they come almost immediately when we notify them of any problem.

Besides, it is easy to learn Japanese. Its much easier than learning Western languages. In terms of technology, we tend to depend on Japanese products, since quality, trust, and after service are far superior than their European and U.S. counterparts. The Japanese workers who are stationed in Korea already speak Korean. On the other hand, Americans never learn any Korean when they come over here. For technical manuals, it is also easier to read them in Japanese. Even high-school graduates who work as technicians seem to have little difficulty in reading and comprehending Japanese manuals. For management and technology, we tend to study the Japanese books much more than English books.

A manager of Kia Motors, a major competitor of Hyundai Motors, also echoed the sentiment expressed by the Hyundai manager. Mr. Chŏng ŭi Hŏn of Kia discussed why Kia was working with Japan's Mazda, rather than with the Ford Motors of the United States during my interview with him on June 20, 1990, from 10:30 A.M.–12:00 noon, at his office at Kia Motors headquarters in Seoul. He said:

First of all, the founder of Kia, Mr. Kim Ch'ŏl Ho had previous working experience with the Japanese in the iron and steel industry. I think Mr. Kim's familiarity with Japan was important when he made the decision to work with Mazda rather than Ford. From my perspective, there are several concrete advantages in working with Mazda. First, the Japanese provide much better after service compared to the U.S. companies. Compared to the Americans who took much longer to respond to our queries and required us to navigate a complicated bureaucracy to receive assistance, the Japanese were much faster to respond to our calls. Furthermore, the Japanese were very precise in their diagnosis and prognosis, and the rate of correction higher. Secondly, U.S. companies were troubled by many labor unrests, which we thought, were undermining the quality and delivery time of their products. Thirdly, we found that the U.S.-made products were sturdy, but that the Japanese-made products were more precise. Although German products were also precise, we decided to go with the Japanese since the geographical proximity helped us to cut costs, and cultural similarity made them easier to work with. And finally, we found the Japanese were much more flexible. They were not only faster but more responsive to our needs.

Mr. Kim Yŏng T'ae of Korea Diesel Industries, which also worked with a Japanese company but was a non-*chaebol* independent medium-sized enterprise told similar stories about why his company works with a Japanese company:[17]

I think the main reason why we emulate the Japanese is because South Koreans want to grow quickly, and the Japanese provides us with a tangible model. In my company, we decided to work with the Japanese because Japan is geographically close to us, because it is easier to learn Japanese than other Western languages, and because there is little cultural differences. In fact, many in the upper management, who have experienced the

Japanese colonial period, still feel comfortable with the Japanese language and culture.

These interviews imply how an MNC affects a subsidiary's organizational structure and functions. In particular, these interviews reveal why high-level managers often decide to work with a Japanese company for FDI or technology transfers. Cultural similarity and ease in learning the language all contribute to this selection. As aptly summarized in Mr. Kim's remark, many South Korean businesses emulate the Japanese companies from which they receive technology or capital.

The case of Hyundai Motor Company and Kia Motors could be placed in the middle of a continuum in terms of MNCs' influence and control of their subsidiaries from complete managerial control by MNCs to loose cooperation with MNCs. The share of ownership and management ideology of the MNC appear to be important factors in determining the level of the MNC's involvement in the management of its subsidiary.

Colonial Legacy

Colonialism can leave lasting legacies on a former colony. For example, an unequal (and often exploitative) relationship between the colonizer and colony can linger on for decades after the formal dismantling of colonialism. And the colonizer's imprint on domestic political and economic institutions can linger on long after the departure of the colonizers (Eckert 1991; McNamara 1990; Woo 1991). This is particularly true when the colony did not have any indigenous institutions or if such institutions were destroyed under colonial rule. However, the effects of colonialism can also be weakened if there are critical breaks after the liberation and/or if there are significant changes in the political and economic leadership and in the economic and political institutions.

Japanese colonialism (1910–45) left an indelible mark on the Korean economy. Among its legacies were a strong state that intervened heavily in the economy and the industrial organization of the *zaibatsu*. These shaped the character of the state and the *chaebol*, as well as the relationship between them.

The dual economic structure, which was put in place by the Japanese, left the divided Korean peninsula in an economic chaos following the liberation in 1945 and became the predicament each economy had to overcome in future decades. The dual economic structure refers to the heavy industries and hydroelectricity generating plants developed in the north and agriculture and light industries in the south by the Japanese colonial government. The northern and southern regions of the Korean peninsula, thus, were not self-sufficient. Each was heavily dependent on the other for basic energy or for food and consumer nondurable products. South Korea has been successful in overcoming this regional dualism by developing both the light and heavy industries. On the other hand, North Korea has not been able to develop the consumer nondurable light industries, due to the industrial structure left behind from the colonial period and the North Korean government's emphasis on building the defense industry.

In 1945 when South Korea was liberated from Japanese colonial rule, its economy experienced a near breakdown. The massive departure of Japanese managers and technicians from Korea paralyzed its factories. The return of more than 2 million Koreans from labor camps and overseas factories further jeopardized this weak economy. Production fell dramatically and prices soared. From June 1945 to December 1949, the number of manufacturing firms decreased by nearly 50 percent, dropping from 9,323 to 5,249; employment in manufacturing declined by nearly 60 percent, falling from 300,520 to 122,159 (*Hanguk Ilbo* April 6, 1991). In 1947–48, manufacturing output was only 15 percent of the level achieved in 1939 (Mason et al. 1980:77). The economy was in complete chaos, and the economic outlook was bleak.

The process of mimetic isomorphism (DiMaggio & Powell 1983) can help explain the adoption of the *chaebol* as the major industrial organization following the Japanese colonial period. Mimetic isomorphism speaks to the uncertainties in the environment and to how those influence organizations to adopt an existing industrial organization in order to minimize risks (Ibid.). In the chaotic aftermath of the colonial rule, it is not difficult to understand why many newly established South

Korean businesses adopted features of the *zaibatsu*—the only form of modern business they had known.

Furthermore, many Koreans had acquired some work experience in the *zaibatsu*, albeit limited to low-level technical jobs or clerical positions. This is because the Japanese colonial government had barred the *zaibatsu* from hiring Koreans in upper-management positions or in high-level technical jobs (Jones & Sakong 1980; Mason et al. 1980). Several future *chaebol* owners gained their first experience in a modern enterprise by working as a low-level technician or a clerical worker for a *zaibatsu*. The founder of the Sunkyong *chaebol*, Ch'oe Chong Kŭn, worked as a technician in the Japanese-owned Sunkyong Textiles before he acquired it from the Korean government in 1953. Haitai's cofounder, Pak Pyŏng Kyu, was employed as a clerical worker in the Japanese-owned Yŏng Kang Confectionery Company before the end of the war. He and two of his coworkers founded Haitai [Haet'ae] Confectionery Company in 1945. Another future founder of a major *chaebol*, Kim Chŏng Hŭi, worked as a chief clerk of a dynamite division in a Japanese explosives company. He later acquired the company, and it became the core company for the Korea Explosives *chaebol*, which was the tenth-largest *chaebol* in 1991 (*Hanguk Ilbo* April 6, 1991; Management Efficiency Research Institute 1992). Thus, when many of these inexperienced men took over their former employer's businesses, they crudely imitated the practices of the *zaibatsu*. Although they did not have much background in management, they became quick studies as they literally walked into the offices and factories, which contained the files, manuals, machinery, and equipment left behind by the Japanese when they fled after World War II.

However, the colonial legacy in South Korea should not be exaggerated. It played an important role in the initial setup of the *chaebol*, but that influence waned over time and with major breaks in South Korea's political and economic history. First, the Korean War (1950–53) destroyed the bases of wealth for many South Korean industrial and landed capitalists. To begin with, relatively few capitalists survived the colonial period, since the colonial government had various measures to hinder the growth of Korean-owned and Korean-managed firms, at which it was quite successful. The small number of the colonial period's Korean firms were further assaulted when houses and factories were burned and destroyed during the Korean War. By the end of the Korean War, many of the colonial period businesses were severely damaged. In the place of the colonial period capitalists, a new group of mercantile entrepreneurs flourished, who took advantage of the chaotic war economy. Second, the Park Chung Hee regime and his economic development plans effectively changed the map of the South Korean businesses. By the end of the 1960s, older colonial period and post–Korean War *chaebol* were phased out as a new group of *chaebol* emerged (see chapter 4 for details). These new chaebol continue to dominate the South Korean economy even today.

The Korean War and President Park's ambitious Five-Year Economic Development Plans brought an end to several colonial period *chaebol*, including Tai Han [Tae Han] and Gaipoong [Kaep'ung]. Furthermore, the current influences of Japanese businesses appear to be largely due to more recent practices of joint ventures with, and technology transfers from, Japanese corporations since the signing of the 1965 Normalization Treaty between South Korea and Japan.

Concluding Remarks

The *chaebol* and the state are two engines of South Korean development. Although the state exerted greater influence on the *chaebol* during the early stages of economic development than vice versa, these two institutions are equally important in understanding the South Korean success story. The alliance formed between the strong developmental state and big business groups in South Korea helped bring about rapid economic development. The economies of scale achieved by utilizing large business groups enabled South Korea to jump-start its economy toward export-oriented industrialization in the early 1960s. The large business groups and the state's tremendous financial support of them, enabled South Korea to move forward from light industries to heavy and chemical industries in the early 1970s, when many scholars, policymakers and businesspeople were skeptical.

The utilization of large business groups for economic development differentiates South Korea among its allies in the Gang of Four. Taiwan, in particular, has relied more on small- and medium-sized enterprises. Taiwan was also very successful in export-oriented industrialization since the 1960s but less so in transforming the economy toward heavy industries. Taiwanese companies also do not enjoy the brand-name recognition like the South Korean *chaebol*.

In this chapter, the main organizational attributes of the *chaebol* were examined. They were: (1) family ownership and management; (2) flexibility in mobilizing and in exchanging capital, technology, and personnel among member firms; and (3) horizontal diversification into unrelated businesses. What emerged from these discussions was an industrial organization, which combined the traditional values of Confucianism and patriarchy, with modern business practices similar to Western enterprises.

The second part of this chapter focused on the domestic and international political and economic factors that helped the *chaebol* become a dominant industrial organization. The state, internationalization, and the colonial legacy were discussed as main factors that contributed to the *chaebol*'s ascendance in the domestic and international markets. DiMaggio and Powell's (1983) theory of isomorphic change was used to illustrate the causes and processes, in which the *chaebol* became an organizational type many South Korean businesses aspired to imitate.

However, South Korea's reliance on the *chaebol* to achieve rapid economic growth did not come without a price. The workers were an important group that was sacrificed in the process: they endured low wages, poor working conditions, and severe restrictions on labor mobilization. These issues are discussed in chapter 6.

The growing prosperity of *chaebol* owners and their families also has become a source of social tension. The *chaebol* families have amassed huge amounts of capital, in the face of meager wages paid to the workers. The growing inequality of wealth between the super-wealthy *chaebol* families and the middle and working classes has become a social problem. Furthermore, the perception (and, in some cases, a reality) that the *chaebol* accumulated their fortune through speculative and nonproductive investments and by unjust and collusive relations with politicians has angered the middle and working classes. These issues are also discussed in chapter 6.

Lastly, the tremendous growth of the *chaebol* also poses an important question in the understanding of the dialectic process of development. The *chaebol*, which owe much of their prosperity (at least during the 1960s and 1970s) to the state, have become a formidable social class that began to ask for reduction of state intervention in the economy in the 1980s. Instead of a developmental state, the *chaebol* demanded a protectionist state, which would continue to provide subsidies but stop the heavy-handed control in the market. The irony is that the developmental state played a large role in creating its challenger.

In Part II, I examine in greater detail how the two institutions of the state and *chaebol*, and the relations between them, changed in the process of economic development: how the state shaped the society and its members to bring about economic development in the 1960s following the military coup in 1961 (chapter 4); how the state and the *chaebol* grew together and how their relations intensified during the 1970s (chapter 5); and how the *chaebol* and labor began to challenge the state in the 1980s (chapter 6).

Part II
History of Development

4

The State and the Remaking
of the Chaebol (1960s)

South Korea's remarkable "rags to riches" story of economic growth during the 1960s is a powerful example of effective state intervention. Contrary to arguments made by advocates of the free market, the changes in the 1960s were clearly led by the state. A comprehensive developmental state was established, and it initiated a series of successful Five-Year Economic Development Plans with export as the newly chosen strategy for industrialization. The state formed a tight working alliance with large businesses. The state disciplined the private sector to conform to its policies by using an effective mix of carrots-and-sticks. This alliance brought forth real economic growth for the nation rather than rent-seeking and corruption as had been in the previous regimes. By the end of the decade, a new group of successful *chaebol* emerged, which included only a few from the 1950s. By 1970, GNP per capita rose to $266.72 from $82 in 1961, an average annual growth rate of 12.6 percent since 1961 (EPB 1978). GNP increased nearly fourfold from $2.33 billion in 1961 to $8.60 billion in 1970 (Ibid.). Over 13 percent of the labor force was working in the industrial sector by 1970 (Ibid.).

The most remarkable growth was in exports, which grew from $53 million to $1,227 million (Ibid.). Furthermore, the composition of export products changed from primarily agricultural and natural resources (86 percent) to largely manufactured products (83.6 percent) (EPB 1978; International Monetary Fund 1979).

This chapter examines the changes that took place in the state, the relations between the state and businesses, and the businesses during the 1960s. The first section of the chapter focuses on the establishment of a comprehensive developmental state, which was simultaneously an authoritarian state. The second section focuses on the ways in which the state demonstrated its authority to the *chaebol* and workers. The nature of the state-business and state-labor relations is explored through an examination of the charges of illicit accumulation of wealth and labor laws. The last part of this chapter addresses the question of how dependent the *chaebol* were to the state. Many state-centered studies of South Korea's development argue that the private sector was a mere puppet of the state. However, evidence in that section will suggest that even during the 1960s, when the state was clearly dominant, the *chaebol* had some limited autonomy. This is a crucial argument of the book: the state and the *chaebol* are separate institutions with varying degrees of autonomy.

Park Chung Hee and the Military Coup of May 16, 1961

Two days after the coup on May 16, 1961, led by Major General Park Chung Hee and Lieutenant Colonel Kim Chong P'il, the entire cabinet of Chang Myŏn resigned, and a day later President Yun Po Sŏn resigned. The United States government recognized the military regime on May 18, and on May 29 the U.S. State Department expressed its willingness to support the new government.

In order to illustrate the magnitude of changes during the 1960s, a brief discussion of the preceding decade is presented. Park came to power in the aftermath of two failed regimes of Rhee Syngman (1948–60) and Chang Myŏn (1960–61). Rhee was the first democratically elected president of the Republic of Korea. His regime's main political goal was reunification of

South and North Korea, with economic development and economic policies taking second place. The economic policies were aimed at establishing a self-reliant economy, with the South Korean economy ridding itself of foreign influence, especially that of Japan. However, despite the nationalistic resolve, the economy under Rhee was heavily dependent on foreign aid, especially following the Korean War. Industrial policies were oriented toward import substitution industrialization (ISI). However, there was little economic growth or ISI during this period, due to the government's lack of managerial and executive expertise to effectively intervene in the economy and rampant corruption among politicians, government officials, and businesses.

Rhee's close aides and government officials were corrupt. Businesses that had close personal ties to Rhee's cronies did quite well through lucrative monopoly and oligopoly rights and through low-interest-rate loans doled out by the government. On the other hand, the economy as a whole suffered from widespread poverty and an inefficient industrial sector. Rhee was out of touch with the public and incapable of controlling his government and his party. Political malaise was deeply intertwined with economic problems. Thus, when the students took to the streets in the spring of 1960 following a badly rigged presidential election on March 15, they demanded "democracy in politics and prosperity in economy." The Rhee regime was ousted following the student revolt of April 19, 1960.

The next regime, that of Chang Myŏn, had two formidable goals: democracy and economic prosperity. However, the Chang regime failed on both accounts. A myriad of political and social groups sprouted throughout the nation, some of which seemed more interested in social unrest than in democratic governance. Dependence on foreign aid and loans persisted as well, since 52 percent of the national budget was supplied by the United States in aid, loans, and agricultural products (Park 1966, 1971). This heavy reliance on foreign aid was perceived as making the South Korean economy perpetually dependent on foreign powers and as alluring the private sector to engage in rent-seeking activities rather than in industrial manufacturing. Illicit activities of politicians and businesses also continued. The Chang regime charged those who engaged in such activities with illicit accumulation of wealth, but it was unable to fully prosecute them due to internal inefficiency and corruption. The Chang regime was considered inept and, despite its noble efforts to bring about democracy and economic prosperity, was seen as basically a holdover of the corrupt Rhee regime.

Thus, when Park led the military coup, claiming that he would bring "economic self-sufficiency and prosperity," he did not face widespread opposition on the streets (Ministry of Public Information 1965). However, this does not mean that he was enthusiastically and warmly greeted by the public. It does reflect the people's recognition of the powerful force of a fully armed military on the streets and the hope that a military regime might be able to bring some order to the political chaos and unrest experienced during the previous regimes.

Sensing such a sentiment, Park justified the principal purpose of his coup in economic rather than political terms. In his speech following the May 16 coup he said the following:

> I cannot think of anything else that would make me more miserable than to be hungry. Priority one of my duties at this moment is to drive poverty away from this chronically poor country, and I believe this is the only way to win the struggle against Communism (P. S. Shin 1970: vii).

On the other hand, democracy was summarily abandoned by Park, since democracy was blamed as the main cause for social instability of the past and an indirect cause of the Korean War. Moreover, a regime that came into power through a military coup could hardly be a strong proponent for democratic rule. Political stability was promoted in the name of engendering an environment for economic prosperity, and thus an authoritarian regime was justified.

In order to enhance government intervention to attain economic development, Park proposed two important strategies: (1) restructuring the government to become a comprehensive developmental state, and (2) elimination of corruption in the political and economic systems. To achieve the former, economic ministries were restructured and the EPB was created to oversee economic development plans. Elimination of corruption was intended to bring forth a new relationship between the state and the businesses. A close working relationship between the state and businesses, yet a distant one in terms of familial and personal relationship, was promoted to bring about economic development (and not to bring about economic stagnation with corruption as was the case during the Rhee and Chang regimes).

Economic development was pursued by Park for several reasons. First, as Park himself pointed out in his speeches, he was committed to eradicating poverty. As a son of a poor peasant, who had been told that his mother had tried to abort him by jumping off of a ladder to avoid having another "mouth to feed," Park had always been concerned with poverty. Park's statement, "I cannot think of anything else that would make me more miserable than to be hungry" (P. S. Shin 1970:vii), is thus based on his own life experience rather than a politician's empty rhetoric. Ridding the society of hunger and starvation was a goal very near and dear to Park.[1] Second, rapid economic development was perceived as a way of justifying the military coup and of earning public support. Park argued that inept and corrupt government officials, politicians, and business people led the nation to poverty in the past. He rationalized that the military was the only organization capable of eradicating poverty and restoring political stability. He argued that the coup was not for his personal gains but borne out of social responsibility. Regardless of how noble the rationale was for conducting the military coup, the Park regime lacked legitimacy. And since poverty was widely believed to be a major social problem of that time, Park shrewdly seized on this issue as his ticket for public support. Thus, economic development was used by the Park regime as a way of earning public recognition and approval in lieu of legitimacy (Koo & Kim 1992).

Comprehensive Developmental State

The Park regime restructured the government bureaucracy to ensure that economic development would be attained rapidly.

The economic goals put forward in the First and Second Five-Year Economic Development Plans represented a dramatic departure from the past. The economy was to be completely restructured and reoriented along the following three dimensions: from agriculture to industry, from mercantilist and rent-seeking activities to industrial manufacturing, and from domestic sales to exports. And the Park regime decided that this restructuring will be led by the state. Therefore, a comprehensive developmental state was created.

The Economic Planning Board (EPB), the Ministry of Finance, and the Ministry of Trade and Industry formed the three economic ministries in charge of South Korea's economic development. The EPB was the leader of the three, consisting of some of the brightest elites in South Korea. Its main missions included formulation of long-term economic development plans, comprehensive implementation and management of the economic development plans, and control of both domestic and foreign capital (through nationalization of banks and control of the national budget).

The EPB was established on July 22, 1961, less than two months after the military coup. The EPB became the most important government ministry in the coordination and control of South Korea's economic development. Its objectives were described in the 1961 law as "to establish comprehensive plans for the development of the national economy, and to manage and to regulate the execution of the development plans" (EPB 1982: 407). It remained as the most prestigious ministry within the government bureaucracy throughout the 1960s and 1970s.

The EPB was established by combining and creating various plan-oriented departments scattered throughout the government bureaucracy. These included the Bureau of Comprehensive Planning and the Bureau of Material Resource Mobilization of the Ministry of Construction; the Bureau of Statistics of the Ministry of Internal Affairs; and the Bureau of Budget of the Ministry of Finance. The EPB was established with four bureaus and nineteen departments, with approximately 600 government officials. In October 1961, the Bureau of Supply was brought under the EPB, allowing the EPB to control the procurement, supply, and management of all domestic and foreign capital and goods. By the end of 1963, the post of assistant minister was created, and the Bureau of Economic Development Planning was established to coordinate the activities of four departments on planning. In 1963, the minister of the EPB's rank was elevated to simultaneously hold the position of deputy prime minister, thus securing the EPB's leadership role among all government ministries (EPB 1982; FKI 1987).

The Five-Year Economic Development Plans

The first project of the EPB was to design comprehensive economic development plans, and the EPB sought the support of South Korean and foreign economists and planners to develop a series of Five-Year Economic Development Plans. The First Five-Year Plan was announced in January 1962, to take effect immediately and remain in place until December 1966. Each plan contained broad goals, specific development strategies, and target rates of economic growth (EPB 1962; FKI 1987). Although previous administrations had put in place economic development plans that ultimately failed, the Park regime went ahead with these plans at the advice of planners and economists. From the very beginning, Park was deeply involved in developing plans and he sat in many of the meetings.

The First Five-Year Plan aimed to lay the basic foundation for an industrial economy. The two goals were correction of the vicious cycle of social and economic malaise and establishment of the foundation for a self-reliant economy ("Chalip Kyŏngje"). Emphases were on building the infrastructure and on promoting ISI. The latter was to eradicate the consumption-oriented, rent-seeking economic structure that had grown out of South Korea's heavy reliance on foreign aid during the 1950s (FKI 1987: 5).

"Chalip Kyŏngje," which was a motto emblazoned on placards and billboards throughout South Korea during the 1960s, did not mean a complete isolation and independence from the world economy. It meant an economy no longer dependent on foreign aid as a major source of revenue, which resulted in a dependency to the aid-providing nations or organizations. In order to overcome this dependency, the South Korean government proposed exports as a way of earning foreign exchange, which could be used at the discretion of South Koreans. Self-reliance had more to do with a sense of autonomy and sovereignty based on the ability to "earn," rather than being detached from the world economy. To the contrary, exports made the South Korean economy quite dependent on the availability and condition of foreign markets.

Exports was chosen as a strategy for economic growth based on advice from the U.S. government and U.S. and South Korean specialists. Unlike many Latin American nations, which pursued the ISI strategy, South Korea did not have a large domestic market nor abundant natural resources. What South Korea had in abundance was a relatively well-educated and well-trained labor force. Exports based on light manufactured products, which were labor-intensive but not capital- or technology-intensive, were chosen by the EPB as a way out of poverty. Thus, South Korea followed the footsteps of its more illustrious neighbor, Japan, and promoted export-oriented industrialization (EOI) as the main strategy for economic growth. This policy choice, Haggard (1990) and others argue, was critical in leading South Korea to remarkable economic development.

The selection of EOI was a prodigious decision made by the South Korean government in the 1960s, which dramatically transformed the economy. However, more important were the changes that took place in the state bureaucracy and in the relations between the state and businesses. Without the comprehensive developmental state, and a newly established working alliance formed between the state and businesses, even good policies could not have been implemented and borne fruit. The South Korean case shows that similar policies that were adopted by different regimes had very different outcomes. The Rhee and Chang regimes had multiyear economic development plans that ultimately failed. The Chang regime was unable to prosecute businesses with illicit accumulation of wealth charges. During the Chang regime the government bureaucracy was inept, and big businesses were able to use their personal ties to politicians and bureaucrats to avoid prosecution. Thus, the changes that took place during the Park regime were not caused simply by selecting the correct policies but by establishing a comprehensive developmental state and changing the way the state and businesses interacted with each other.

Based on the motto of "Chalip Kyŏngje," the state promoted specific goals and targets to be attained by the First Five-Year Economic Development Plan. The target for the economy's annual average growth rate was set at 7.1 percent, which was far higher than during the Rhee and Chang regimes and far surpassed the growth rate of other developing nations. The six development strategies were as follows:

1. Correction of structural imbalance in the national economy, caused by an increase in agricultural productivity.
2. Securing of resources, supplies, and energy.
3. Expansion of basic industry and sufficient supply of social overhead capital.
4. Utilization of idle resources.
5. Improvement of the balance of payments.
6. Promotion of technology (FKI 1987: 6).

Although the First Five-Year Plan had to be revised due to many imperfections in the plan itself as well as to unforeseen domestic and international economic problems, it was a phenomenal success. Between 1962 and 1966, the South Korean economy grew at an annual average rate of 8.9 percent, far exceeding the initial goal of 7.1 percent. The manufacturing sector grew at an annual average rate of 15.1 percent, and exports grew at 29.2 percent (EPB 1978; International Monetary Fund 1979).

Boosted by the enormous success of the First Five-Year Plan, the Second Five-Year Economic Development Plan (1967–71) aimed to promote exports as a way of earning foreign exchange to pay off foreign debt incurred during the 1950s and early 1960s. Rapid economic development and export-oriented industrialization became two important goals of this period.

The Second Five-Year Plan's goals were modernization of the industrial structure and acceleration of attaining a self-reliant economy through export. The target for the economy's annual average growth rate was set at 7 percent. The six development strategies were as follows:

1. Self-sufficiency in food and development of water resources.
2. Establishment of the foundation for rapid development of industries (chemical, iron and steel, and machinery).
3. $700 million worth of export performance, and acceleration of import substitution industries; improvement in the balance of payments.
4. Increase employment, expedite family-planning measures, and restrain population growth.
5. Diversification of farming and increase of farm income.
6. Promotion of science and management technology and increase in productivity (FKI 1987: 6).

Exports of light manufactured products became the key to remarkable economic growth during this period. The entire economy grew at an average annual rate of 11.1 percent, once again far exceeding the target. The manufacturing sector grew at an average annual rate of 21.1 percent. Exports grew dramatically, at an annual average rate of 28.7 percent—one of the fastest growth rates in the world. Exports accounted for 15.8 percent of the GNP in 1971, up from 5.3 percent in 1961 (EPB 1978; International Monetary Fund 1979).

Control of Domestic and Foreign Capital

The Park regime correctly recognized that it needed to be in control of the single most important resource—i.e., capital—in order to persuade (or coerce) the private sector to cooperate with the state. The ministries that were selected to oversee the procurement and distribution of capital were the Economic Planning Board and the Ministry of Finance. Woo (1991) argues that the state's nationalization of banks, and its effective use of these banks, befits the popular image of "Korea, Inc."

The private banks in Seoul were nationalized in October 1961 and were put under the control of the Ministry of Finance (M. Y. I 1985: 318). Several specialty banks were established and strengthened by the government, including the Bank of Medium- and Small-Enterprises and the Korea Development Bank. The nationalized banks were used by the Park regime as a carrot to attract private businesses to conform to the state's directives in the economy and as a stick to punish those that did not follow by threatening a withdrawal of capital assistance. The so-called policy loans were offered to private businesses at an interest rate substantially lower (by one-half to one-third) than regular bank loans (S. K. Kim 1987).

Foreign capital was also put under the state's control. The Park regime actively sought to attract foreign capital to finance its economic development plans, since there was very little accumulation of domestic capital. However, it had to be very careful not to jeopardize the goal of a "self-reliant" economy, which meant independence from foreign control of the domestic economy. Thus, the South Korean government sought foreign loan capital, in which the responsibility of distribution and management was in the hands of the borrower. This is in contrast to foreign direct investment (FDI), in which the lender (e.g., MNCs) is in charge of distribution of capital and management. This partly explains the government's lukewarm receptivity toward FDI during the early phase of development. On the surface, the Foreign Capital Inducement Law did not appear to discriminate FDI from other types of foreign capital. However, in practice, there were many overt and covert obstacles for FDI, including laws on which industries were allowed for FDI.[2]

Various changes in the law and in the organization of government bureaucracy were made in order to attract foreign capital. The Foreign Capital Inducement Law was revised and expanded in August 1961 and again in December 1961. A new Bureau of Foreign Capital was established within the EPB in 1961. This bureau was later expanded and renamed the Bureau of Economic Cooperation. With an expanded budget and increased personnel, the Bureau of Economic Cooperation actively sought foreign capital loans and, to a lesser degree, foreign direct investments. More substantial restructuring of the law and government offices took place between 1964 and 1965, when export was promoted heavily. The EPB and its Bureau of Economic Cooperation played a major role in acquiring and distributing foreign loan capital and foreign direct investment during the early phase of South Korean development.

There are three types of foreign capital: aid, loan capital, and FDI. It is important to differentiate the type of foreign capital. In earlier dependency writings about Latin American cases, foreign capital was synonymous with foreign direct investment from MNCs. This type of foreign capital involves foreign control, thus diminishing the independent decision making by the domestic corporation and by the recipient state. The concept of "dependency" refers to such dependence on foreign capital and technology, which inhibits long-term economic growth in the Third World by engendering a cycle of permanent dependency of the borrower to the lender. More recent writings on foreign capital, however, differentiate the types of capital and discuss their varying effects on the recipient state and domestic businesses (Frieden 1981; E. M. Kim 1989; Mardon 1990; Stallings 1991).[3] The first type (aid) can be further specified as economic and military aid. In South Korea, the second type (loans) includes public and commercial loans, in which the former is often provided to the government, while the latter is provided to private businesses (Ministry of Finance 1990b). The second and third types (loans and FDI) required the EPB's prior approval and close supervision in their distribution. This remained relatively unchanged throughout the 1960s and 1970s.

South Korea received large sums of military aid from the United States since the eruption of the Korean War in 1950. However, military aid dwindled after the end of the war. On the other hand, economic aid from the United Nations and the United States continued to pour in through the 1950s. The United Nations provided a total of $120 million, and the United States provided a total of $1,745 million, including foodstuffs (Bank of Korea 1986a). U.S. economic aid was very important for sustaining the economy during the Rhee regime. However, this aid was also cut off in the early 1960s, and the Park regime had to seek other sources of foreign capital.

Foreign direct investment was not a viable option for South Korea in the early 1960s. On the one hand, FDI was not very appealing to the government, which wanted to demonstrate its sovereignty. South Korea's bitter experience of foreign domination during the Japanese colonial period made FDI a politically unpopular option. On the other hand, the MNCs did not see South Korea as an attractive investment site either. A nation that had a GNP per capita of less than $100, no natural resources or cash crops, and a rather unstable political environment was hardly a choice setting for FDI. As a result, between 1962 and 1966 FDI amounted to only $22 million, or 7.3 percent, of all foreign capital input. Between 1967 and 1971 the amount increased to over $70 million, but the share decreased to 3.2 percent of all foreign capital, due to the rapid rise of commercial loans from Japan following the 1965 signing of the Normalization Treaty between South Korea and Japan.

Foreign loan capital, unlike aid or FDI, was readily available to South Korea in an expanding international economy of the 1960s. The United States saw South Korea as a strategic area for the containment of communism in Pacific Asia during the cold war (Mardon 1990). It was thus in the best interests of the United States to have a sound capitalist economy in South Korea (Cumings 1991). And from the standpoint of the Park regime, this type of loan—especially a public loan—represented relatively little foreign control in comparison to FDI. As a result of these conditions, massive amounts of foreign loan capital were provided. Foreign loan capital, which includes public and commercial loans, accounted for over 96 percent of all foreign capital input in South Korea between 1962 and 1971 (Bank of Korea 1986a; E. M. Kim 1989). The actual amount was $2.55 billion (Ministry of Finance 1986).

Since public loans were provided to the South Korean government, their distribution was decided by the government. The EPB distributed public loans to sectors that had been neglected by the private sector but had been crucial for economic development. Between 1959 and 1979, 25 percent of all public loans were invested in agriculture and 46 percent in the infrastructure (i.e., electricity, gas, water, and construction) and in industrial and service sectors where state-owned enterprises dominated (e.g., iron and steel, and communications). Channeling these loans to the infrastructure and state-owned enterprises reflected the government's extensive involvement in the actual procurement and disbursement of such loans.

Commercial loans, on the other hand, are provided to the private sector. In theory, this type of loan should involve less direct state control relative to public loans. However, in South Korea, due to the state's determination to control foreign capital and due to the relative inexperience of the private sector, the EPB was active in procuring and distributing commercial loans as well. The government provided government-guaranteed repayment in 90 percent of all commercial loans. Forty percent of commercial loans between 1959 and 1968 had government-guaranteed repayment and 50 percent had state-owned local bank–guaranteed repayment. In only 10 percent of commercial loans were the private recipients responsible for repayment (C. P. Kim & C. R. Pak 1968). Without this government backing, it would have been impossible for South Korean companies to receive any foreign commercial loans, and the distribution of commercial loans strongly suggests the government's control of their distribution process. Between 1959 and 1979, about 45 percent of all commercial loans were invested in six target industries designated by the state for promotion and growth (Bank of Korea 1986a; Ministry of Finance 1986). These included iron and steel, nonferrous metal, machinery, shipbuilding, electrical appliances and electronics, and petrochemicals (E. M. Kim 1989).

In light of failures during the Rhee and Chang regimes, the Park regime's success in attaining economic development was based partly on three important restructuring efforts in the state. First, economic development was promoted as the top priority of the government. A series of comprehensive economic development plans were developed and implemented. Second, the government bureaucracy went through structural reforms in order to effectively implement economic development plans. In particular, the EPB was created, and its offices were expanded and strengthened throughout the 1960s. Third, the state took control of the vital resources for economic development, including domestic and foreign capital, allowing the state to intervene in the economy effectively.

The last two institutional reforms differentiated the Park regime from the previous regimes. These reforms constitute the establishment of a comprehensive developmental state in South Korea, which largely stayed in place until the early 1980s. The institutional reforms produced a troika of economic ministries, with the EPB at its front and the Ministry of Finance and the Ministry of Trade and Industry forming the two "back horses" supporting the EPB. The relative freedom in decision making provided to these ministries and the centralized control and coordination by the EPB were similar to the privileges and power given to the Ministry of International Trade and Technology and the Ministry of Finance in Japan (Johnson 1982).

The Relationship between the State and the Private Sector

A change in the state-business relations took place in 1961, which was critical in the effective implementation of the state's development plans. The institutional reforms within the government ministries and establishment of the finest development plans would not have borne the fruit of economic growth, unless they had the vehicle of implementation. To this end, the reforming of the relations between the state and business was important. Several changes took place: (1) the state formed a tight working partnership with large private enterprises in pursuit of a common goal—i.e., economic development; (2) the state was, at least in the beginning, the dominant partner, often exerting its influence in an authoritarian manner; and (3) the nature of their relationship became formal and institutionalized (compared to a more personal and collusive relationship during the Rhee and Chang regimes). These changes clearly show the different *modus operandi* between the Park regime versus the Rhee and Chang regimes. They are also important in helping us understand why some other less developed countries are unable to attain development, even when they have economic development plans. There are various reasons for failure, but a lack of an effective vehicle of implementation is probably as important as the existence of sound economic development plans.

The state and the businesses formed a close working relationship, yet a distant one. When we simply look at the closeness of the state and business, the Rhee and Park periods do not show much difference. Some politicians and businesses had a very cozy relationship during Rhee. During Park, this closeness can be found in the working relationship. The difference was in the *nature* of the relationship: during Rhee it was personal and collusive, while during Park it became more of a formalized working relationship without shared class backgrounds.

The distance resulted from the different class backgrounds and different familial and personal networks of those in government and businesses. This distance allowed the state to be autonomous from the interests of the landed and industrial classes. Closeness was important, since this was an alliance for economic development that required constant consultation and cooperation. The concept of state autonomy, which is used by development scholars to explain the success of East Asian NICs, conceals the significance of the close working relation that evolved between these two actors (Evans 1987; Koo 1987; Rueschemeyer & Evans 1985). A delicate balance in the relations was achieved, in which each of the two partners was autonomous, yet there was a formalized and close working relationship (Evans 1995). Evans developed the concept, "embedded autonomy" to refer to this relationship. This type of partnership helped prevent corruption as it led to economic development.

This close and yet distant relationship appears to have helped the implementation of economic development goals:

- The autonomy of the state allowed the state to design and implement industrial policies that required a drastic restructuring of the economy without much objection from the capitalist class.
- The disciplinary relationship that was established by the authoritarian state made it extremely difficult (although not impossible) for the private sector to object to the state's plans.

The Charges of Illicit Accumulation of Wealth

Park argued that South Korea's stagnant economy under Rhee and Chang had resulted from a lack of political leadership and from corruption committed by both politicians and businesses (Park 1966, 1971). The Park regime demonstrated its power to the private sector with the charges of illicit accumulation of wealth. These charges were in place during the Chang regime, but they were not executed effectively. The Park regime took control of these charges and utilized them for important political gains. One was to force compliance from the private sector. The other was to demonstrate to the public that it was serious and effective in eliminating corruption.

A brief discussion is presented of the state-business relations and the *chaebol* during the Rhee and Chang regimes. This will help one to understand the extent of the changes that Park initiated in the private sector after the coup. During the Rhee and Chang regimes, personal ties to government officials and politicians were key to a business's success. Once these ties were established, lucrative deals were doled out to businesses. Kickbacks to political patrons were not uncommon. Most of the recipients of preferential treatment were either members, or relatives of members, of Rhee's Liberal Party. K. D. Kim (1979) refers to the *chaebol* leaders as "political capitalists." Kim describes them as:

[who] accumulated capital mainly through such "non-rational" processes as speculation, price fixing, tax evasion, and taking advantage of cumulative inflation. More crucial to this process, however, was that they played on political connections to gain economic favors in exchange for political contribution (1979: 469).

Many members of the Liberal Party were also founders, owners, and large stockholders of the *chaebol*. Jones and Sakong report two such cases where the members of the Liberal Party received preferential treatment:

. . . by 1960, the controller of the Liberal Party "was estimated to have large interests in twenty-nine projects, and the party was believed to have a large interest in at least 50 percent of all private projects receiving American aid."
Domestic credit seems to have been likewise distributed to the advantage of the Liberal Party. It is reported

that, just prior to the 1956 election, the Commercial
Bank of Korea made loans of 17 billion hwan (the
pre-1961 currency unit) to twelve industries which then
kicked back as much as 100 percent of the loans to party
campaign officers (Jones & Sakong 1980: 273).

These cases show the close and collusive relationship
between the Rhee regime and the *chaebol*. It was more profitable
to take advantage of low-interest-rate loans than to actively
engage in productive activities, especially when the government
could not effectively regulate corrupt or unfair business practices
(Jones & Sakong 1980; Koo & Kim 1992). Since there were
ample opportunities for rent-seeking, businesses during the
Rhee and Chang regimes were primarily engaged in commerce
rather than in manufacturing.

Of the fifty largest *chaebol* as of 1983, forty had been established after the end of the Japanese colonial period, and of the
forty, nineteen had been established from 1951 to 1960. Thus,
we can see that quite a few *chaebol* were established during the
Rhee (1948–60) and Chang (1960–61) regimes. However, their
most rapid growth occurred since the 1960s, and a number of
Rhee- and Chang-period *chaebol* disappeared from the top ten
list by the late 1960s.

The Park regime set out to change the corrupt state-business
relations of the past. Park demonstrated the supremacy of the
state over the private sector and redefined the nature of relations between them. The fact that the state was in a position to
provide lucrative business opportunities to the private sector
could have led to rent-seeking and political corruption as were
the case in the past. However, as Amsden (1989) argues, the
private sector was disciplined by the state, and this resulted in
economic performance rather than corruption.

On May 28, 1961—just twelve days after the coup—the
Supreme Council for National Reconstruction (headed by Park)
announced the formation of a committee for the investigation
and execution of the Charges of Illicit Accumulation of Wealth.
On the same day, presidents of the major *chaebol* were arrested
and jailed. The swiftness in acting against the *chaebol* and the
seriousness of the charges strongly indicate that the Park regime

had established fairly detailed plans to prosecute the *chaebol* prior to the coup and that these charges were seen as urgent and important measures for the new regime. The charges were meant to bring a clean sweep of the government and of businesses.

Illegal activities under the charges included the following:

1. illegal acquisition of government-invested properties;
2. unjust loaning of government-owned foreign capital;
3. giving political funds to government officials (bribery);
4. profiting from unjust bidding;
5. unjust profiting from foreign loan capital;
6. tax evasion;
7. transferring property to foreign countries; and
8. others (Korea Yearbook 1961, 1962).

Those who were charged were to pay a hefty fine and, in some cases, to serve a jail sentence.

The Park regime cast the net wide to include all the major *chaebol* and large businesses. Since the *modus operandi* during Rhee was to utilize personal ties and to engage in often illicit rent-seeking activities, most of the successful businesses were subject to these charges, especially those engaged in the businesses of "Three Powder Products" (Korea Yearbook 1962). These businesses were the manufacturing and sales of flour, sugar, and cement, which were protected by the government to ensure oligopoly of the market. Thus, for a select few *chaebol*, these were extremely lucrative businesses. In the end, the two most prominent businessmen of that time were charged: I Pyŏng Ch'ŏl, the chair of Samsung, whose illicit wealth was officially estimated as 800 million Won, or 19 percent of the national total; and Hong Chae Sŏn of Keum Sung [Kŭm Sŏng] Textiles, which later became Ssangyong (Jones & Sakong 1980: 353).

Politicians and military officers who were involved in aiding businesses or themselves profiting from illicit business activities were also charged and arrested. Many high-ranking government officials in the Rhee regime were arrested, including the minister of finance, mayor of Seoul, President Rhee's security officer, and many high-ranking officers in the military.

The prosecution of government officials and other politicians took on a very moralistic tone, as expressed in the announcement of the charges by the Supreme Council for National Reconstruction:

> The purpose is to prosecute government officials, political party members, and others in important government posts who used their position and power to illegally acquire the nation's property, or businessmen or the sort who collaborated with the above to illegally accumulate capital, with charges of administrative and criminal offence. The acts of these people have caused confusion in moral ethics and business ethics, have resulted in poverty of the nation by disrupting the order of the national economy, and caused much shame for this nation. So by prosecuting them with severe punishment, we will restore this nation's fundamental principles and provide a basis for reconstruction of this nation (Korea Yearbook 1962: 200).

According to this statement, all past economic problems rested in the hands of corrupt politicians. The Park regime, lacking political legitimacy, saw the expulsion of corrupt Rhee regime officials (who had been put in office through democratic elections, thus having legitimacy) as a justification of its coup. Since the democratically elected officials were corrupt, political legitimacy could be refuted as not necessarily having served the needs of the public. If the Park regime could show that it was indeed working for the people and capable of correcting the most serious social ill of that time—poverty—then it could be accepted as a legitimate government by the public even if it had not been elected in a democratic manner.

Thus, the charges of illicit accumulation of wealth were important for both political and economic reasons. First, as just discussed, by prosecuting the corrupt government officials of the Rhee and Chang regimes, the Park regime was able to gain some political support from the public. The Park regime could claim a sense of moral purity over the corrupt Rhee regime. And, perhaps more importantly, the Park regime demonstrated a sense of superiority over a democratically elected and legitimate regime. A military government that took power by force, Park wanted to show, was better than a legitimately elected government that was corrupt. Second, the Park regime demonstrated that it was capable of punishing the *chaebol*, which were seen as untouchable during the previous two regimes. By punishing the *chaebol* owners with jail sentences, it showed that it could discipline and punish the *chaebol*. The state was clearly in charge.

Selection of Large Businesses as New Partners for Economic Development

Once the military regime had demonstrated its might to the public and the *chaebol* with the charges of illicit accumulation of wealth, it began to soften its tone. It had to foster a cooperative relationship with the private sector. Nevertheless, the state was clearly the dominant partner, with capital under its control and with an expanded and reformed economic bureaucracy. Thus, the state had the prerogative to choose its partner. We first discuss the issue of who influenced whom in the state-business alliance in the early 1960s. Then, we discuss what other options were available to the South Korean state besides the state–big business alliance. This will help us understand further the reasons for the state's decision and the limitations within which the state made this decision.

An interpretation different from the one I offer here regarding the state's decision to work with large private businesses could be that the state was forced to negotiate with the *chaebol* due to the latter's enormous influence. However, evidence from the early 1960s suggests that the *chaebol* were unable to manipulate the Park regime and that the *chaebol* had no other choice than to cooperate with the state. The Park regime's decision to work with the *chaebol* was a practical decision to utilize existing businesses and to provide economies of scale for the newly embarked economic development plans. And the Park regime's decision was a political one to earn public support by demonstrating that there will be no conflict-of-interest—i.e., the Park regime will not use power for personal monetary gains.

Several factors help explain why the state was able to dominate its relations with the *chaebol* in the early 1960s. First, as noted earlier, the key members of the Park regime did not come from the capitalist class. Many members, including Park, were from peasant families. Thus, the Park regime did not share the class interests of the capitalists. This class distinction helped the state focus on national interests, rather than on narrowly defined class interests. Second, the Park regime clearly demonstrated its power to the private sector by jailing many leading businessmen. The military regime had declared a state of emergency, giving itself tremendous latitude in disciplining and punishing the *chaebol*. A military regime under a state of emergency did not readily lend itself to manipulation by the private sector. Third, the businesses themselves were not very well organized to represent their class interests. The businesses were in disarray. Few formal organizations among businesses existed at the time. Each business was busy fending for its own survival against a military regime intent on punishing it. The businesses, either collectively or individually, were simply unable to effectively protest and object against the state. Finally, the state controlled a vital resource for the businesses—i.e., capital. Nationalization of the banks in 1961 meant that the businesses had to become more dependent on the state for their survival compared to previous regimes. As a result of these factors, the Park regime was able to control the relations between the state and businesses.

What were the options available for the Park regime other than collaborating with the large private businesses? I argued that it was the Park regime who decided to work with the businesses, and not vice versa. As noted earlier, the businesses were not in a position to influence the newly empowered military regime. There were three other options that the Park regime could have chosen: (1) establishing state-owned enterprises, (2) attracting MNCs to form joint ventures with domestic corporations or to establish subsidiaries, or (3) selecting medium- and small-sized businesses. However, the Park regime deemed that these options would hinder the process of attaining rapid economic growth and/or would be detrimental to its political survival.

First, establishing state-owned enterprises was not an impossible option, since Park controlled both the domestic and foreign capital. However, the members of Park's regime had little experience in business, since none of them were from the capitalist class. But, more importantly, they could not risk the chance of "appearing" to work as businessmen: since corruption under Rhee had involved government officials running businesses for their personal interests, any appearance that the Park regime was running business would be seen as politically risky.

Second, working with MNCs would have been politically suicidal. South Koreans were very sensitive to any hint of foreign domination, whether military or economic. This nationalistic sentiment had been strengthened as a result of thirty-five years of Japanese colonialism (1910–45), which had ended only sixteen years prior to Park's ascendance to power. Foreign aid provided after independence and the Korean War left the South Korean economy dependent on the aid-providers. Although South Koreans were thankful for the assistance they received from abroad in times of need, their national sovereignty was perceived to be at stake. This is why Park proposed to bring about a self-reliant economy, capitalizing on this nationalist sentiment to justify his coup. Attracting MNCs would have clearly jeopardized this objective. Furthermore, foreign direct investment by MNCs required the latter to see South Korea as a profitable investment site, and South Korea in 1961 was hardly that. Political stability was uncertain, and the economic outlook was bleak.

Third, forming a partnership with medium- and small-sized businesses could not provide measurable gains in economic development in a short period of time. The Park regime needed to demonstrate to the public that it could attain economic development as it promised. The Park regime did not enjoy the luxury of a fixed term of a legitimate government. Its time could be up at any time, and hence there was an added urgency in attaining economic development (Koo & Kim 1992). If it was not able to perform it could be ousted by public protest or another coup. Nobody knew this better than those key figures in the Park regime, since they themselves had come into power by force.

Once the large private businesses had been chosen by the Park regime, they were provided with generous loans. On January 12, 1962, the Supreme Council for National Reconstruction announced that those charged with illicit wealth accumulation could build factories necessary for national reconstruction and donate them to the state instead of paying fines (Korea Yearbook 1962, 1963). And on May 9, 1962, the Ministry of Trade and Industry approved ten companies that were to be donated to the state in lieu of payment of fines (Korea Yearbook 1962, 1963). These included cement, electrical machinery, iron and steel, machinery, fertilizer, PVC, electrical cable, and refrigeration and freezing companies. Wulsan Fertilizer Company, which was to be built by Samsung and others, was originally planned to have 75 percent of its assets provided by US AID and 25 percent of its assets provided by a U.S. company as foreign direct investment. Ssangyong Cement, which was to be built by Hong Chae Sŏn, was originally planned to have $6.5 million in foreign loan capital from Kloekner-Hambold Deutz Company of West Germany and 300 million Won from domestic loans. All foreign capital had to be approved by the Supreme Council for National Reconstruction, and it was the state that took the initiative in finding the loans for the *chaebol* to build these factories (Korea Yearbook 1962, 1963). As a result of the state's intervention in the private sector to the extent of procuring domestic and foreign capital loans, the wealth among the large businesses was redistributed effectively. And the state controlled that process.

Repression of Labor

The comprehensive developmental and authoritarian state was repressive toward labor: it kept wages low and suppressed labor union activities. The authoritarian state was perhaps harshest when it dealt with the workers. The workers, unlike the *chaebol*, had little to offer the state. They were seen by the state as dispensable, since there was a job shortage, not a labor shortage. Export based on light manufactured products required a large labor force, but with relatively little skill and low wages. The state in collaboration with big businesses suppressed wages in order to make South Korean products price-competitive in the world market. South Korea's popular export products during the 1960s, which included textile, clothing, foot apparel, stuffed toys, wigs, and plywood, were targeted for the lower end of the world market where price, not quality, mattered.

Furthermore, labor union laws made it difficult for workers to form independent labor unions for collective bargaining. Labor union activities were severely restricted under the Park regime, and Jang Jip Choi concludes that the 1963 amendments to the labor law represented "a considerable regression from the first [labor] law [of 1953]" (1989: 85). The 1963 amendments are as follows:

(1) [A] union had to be legally recognized. For this to occur, a newly organized union had to obtain "a certificate of report" by filing a report with an appropriate administrative agency wherein the items the law required were enumerated; (2) a union would not be granted legal recognition if its purpose was to hamper the ordinary operation of a previously established union. That is, any second union, was automatically disapproved; (3) the unions were to be restructured in the form of industrial unions organized along industrial lines and unified under a single national industrial union within the same industrial sector; (4) penalties for employers' unfair labor practices were much abated; (5) a bilateral labor-management cooperation for industrial peace; (6) 'union shops' were recognized, legally allowing compulsory membership; (7) state intervention in the internal and operational matters of labor unions was expanded in scope (for instance, administrative authorities were granted the right to convene extraordinary meetings or to audit union finances) (J. J. Choi 1989: 84–85).

In particular, the amendments made it more difficult for labor unions to organize. As a result, by the end of the 1960s, dissident labor unions gradually disappeared and government-sponsored and company-approved labor unions took their place

(Ibid.: 86). Labor unions lost its militancy and, more importantly, did not represent the interests of the workers in their negotiations with management. Rather, they acted as the mouthpiece for the management. The new amendments also allowed broad latitude for state intervention in union activities. The state was able to use this clause to obstruct and scrutinize the activities of labor unions and of workers in general.

Working conditions were also very poor. In many of South Korea's small sweatshops, which produced cheap textiles and clothing, heating and ventilation were virtually nonexistent. In many sweatshops in the Peace Market in Seoul, the ceilings were too low (4 to 5 feet) for the workers to stand up straight (Ogle 1990: 72). This was apparently to prevent the workers from standing up and taking too many breaks during work hours.

In spite of the repressive labor law, a small number of workers mobilized and protested. However, police used extensive force to crack down on such labor activities. And finally, the 1960s ended with a tragic event in South Korea's labor history: in 1970, a labor leader in the garment makers union, Chŏn T'ae Il, committed suicide by dousing himself with gasoline and lighting fire in protest of the government's repressive labor policies (Ibid.: 72–73). Before his death, Chŏn had fought for the improvement of the working conditions and for the government's enforcement of the Labor Standards Act. This act included the following clauses: the workers should not work more than forty-eight hours per week; children under the age of fourteen should not be employed; and overtime work should be compensated with one-and-a-half-time pay. However, none of the owners of the sweatshops in the Peace Market complied with these rules, and proper state authorities did not monitor or punish those who violated these rules.

South Korean workers' wages did not increase much during the 1960s, even after a decade of record-breaking economic growth for the nation, due to the state's repressive labor policies and the businesses' taking advantage of them. And this happened despite the fact that South Korean workers were working the longest hours in the world: 52.3 hours a week in 1970, which was up from 50.3 hours a week in 1960. In 1970, the average monthly wages went up to only $45.16 from $35.85

in 1960 (International Labour Office 1970, 1980; International Monetary Fund 1980). The percentage figure for South Korean wages as a proportion of U.S. wages actually decreased, from 9 to 8 percent from 1960 to 1970 (E. M. Kim 1993: 237). During the same period, another member of the Gang of Four, Hong Kong, experienced more than a doubling of its workers' wages from $67.92 in 1960 to $136.24 in 1970 (Ibid.). The relatively small gain made by South Korean workers is a painful reminder that South Korea's economic development came at the price of repressing labor. The workers, who toiled long hours under poor working conditions, did not enjoy the fruits of economic development, and their right to form and mobilize labor unions was severely hampered.

Changes in the Private Sector:
The Remaking of the *Chaebol*

The story of South Korea's remarkable economic achievement is not simply that the state summarily reformed itself and gave marching orders to the private sector and that the private sector complied. The success was in part due to the private sector, which went above and beyond the state's mandate and actively took advantage of the favorable economic environment created by the state. They did not react to the state's initiative for rapid economic development as some state-owned enterprises would in a planned economy. The private sector did show some initiative, albeit in a limited degree during the earlier phase of development. Those *chaebol* that grew most rapidly did more than simply invest in sectors that the state had recommended; they employed their shrewd entrepreneurial skills.

A large number of independent—i.e., non-*chaebol* affiliated—small- and medium-sized enterprises thrived during the 1960s and contributed to the export drive (Lim 1981). However, the *chaebol* and their member firms began to dominate the domestic economy as they had never before. The large businesses, which were often members of the *chaebol*, received disproportionate amount of government support, including low-interest-rate loans. Partly as a result, they grew much faster

Table 4.1
Ten Largest *Chaebol*, 1950s–90s

Rank[a]	Late 1950s	Mid-1960s	1974	1983	1988	1991	1994
1	Samsung	Samsung	Samsung	Hyundai	Daewoo	Samsung	Samsung
2	Samho	Samho	Lucky-Gold Star	Samsung	Samsung	Hyundai	Hyundai
3	Gaipoong	Lucky-Gold Star	Hyundai	Daewoo	Hyundai	Lucky-Gold Star	Daewoo
4	Tai Han	Tai Han	Han Jin	Lucky-Gold Star	Lucky-Gold Star	Daewoo	Lucky-Gold Star
5	Lucky-Gold Star	Gaipoong	Ssangyong	Ssangyong	Ssangyong	Lotte	Sunkyong
6	Dongyang	Samyang	Sunkyong	Sunkyong	Hanjin	Sunkyong	Lotte
7	Keukdong	Ssangyong	Korea Explosives	Korea Explosives	Korea Explosives	Hanjin	Hanjin
8	Hankook Glass	Hwashin	Dainong	Han Jin	Sunkyong	Ssangyong	Ssangyong
9	Donglip	Panbon	Dong Ah Construction	Kukje	Dong Ah	Korea Explosives	Korea Explosives
10	Tai Chang	Dongyang	Hanil Syn. Textile	Dae Lim	Kia	Kia	Kia

Note: a. Rank order of the *chaebol* for 1983, 1988, 1991, and 1994 is based on total assets. The basis of rank order for other years was not specified in original sources.

Sources: Bankers Trust Securities Research 1989; Maeil Kyŏngje Shinmun 1984; Management Efficiency Research Institute 1992; Pak 1975, 1982; Shin Sanŏp Kyŏngyŏngwŏn 1996.

than other non-*chaebol* firms. And unlike in Japan or Taiwan, South Korea's export was dominated by the *chaebol* and large businesses (Amsden 1989).

The remaking of the *chaebol* in the 1960s was not so much in the internal industrial organization. Rather, it involved the following: the state initiated a close working relationship with large enterprises, many of which later became *chaebol*; and the rules of the game that governed business activities changed from collusive, rent-seeking activities to production. Thus, as a result, there was a redistribution of wealth among the largest *chaebol* during the Park regime. A new group of Park regime *chaebol* was created by the end of the 1960s. And by the mid-1970s, all of the Rhee- and Chang-regime *chaebol* were gone from the list of the ten largest *chaebol*, except for Samsung and Lucky–Gold Star (see Table 4.1).

The overall growth of the *chaebol* during the 1960s is difficult to document with firm-level information. Statistical information on the *chaebol* is not available for the 1960s. Business directories, which contain financial balance sheets, were not published until 1971. Since information prior to that year is sketchy, at best, I use information available in my data set, which covers the period from 1970 to 1983. In order to shed some light on the growth and changes in the *chaebol* during the Park regime relative to those during Rhee, I grouped those member firms established during Rhee versus those established during Park.

The foundation date of the fifty largest *chaebol* (according to total assets in 1983) are presented in Table 4.2. It shows that more *chaebol* were founded during the Rhee regime than any other period in South Korea's modern economic history. In spite of this, the following figures show that the *chaebol* and firms that were founded during that period have not been the most active ones.

First, more firms were founded during the Park regime than the Rhee regime (see Table 4.3). One hundred and forty-four firms were established by the ten largest *chaebol* during the Park regime compared to twenty-six during the Rhee regime.

Moreover, within each *chaebol*, Park-period firms contributed a significantly larger share of total assets compared to the

Table 4.2
Foundation Date of the Fifty Largest *Chaebol*[a]

Rank	Before 1910	Japanese Colonial Period (1910–45)	U.S. Occupancy (1945–July, 48)	Rhee Regime (August, 1948–60)	Park Regime (1961–79)
		(Number of *Chaebol*)			
1–10	0	1	3	5	1
11–30	1	1	4	8	6
31–50	0	3	4	7	6
Total	1	5	11	20	13

Note: a. Fifty largest *chaebol* as of 1983.
Source: Hanguk Ilbo 1984.

Table 4.3
Average Assets and Number of Firms of the Ten Largest *Chaebol* Founded During the Park Regime, 1983

Light	Heavy	Construction	Finances	Trade	Other Services
		(average assets in $ million)			
105	209	195	183	51	82
		(number of firms)			
13	65	18	8	7	33

Rhee-period firms in spite of the former's shorter history. On average, the former were responsible for 67 percent of each *chaebol*'s total assets in 1983 (Table 4.4), while the latter were responsible for 22 percent (Table 4.5). Five out of the ten largest *chaebol* had more than 70 percent of their assets from Park-period firms (Table 4.4). On the other hand, seven *chaebol* had less than 30 percent of their assets from Rhee-period firms (Table 4.5). Finally, diversification into a wide-range of business activities occurred in more *chaebol* during the Park regime. Figures in Tables 4.3 and 4.4 indicate that most *chaebol* had diversified into four to five (out of six) sectors during Park, compared to only one or two during Rhee. This growing horizontal diversification of businesses into often unrelated sectors

Table 4.4
Total Assets of Firms Founded During the Park Regime, 1983
(in $ million)

Chaebol	Light Manufacturing	Heavy Manufacturing	Construction	Finances	Trade	Services	Tot
Hyundai	180.1	3296.9	277.8	0	175.9	605.1	453o.o 63%
Samsung	319.2	1792.6	5.8	0	0	151.2	2268.8 42%
Daewoo	33.4	1931.7	1893.1	770.1	25.0	61.5	4714.8 88%
Lucky–Gold Star	10.7	1945.2	213.9	316.4	0	53.1	2539.3 58%
Ssangyong	327.6	1678.6	329.0	0.2	0	114.7	2450.1 89%
Sunkyong	216.3	1151.5	14.9	0	0	215.2	1727.9 73%
Korea Explosives	89.8	925.9	32.9	120.0	71.6	65.5	1615.7 86%
Han Jin	0	0	296.0	258.3	0	1396.7	1951.0 91%

Table 4.4 (continued)

Chaebol	Light Manufacturing	Heavy Manufacturing	Construction	Finances	Trade	Services	Total[a]
Kukje	185.3	350.8	0	0	51.5	28.8	616.4
							43%
Dae Lim	0	488.2	13.4	0	35.5	4.3	541.4
							36%

Note: a. First row is total assets of firms founded during the Park regime (1961–79), and the second row is the percentage share of total assets of firms founded during the Park regime of total assets in 1983.

Table 4.5

Total Assets of Firms Founded During the Rhee Regime, 1983
(in $ million)

Chaebol	Light Manufacturing	Heavy Manufacturing	Construction	Finances	Trade	Services	Total[a]
Hyundai	0	400.3	0	87.9	0	0	487.2 7%
Samsung	604	0	268.4	1709.3	0	120.0	2701.7 50%
Daewoo	——— (Daewoo was not founded until 1967) ———						
Lucky–Gold Star	0	595.9	0	97.6	208.7	0	902.2 21%
Ssangyong	0	6.3	223.4	71.4	0	0	301.1 11%
Sunkyong	0	0	0	0	635.8	0	635.8 27%
Korea Explosives	0	205.2	0	65.6	0	0	270.8 14%
Han Jin	0	0	0	0	0	119.5	119.5 6%

Table 4.5 (continued)

Chaebol	Light Manufacturing	Heavy Manufacturing	Construction	Finances	Trade	Services	Total[a]
Kukje	40.1	0	0	268.2	516.3	0	824.6 57%
Dae Lim	0	0	0	97.7	0	0	97.7 6%

Note: a. First row is total assets of firms founded during the Rhee regime (1948–60), and the second row is the percentage share of total assets of firms founded during the Rhee regime of total assets in 1983.

is indicative of a *chaebol*. It is safe to conclude that many
currently largest *chaebol* had reached the *chaebol*-dom d
the Park regime. All these indicate that the period durir
Park regime (the 1960s and 1970s) was critical for the expansion and growth of the large *chaebol*.

The cases of Hyundai and Samsung illustrate how individual *chaebol* responded somewhat differently to the favorable
investment environment created by the government's
economic ministries. They also imply that their growth is not
entirely a result of state intervention.

Hyundai, which was not even on the top ten list during the
1950s and 1960s, had emerged as the third largest by 1974. It is
a good example of a business that took advantage of the
supportive environment created by the state but that went
beyond the state's directive. The Hyundai Engineering and
Construction Company was founded in 1947 by Chŏng Chu
Yŏng. Hyundai's remarkable success in the 1960s resulted from
government projects and low-interest loans provided by the
government and from its vigorous overseas construction
projects. Important government contracts Hyundai received
during the 1950s and 1960s included the First Han River Bridge
in 1957, the Kimp'o International Airport project in 1967, and
the first major freeway in South Korea (linking Seoul and Pusan)
in 1968. Hyundai did not stop with these lucrative government
construction contracts. It was the first South Korean construction company to go abroad. It went to Southeast Asia (Vietnam
and Thailand) in 1966 and then to the Middle East. Largely as a
result of the lucrative construction boom in the Middle East,
Hyundai became the largest *chaebol* by the end of the 1970s.
Clearly, these overseas construction projects were not a direct
result of the South Korean government's preferential treatment.
Hyundai's success story is a reminder that *chaebol* are not mere
puppets of the state but are private corporations that make
their own decisions, albeit within the confines of state policies
and regulations.

The story of Samsung is somewhat different from that of
Hyundai. Samsung, which was the largest *chaebol* during the
1950s and 1960s, had a different trajectory of growth. Instead
of taking full advantage of governmental support, Samsung

tried to maintain a healthy distance from the state after being embroiled in a scandal involving a member company, Hanguk Fertilizer Company (established in 1964). In September 1966, Samsung was accused of smuggling an ingredient for saccharin, which was illegal at that time, to use at the fertilizer plant. This escalated into a major social problem and caused the public to become leery of the Park regime's commitment to eradicate corruption. Responding to the public's outcry, the Park regime arrested the founder's son, I Ch'ang Hŭi, and requested that Hanguk Fertilizer Company be donated to the government in lieu of its paying a fine. On April 20, 1967, the company was presented to the government, and I Pyŏng Ch'ŏl resigned from his post as chair of the Samsung *chaebol* (Korea Yearbook 1967).

I Pyŏng Ch'ŏl himself, along with many who have known and studied Samsung, argue that this incident left a lasting impression on the Samsung *chaebol*. Although Samsung continued to be a major player in the South Korean economy, its involvement in the government's target industrial sectors has been limited compared to other large *chaebol*. For example, it was one of the last to invest in the heavy and chemical industries when these were actively promoted by the state in the 1970s. And even in those industries, Samsung invested largely in electrical and electronic appliances, which the state designated as a target sector but for which it also decided to limit subsidies (E. M. Kim 1987). Samsung actively sought FDI from MNCs instead of loan capital distributed by the state when the other *chaebol* were less active in acquiring FDI. Many Samsung companies established joint ventures or became subsidiaries of Japanese MNCs. Samsung's case is an important reminder that a sufficiently large and entrepreneurial *chaebol* could succeed without complete dependence on the state subsidies, even during the 1960s.

Concluding Remarks

The story of South Korea's success in the 1960s highlights the significance of the creation of a comprehensive developmental state as well as changes in the state-business relations in order to attain rapid economic development. The 1960s was a period in which the South Korean economy based on exports of light manufactured products expanded by leaps and bounds. The state was restructured and became a comprehensive developmental state. Economic development was pursued as a national goal by the Park regime, and the state formed an alliance with large businesses, many of which became sprawling *chaebol* by the end of the 1960s.

The stories of the Hyundai and Samsung *chaebol* illustrate the varying responses from the private sector to the state's economic development plans and policies. State-centered studies too quickly dismiss the role of the private sector, especially that of the *chaebol* in seeking to understand South Korean development. Although the *chaebol* may have started out as junior partners in the state-business alliance, that will change with time. The fact that the establishment and growth of many large *chaebol* is directly tied to the state's preferential treatment does not preclude that these same *chaebol* will challenge the state.

Unlike the mutually reinforcing and reciprocal relation between the state and the *chaebol*, the state-labor relation was one in which labor had little leverage. Repression of labor represents a darker side of South Korea's phenomenal economic growth. Workers could not mobilize themselves to demand higher wages due to the 1963 amendments in the labor law. Because the state was directly involved in suppressing wages and restricting labor union activities, it became the target of violent labor movements in the late 1980s. (See chapter 6 for details.)

The state's dominance in its relations with the *chaebol* and labor, which was shaped during the 1960s, changed in the following decades. The next two chapters explore how these relationships changed, which economic development strategies were pursued, and how the society changed as a result.

5
The State-Chaebol Alliance for Development (1970s)

The 1970s witnessed a deepening of the industrialization process, with the development of the heavy and chemical industries dominating economic growth in that decade. This development was clearly initiated by the government and, more specifically, by President Park's staff at the Blue House, without much consultation with other economic ministries. It was pushed vigorously, despite the objections of domestic and international capitalists. If neoclassical economists still have doubts about whether the South Korean state played an important role in economic development, the history of 1970s should remove those doubts. The state promoted heavy and chemical industrialization (HCI) to develop its own defense industry and to forge a closer alliance with a few *chaebol*. The changing geopolitical conditions with the United States troops beginning a partial withdrawal from South Korea after President Nixon's Guam Doctrine in 1969 and President Park's narrow victory in the 1971 presidential election provided important political—i.e., noneconomic—justifications for the Park regime's pursuit of HCI. Thus, although domestic and international market conditions were not ripe, President Park pushed HCI with firm conviction.

However, the story of the 1970s is not completely clear-cut as would the state-centrists argue. They tend to assume that the state is always in charge of the economic development process and that the private sector merely follows orders. Quite contrary to that assumption, in the 1970s, the relationship between the state and the largest *chaebol* became more *interdependent*. The leverage the *chaebol* had increased because they had grown so successfully in the 1960s and because they were the only entrepreneurs who could afford to invest in the heavy and chemical industries, which were capital- and technology-intensive. Furthermore, the cooperation and support of the largest *chaebol* were important for political purposes. After Park won a narrow victory in the 1971 presidential election, there was a growing need to forge a conservative coalition with the large *chaebol*.

The close alliance formed between the Park regime and a select *chaebol* brought about a decade of robust economic growth. During the 1970s, South Korea's industrialization continued at a rate much faster than that of most other countries. Despite the two oil shocks in 1973 and 1979, South Korea's average annual growth rate of real GNP was 7.9 percent during this decade. GNP per capita rose from $285 in 1971 to $1,589 in 1980, producing an impressive average annual growth rate of 18.75 percent during this decade (EPB 1986). In 1971, 13.3 percent of the labor force were employed in the manufacturing sector; that number had increased to 21.7 percent by the end of the decade. The number working in agriculture, fishing, and mining decreased from 49.3 to 34.9 percent (Ibid.). Exports continued to grow, rising from just over $1 billion to more than $17 billion (Ibid.). South Korea's average annual growth rate of exports was one of the fastest in the world. Exports as a share of GNP continued to rise, reaching 34.7 percent in 1980 (EPB 1990). By 1980, over 92 percent of all export products were manufactured goods, and 20.3 percent of all export goods were machinery and transport equipment (up from 8.1 percent in 1971). All these illustrate that the South Korean economy made a successful transition from being dominated by light industries to having a growing share of heavy industries.

In the midst of a rapidly growing economy, the ten largest *chaebol* grew even faster, with average annual growth rates five to nine times faster than the economy as a whole. The stories of the largest *chaebol* indicate that none relied solely on state subsidies for their tremendous business success during the 1970s, although most benefited from them (some more than others). Those that conformed to the state's initiative for the development of heavy and chemical industries grew most rapidly and displaced some of the older and larger *chaebol*. Others investing in sectors that were not highly subsidized by the state also did quite well, and some successfully attracted MNCs to help with the needed capital and technology. The variations in the success stories of the *chaebol* offer additional support to the argument that an analysis of South Korean industrialization from either a neoclassical economics or a state-centered approach cannot help us to understand the complex and interactive process of development.

This chapter looks at the social structural changes that occurred in the 1970s. The deepening of the industrialization process and the roles played by the state and the *chaebol* are examined. The growing significance of the *chaebol* to the state and the changing relations between them are explored through policy changes. Lastly, the diversity in the different *chaebol*'s investment patterns is examined to shed light on their growing autonomy.

The State's Drive for Heavy and Chemical Industrialization

The Park government announced that the goal of the Third Five-Year Economic Development Plan (1972–76) was a "balanced economy": a balance was to be achieved between the light and heavy industries and between the urban and rural areas (EPB 1972; FKI 1987). The stated rationale was that economic growth during the 1960s had brought growth to light industries and urban areas only. Between the two goals, the drive for heavy and chemical industrialization was pushed much more vigorously than the development of rural areas and received more resources. Heavy and chemical industrialization received the strongest possible endorsement from the government, with

President Park making the Pronouncement for the Development of the Heavy and Chemical Industries during his State of
the Nation message on January 13, 1973.[1] Most industrial policies were announced by relevant ministries, not by the president during the State of the Nation message. That Park would
use the occasion to make this pronouncement demonstrated
his strong conviction to promote HCI. It was also a way of
dispelling any criticism that could have come from various
ministries by putting the president's stamp of approval on the
plan (Chŏng 1985).

In the early 1970s, HCI was widely seen as premature for an
economy with only a decade of growth based on light manufacturing and with few natural resources. Sŏ, an EPB official
discussed in an interview with me in 1988 that HCI's rationale
could be found primarily in military terms and not in economic terms.[2] He argued the following as to why the promotion of HCI did not make any economic sense.

> The dilemma of the heavy and chemical industries is
> that if it is promoted for the domestic market alone, the
> economies of scale cannot be achieved [due to the small
> size of the South Korean market]. On the other hand, if
> the heavy and chemical industries are developed to
> meet the demands of the international market, we do
> not have adequate capital or technology.

Furthermore, the private sector was not capable of investing in
the heavy and chemical industries. Kim Kwang Mo, the vice
chair of the Committee for the Development of the Heavy and
Chemical Industries from 1978 to 1980, argued that the private
sector lacked the capital and technology. He cited that even
Samsung, which was the largest *chaebol* in the mid-1960s, did
not have enough capital to build a fertilizer company. The
International Monetary Fund and the Federation of Korean
Industries also opposed HCI when the policy was first
announced (FKI 1985).

However, the Park regime promoted HCI vigorously. There
were several reasons why HCI was promoted with such vigor in
spite of unfavorable economic conditions and why HCI's initial

plans were developed under secrecy by the Blue House staff. First, the HCI plan was seen as vital for South Korea's self-defense. The changing geopolitical conditions in the Asia Pacific in the late 1960s and early 1970s provided justification for South Korea to develop its own defense industry and the heavy and chemical industries. International geopolitical conditions changed when President Richard Nixon of the United States made an announcement regarding the defense of the Pacific during his visit to the Guam Islands in 1969 (which later became known as the Nixon Doctrine or the Guam Doctrine) and with the defeat of the United States in the Vietnam War. President Nixon announced that the defense of the Pacific must lie in the hands of the people in the Pacific and declared that U.S. troops would gradually be withdrawn from various bases in Asia, including South Korea. Between 1970 and 1971, there was a partial withdrawal of U.S. military personnel from South Korea. This was perceived by South Koreans as a grave threat to their defense from North Korea, and President Park therefore was able to justify his plans for developing a self-reliant military and the defense industry. HCI was seen as an important base—e.g., iron and steel, heavy machinery, and transport equipment—to develop the defense industry. And, more importantly, development of the defense industry fit with Park's own firm conviction in the anticommunist ideology. Interview with Pak Yŏng T'ak, who worked closely with Kim Kwang Mo on HCI during the 1970s, reveals President Park's personal commitment toward HCI:[3]

Another important reason[4] to promote HCI was for the development of the defense industry. "Military self-defense" became one of the two policy objectives of the state, and HCI was seen as a vital step for the development of the defense industry. And, if you only consider economic profitability, it is impossible to promote the defense industry. The firm determination to become independent from the U.S. was behind HCI. President Park personally conducted inspections on all new defense industry products.

I argue that Park used the Guam Doctrine to further his plans for developing an indigenous defense industry in South Korea. To suggest that HCI was a mere reaction to the changing geopolitical and security conditions is somewhat misleading. Park worked hard for several years to establish South Korea's own iron and steel mill, which was seen as a cornerstone for the defense industry. The Pohang [P'ohang] Iron and Steel Company (POSCO) was finally established in 1968, largely with Japanese financing after years of work by Park to finance it. Thus, POSCO's foundation predates the 1969 Guam Doctrine. And if Park was simply reacting to the Guam Doctrine, it is not clear why he chose to develop South Korea's own defense industry, rather than to import military equipment in light of South Korea's poor financial situation and lack of necessary technology. I argue that the Guam Doctrine provided additional justification to promote HCI, and that HCI was already underway as part of Park's master plan to develop a defense industry.

Domestic political conditions also changed in the early 1970s, and gave Park additional rationale for promoting HCI. President Park won a narrow victory against a leading opposition party leader, Kim Dae Jung [Kim Tae Chung], in the 1971 presidential election garnering 51 percent of the votes against Kim's 44 percent.[5] This precarious victory amid rumors of extensive vote-buying caused Park to announce the Yushin Reformation in October 1972, changing the constitution to allow himself a life-term presidency.[6] To earn public support and appease the public prior to the promulgation of the draconian Yushin Reformation, Park announced the economic goals to be achieved by 1981 as "GNP per capita of $1,000, and $10 billion in exports." This was another attempt to earn public support and political legitimacy with economic delivery, as in the aftermath of the 1961 military coup (Koo & Kim 1992).

More importantly, through HCI, Park could forge a closer alliance with a few select heavy and chemical-industries' *chaebol*. The state's generous plans to support these *chaebol* could engender a strong relationship between the two and ultimately provide incentives for the businesses to contribute political financing for the state. Thus, military self-defense and domestic political survival were important political justifications for promoting HCI in the 1970s.

The significance Park attached to HCI was evident from the fact that he actively participated in developing the blueprints for HCI in the Blue House. The custom was that economic policies and, in particular, important industrial policies were developed jointly by the EPB and the Ministry of Trade and Industry. However, HCI was developed without the EPB in charge or with the Ministry of Trade and Industry involved until HCI was promulgated in 1973. Only after its official announcement were the EPB and the Ministry of Trade and Industry brought into the picture.

The Blue House staff was involved in designing the plan under secrecy as early as 1971, two years before the official Pronouncement for the Development of the Heavy and Chemical Industry in 1973. O Won Ch'ŏl and Kim Kwang Mo were appointed as senior staff at the Blue House at the time. As new members of the Blue House, they prepared plans to develop the heavy and chemical industries, as a way of developing the defense industry in close consultation with President Park. By 1972, a series of preliminary examinations for the possible sites and target industries for HCI were already conducted by the Blue House staff.

President Park argued that he must take full control of the HCI for two reasons. Kim Kwang Mo discussed these reasons.[7]

> President Park took personal interest in, and personally controlled, the developments of the defense industry and HCI. First, President Park argued that this industrial policy will be difficult to implement due to objections from the military as well as other ministries. Second, this policy is vital for South Korea's self-defense and long-term economic development. It was too important for President Park to delegate it to other ministries.

Kim elaborated on Park's perception of objections from various sectors, which Park argued could derail the whole project (HCI) before it was announced. This anticipation of objections appeared to have led Park to develop the plans for HCI under secrecy so that they could be advanced enough to heed off any criticism when promulgated. Kim summarized Park's opinions regarding the Ministry of Defense and HCI.

> The Ministry of Defense is against manufacturing military equipment domestically. They [the officials in the Ministry of Defense] distrust Korean-made military equipment, since Koreans have had no experience or expertise in manufacturing these products. And since these military men [the large number of ex-military officers in the Ministry of Defense] are opposed to this, President Park argued that he must take control of HCI in order to see that it succeeded.

Furthermore, not only did Park anticipate his important support group from the military and the Ministry of Defense opposed to the idea, he also thought premature disclosure of the plans for HCI could invite a divisive competition between the Ministry of Defense and the Ministry of Trade and Industry. Kim noted that the competition between the two ministries could have led to a stalemate, which Park could not tolerate:

> The Ministry of Defense would want to import military equipment, which would be under its control. On the other hand, the Ministry of Trade and Industry would argue that the military equipment must be manufactured in South Korea. It would argue that it is difficult for South Korea to acquire technology or other rights from the U.S. In a recent case, it argued that the U.S. would not allow South Korea to assemble F-16 in South Korea. Citing such cases, the Ministry of Trade and Industry would argue that we must develop our own defense industry.

Although Kim did not mention it in his interview, it is not difficult to see why the two ministries would have different opinions regarding the defense industry. If South Korea were to manufacture military equipment, the Ministry of Trade and Industry would be able to finally step into the limelight, taking it away from the EPB, as the most important economic ministry. Unlike Japan where the Ministry of International Trade and Industry—the counterpart to South Korea's Ministry of Trade and Industry—was the most prestigious and influential ministry involved in industrial policy-making, South Korea's Ministry of Trade and Industry had always been second-in-command to the EPB. For the Ministry of Defense, importing could guarantee a powerful position in relation to the military and to the private sector. Thus, aside from the rationales provided here, the decision to manufacture or to import would have grave consequences on the relative power and prestige of these ministries. The chosen ministry would undoubtedly expand in terms of personnel and budget, greatly enhancing its position within the government. It appears that Park anticipated a cut-throat competition between these ministries and that HCI would be caught in the middle and be derailed even before it was launched. Thus, Park took charge of developing HCI, at least in the beginning, in order to prevent competition between ministries. Park's strong commitment toward HCI is reflected in the use of the authority and power of the Blue House, which stood above and beyond the reaches of economic ministries (Chŏng 1985).

Strengthening and Restructuring of the Comprehensive Developmental State

Immediately following the January 1973 pronouncement, Park appointed O Won Ch'ŏl (who was the Chief of Staff of the Blue House) as the head of the Committee for the Development of Heavy and Chemical Industries. With the Blue House at the center, other economic ministries were finally brought in to develop more detailed and long-term plans for heavy and chemical industrialization. In August 17 of that year, the "Long-Term Plans for the Development of the Heavy and Chemical Industries" were announced, and various institutional reforms took place. Within a year after the January 1973 pronouncement, numerous plans were announced by the economic ministries, including the following:

March 1973:	Long-term human resources development plan was announced.
May 1973:	Ministry of Trade and Industry announced basic principles for the development of the heavy and chemical industries.
August 1973:	The law for public investment fund was promulgated.
October 1973:	A new long-term plan for energy was announced.
November 1973:	A plan for effective business management for the heavy and chemical industries was announced.
January 1974:	A new plan to reduce taxes for heavy and chemical industries was announced (Chŏng 1985: 51).

Economic ministries underwent institutional reforms to help assist in the development of the heavy and chemical industries. Within the EPB, the Department for Foreign Capital Management and the Department for Promoting Investment were both formed in 1973 to assist with attracting foreign capital (i.e., public and commercial loans and foreign direct investment). Similar departments within the Ministry of Finance were also expanded. In the Ministry of Construction, the Department of Industrial Plants was created in 1973.

The Ministry of Trade and Industry underwent the greatest changes. The Department for Industrial Development and the Department for Management of Industrial Plants were expanded and promoted to higher status within the ministry. Many defense-related departments and heavy and chemical industries–related departments were created, and old ones were expanded to give them more prominence within the ministry.

A new Bureau of Science and Technology was established in 1973 to consolidate and expand the research and development efforts for the heavy and chemical industries. In January 1974, the Development Association for Marine Resources was expanded and renamed the Development Association for Industrial Parks. Its new responsibility was to oversee the establishment and development of industrial parks for heavy and chemical industries.

With the comprehensive developmental state restructured and strengthened for the promotion of HCI, the state set new targets for the economy. These targets promised that the South Korean economy would complete a transition toward heavy and chemical industries by the beginning of the 1980s. The goals for the industrial restructuring, which were to be attained by 1981 were as follows: the primary sector was to decrease to 15.9 percent from 25.5 percent in 1972; the secondary sector was to increase to 42.9 percent from 26.3 percent in 1972; and the tertiary sector was to decrease to 41.2 percent from 48.2 percent in 1972. In terms of manufacturing alone, the share of heavy manufacturing within it was to increase from 35.2 percent in 1972 to 51.0 percent by 1981. The export structure would change toward exports of more heavy manufactured products. Other more general economic goals included increasing the GNP per capita to $983 by 1981 and increasing foreign capital holdings to $2.7 billion (Chŏng 1985; P. H. Pak 1980).

Specific plans for the development of the heavy and chemical industries were to select a few target industries and provide them with generous government support. Six target industries were selected based on the following factors:

1. forward and backward linkages
2. contribution for the whole country's economic development
3. possibility of foreign capital earnings through exports, and foreign capital savings through import substitution
4. usage of natural resources
5. inducement effect of foreign capital.

The six target industries chosen were *iron and steel, nonferrous metal, machinery, shipbuilding, electrical appliances and electronics,* and *petrochemicals.*

Several state-owned enterprises were established following the HCI. The Pohang Iron and Steel Company was founded in 1968 and began production in 1973. It took several years for

POSCO to begin production since it was difficult to secure the necessary foreign capital loans to build factories. It was only after the Pronouncement for the Development of the Heavy and Chemical Industries that POSCO finally began production (Y. H. Kim 1976; Nam 1979). Another state-owned enterprise, the Korea Chemical Company, was founded in March 1973.

Along with the state-owned enterprises, the private sector also received preferential treatment from various economic ministries. It received financial assistance through foreign capital loans, the newly created National Funds, domestic loans, tax cuts, technology, and infrastructure. An annual average of 14.5 percent of total development finances was used for the development of the heavy and chemical industries between 1971 and 1981 (Chŏng 1985). The law for tax cuts for the heavy and chemical industries was passed in 1974, and 40.1 percent of tax cuts were subsequently given to the heavy and chemical firms. Other protective measures were provided, such as removing tariff barriers and banning imports of certain heavy and chemical products. Of the six industries, electrical appliances and electronics received the least financial assistance from the government, since the state claimed that the industry had already reached a satisfactory level of international competitiveness (Korea Yearbook 1975).

In addition, heavy and chemical firms received preferential treatment for FDI. Before other manufacturing firms were allowed to receive 100 percent foreign ownership, which would have made a firm a wholly owned subsidiary of an MNC, many heavy and chemical firms were allowed by law to do so. By 1974, metal, machinery, and electronics firms were allowed to accept 100 percent, and by 1978 all six target industries were allowed to acquire 100 percent foreign ownership.

The EPB and the Ministry of Trade and Industry specifically sought the support and cooperation of the large *chaebol* in order to promote HCI. These *chaebol* were capable of financing—at least partially—the capital- and technology-intensive industries, and they had a proven track record of growth during the 1960s. The stories of *chaebol* collaboration are discussed later in this chapter.

Changing Relations Between the State and the Chaebol*:*
President's Emergency Decree for Economic Stability,
August 3, 1972[8]

A clear example that the relations between the state and the
chaebol had become more symbiotic and interdependent by the
early 1970s is the president's Emergency Decree for Economic
Stability, announced on August 2, 1972, effective the next day.[9]
On the surface, this emergency decree was supposed to bail out
all private enterprises under economic hardship from curb
market loans.

Curb market loans are from outside of the legal financial
institution and were considered illegal by the South Korean
government. Both the lender and borrower were subject to
punishment. Curb market loans were popular among businesses
when regular financing was unavailable or when businesses
wanted a quick loan without extensive paperwork and a quick
turnaround time. Curb market loans could come from commercial capital, loan sharks, or individuals. Individuals could be
anybody from a relative, friend, or a business associate (Cho,
Chŏng et al. 1984: 108). In some cases, the owner of a business
loaned his/her private funds to his/her own business to accrue
high interest, and this was called a "disguised curb market loan."

Curb market loans were usually for the short term, from one
to three months. Interest rates were very high, far exceeding
that of regular bank loans. The yearly interest rates ran between
40 and 70 percent (Ibid.: 108). These illegal loans were very
popular in spite of the government's sanctions against them. A
survey conducted in 1963–64 by the Bank of Korea found that
about 75 percent of businesses questioned said that they used
curb market loans during the time of the survey (Ibid.: 110).
Other studies conducted in the late 1960s showed that almost
60 percent of large manufacturing firms and a little less than
half of small- and medium-sized manufacturing firms used curb
market loans (Ibid.: 111–12). It appears that a large majority of
manufacturing firms relied on curb market loans throughout
the 1960s.

Financial trouble for the businesses began at the end of
1969 when the new Deputy Prime Minster[10] Kim Hak Ryŏl and

the Minister of Finance Nam Tŏk Wu administered a retrenchment policy to rectify a chronic inflation. The inflation was a
result of generous financial assistance provided to businesses
during Deputy Prime Minister Chang Ki Yŏng's tenure in office
between 1964 and the end of 1967. The retrenchment policy,
which was announced to control the inflation, began in 1969
and continued for two years. Many businesses went bankrupt
during this period. They had grown so accustomed to receiving
financial assistance from the state that they were unable to
survive once that assistance was gone.

   Thus, in an effort to save the failing businesses, President
Park turned toward a contingency policy. Park ordered Kim
Yong Hwan, the president's secretary on foreign capital at the
Blue House, to secretly develop policies to freeze the curb
market loans and to provide relief funds to businesses. He
formed an Ad-Hoc Committee on Economic Policies comprised
of his closest aides and excluded the EPB and Ministry of Trade
and Industry, which had been central in developing other
economic policies. The Ad-Hoc Committee on Economic
Policies consisted of President Park's Senior Secretary Kim
Chŏng Ryŏn, Minister of Finance Nam Tŏk Wu, the president
of the Bank of Korea Kim Sŏng Hwan, and the president's secretary on foreign capital Kim Yong Hwan.

   The Emergency Decree prepared by the Ad-Hoc Committee
included the following articles: (1) freeze curb market loans and
transfer them to bank loans at a monthly interest rate of 1.35
percent (or, 16 percent annually), with a repayment period of
five years with a three-year grace period; (2) banks will issue
special financial bonds worth 200 billion Won, which will be
used to replace 30 percent of short-term loans for businesses;
(3) the government will contribute 1 billion Won each to the
Trust Guarantee Funds for Small- and Medium-sized Businesses,
and the Trust Guarantee Funds for Agriculture and Fisheries;
and (4) establish the Fund for Industrial Rationalization at the
Korea Development Bank. Long-term, low-interest-rate loans
were provided to businesses based on standards decided by the
Committee on Industrial Rationalization (Bank of Korea 1973).
Other related economic policies included lowering the annual
interest rate for local bank loans by 3.5 percent from 19 to 15.5

percent, stabilizing the exchange rate at 400 Won to $1 and stabilizing public utility rates and retail prices (Ibid.).

The Emergency Decree was secretly prepared by the Blue House without much consultation with the technocrats in the EPB. It appears that the Emergency Decree was more a political gesture by the Park regime to solidify its ties to large businesses. By helping these businesses, the Park regime could expect the businesses to be loyal to the regime and to provide the regime with political financing.

Although this Emergency Decree was meant for capitalists in general, the results show drastic differences between capitalist groups. The large *chaebol* were the main beneficiaries of the Emergency Decree, while the small- and medium-sized enterprises were not helped substantially. There are at least three incidents that support this argument.

First, according to reports made during the 84th National Assembly Meeting, some 600 large firms accounted for 60 percent of total curb market loans made. Furthermore, in only 547 cases (1.5% of total number of cases) did firms contract for more than $252,000 (100 million Won), but the total amount of these loans was $460 million (193 billion Won), accounting for 52.9 percent of total curb market loans (S. H. I 1985).

The second incident concerns the appropriation of the Fund for Industrial Rationalization, which was established by the decree. This fund was used mostly for strategic industries and foreign capital–earning industries, which were important businesses for the *chaebol*—i.e., iron and steel, nonferrous metal, shipbuilding, electronics, electrical machinery, and coal. Seventy-three percent of the total fund, or 48.1 billion Won, was released between 1972 and June 1975 and was invested in these industries (Ibid.). These sectors were heavily dominated by the large *chaebol*. They are capital- and technology-intensive industrial sectors in which medium and small firms could not participate.

The third case involves bank loans. The interest rate for bank loans was lowered from 19 to 15.5 percent and was mostly used by firms with high debt—i.e., engine, turbine, automobile, and basic pharmaceutical companies. These industries were also dominated by the large *chaebol*. They are capital- and technology-intensive, and the *chaebol* were the only ones who could afford such businesses. Therefore, the large *chaebol* became the largest recipients of these loans.

Another example that illustrates the development of close linkages between politicians and the *chaebol* was the case of "disguised curb market loans." Since the interest rate was higher for curb market loans, it was a lucrative business if one had capital to lend. For instance, the company chair would lend his/her money to his/her own company as a curb market loan and receive high interest. This was called "disguised curb market loan," since it was capital accumulated in the business but went back into the business "disguised" as a curb market loan to accrue high interest.

There is some evidence that the news of this decree was secretly provided to a few *chaebol* by politicians closely involved in the policy. Partially as a result of this, 30 percent of reported curb market loans came from major stockholders or from members of the board of directors as disguised curb market loans. A report from a national assemblyman from the opposition party claimed that eight of the ten largest creditors' loans were disguised curb market loans (S. H. I 1985:273–74). For example, Shinjin Machinery had a bank account of more than $7.5 million (3 billion Won) but borrowed over $17.16 million (7 billion Won) from the curb market. Rumors are that an influential politician and patron of Shinjin revealed the secret of the decree to Shinjin before it was announced, and Shinjin acquired massive amounts of curb market loans before the freeze. Other large *chaebol* that had not borrowed from the curb market prior to the decree also suddenly acquired large loans between the end of July and the beginning of August (Ibid.). These curb market loans were quickly transferred into low-interest bank loans with the announcement of the Emergency Decree and resulted in increasing the total assets of the involved *chaebol*.

All these incidents resulted in aiding the large *chaebol* to acquire more funds to expand. The relationship between the state and the *chaebol* could no longer be characterized as antagonistic or remote as in the early 1960s when major *chaebol* leaders were jailed for illicit accumulation of wealth. These incidents imply that collusive relations were developing between some politicians and businesses. Whether the state initiated the decree in order to bail out the *chaebol* or whether the *chaebol* influenced the state to act on their behalf, the point remains that the relationship between the state and the *chaebol* had changed from an antagonistic to a more amicable one.

The consequences of the decree need to be examined from two perspectives—political and economical. Politically, the decree seemed to have solidified the ties between the state and the *chaebol*. The Emergency Decree implies some interesting changes. Evidence that suggests that the decree was leaked to a handful of *chaebol* prior to the announcement implies that the relations between the state (or, at least some members of the state who were involved in formulating this policy) and some *chaebol* have become quite close and collusive. Secondly, the fact that the decree had many provisions to protect the heavy and chemical firms, which were disproportionately owned by the large *chaebol*, indicates that the state was willing to forge a much closer tie with a select *chaebol*. These largest *chaebol* were important because they could not only finance the HCI but the political parties as well.

The economic consequences of the decree was to expedite and to further the oligopolization process in certain key industrial sectors—the heavy and chemical industries. The *chaebol* were left free to expand without competition from small- and medium-sized firms. Capital had been effectively reallocated within each industrial sector in favor of the *chaebol*. In the short run, the Emergency Decree solidified the government's relations with the *chaebol* and guaranteed the *chaebol*'s support for the state. However, in the long run, the *chaebol* were able to amass economic as well as political power that would help them challenge the state.

In sum, a comprehensive developmental state underwent restructuring during the 1970s in order to promote HCI. HCI was vigorously pushed initially by the Blue House and later by the Blue House, the EPB, and the Ministry of Trade and Industry with the assistance of the Ministry of Finance. This was clearly a case in which the state intervened and actually led the market in spite of objections from the market. Quite contrary to neoclassical economists, who suggest that the state only played a supporting role to the private sector, the 1970s' HCI was clearly led by the state.

The president's Emergency Decree of August 3, 1972, and HCI show that in the 1970s the Park regime clearly favored the large *chaebol* and, in particular, those that invested in the heavy and chemical industries. Through the generous support provided to promote HCI and through the Emergency Decree, the large *chaebol* were given an unusual competitive edge over the other *chaebol* and small- and medium-sized firms. In the next section, we examine what these "chosen" *chaebol* did to further their advantage and how the other less fortunate *chaebol* also grew based on their ingenuity and entrepreneurship.

The Concentration of Wealth and the Growth of the *Chaebol*

Many large enterprises grew and became *chaebol* during the 1970s. The *chaebol* acquired and founded many member firms, and they diversified businesses into related as well as unrelated sectors. The ten largest *chaebol* grew very rapidly during the 1970s, at a rate five to nine times faster than the economy as a whole (see Table 5.1). The list of the ten largest *chaebol* changed significantly since the early 1960s when Park came to power and promoted rapid economic development (see Table 4.1). By the end of the 1960s, a new group of Park-regime *chaebol* had appeared, and this list has remained fairly stable ever since.

The heavy and chemical industrialization and domestic political needs to garner support from the large *chaebol* prompted the state to forge a tight alliance with the leading *chaebol*. In return for the *chaebol*'s compliance, the state provided them with low-interest-rate loans and other protective measures. Those *chaebol* that invested heavily in state-targeted heavy and chemical industries grew at a phenomenal rate during the 1970s. The other *chaebol*, which invested only modestly in heavy and chemical industries, sought other sources of capital, especially from MNCs. The variations in the trajectory of the growth in the largest *chaebol* in the 1970s indicate that we need to seriously examine the role played by the *chaebol*, apart from the state's economic development plans and industrial policies.

Table 5.1
Basic Indicators of the Ten Largest *Chaebol*, 1971–80

Rank[a]	*Chaebol*	Foundation Year[b]	Total Assets[c] (in million Won) 1971	Total Assets[c] (in million Won) 1980	Average Annual Growth Rate of Total Assets (%) 1971–80
1	Hyundai	1947	158,261	2,874,114	38.0
2	Samsung	1951	415,978	1,901,127	18.4
3	Lucky–Gold Star	1947	437,060	1,825,429	17.2
4	Daewoo	1967	34,679	1,663,400	53.7
5	Ssangyong	1954	310,424	1,255,876	16.8
6	Han Jin	1945	83,734	1,085,337	32.9
7	Kukje	1949	153,489	772,993	19.3
8	Dae Lim	1939	64,522	748,795	31.8
9	Korea Explosives	1952	256,424	695,363	11.7
10	Sunkyong	1953	40,049	666,359	36.7

Notes: a. Rank order based on total assets in 1980.
b. Foundation year of a mother firm.
c. Total assets in 1980 constant Korean million Won.

The growth of the largest *chaebol* parallels the South Korean state's drive for HCI. Those *chaebol* that conformed to HCI seemed to have grown faster than others who did not. Most of the successful large *chaebol* received generous support from the state, but they also were led by entrepreneurs who were aggressive risk-takers, perhaps with the exception of Samsung's I.

The next section is organized around the following four issues to describe and analyze the growth patterns of the largest *chaebol* during the 1970s. First, we examine the growth of the state-targeted heavy and chemical firms within the *chaebol*. The *chaebol*'s growth during the 1970s depended in large measure on the growth of these firms. Second, we examine the construction industry as an example of an industry that was not a state target sector. The growth of this industry, and the *chaebol*'s involvement in it, illustrate that the growth of the *chaebol* is not solely dictated by the state. Third, we examine the horizontal diversification of the *chaebol*, a feature that is uncommon among business groups elsewhere, except the Japanese pre–World War II *zaibatsu*. Diversification into unrelated sectors increased during the 1970s, and it was partly an effort by the *chaebol* to become less dependent on the state. Lastly, we examine the MNCs' involvement with the *chaebol*. Again, the evidence suggests that the *chaebol* had more room to maneuver outside of the state's tight control than the state-centrists would argue. MNCs, although only a few in number in South Korea during the 1970s, were an important alternative source of capital and technology for the *chaebol* that did not seek, or receive, state support.

These four issues highlight several important arguments in this book. First, the *chaebol*'s growth patterns are more heterogeneous than assumed by the state-centrists. Second, the *chaebol*'s diversification and seeking out MNCs imply that the *chaebol*'s relations to the state is colored with contradiction and tension. On the one hand, the 1970s' largest *chaebol* were indebted to the state for its generous support during the 1960s and 1970s. On the other hand, the *chaebol* were at the same time trying hard to become less dependent on the state. The tension between these two tendencies will increase as the *chaebol* continue to grow.

The State-Targeted Heavy and Chemical Industries[11]

The growth rates of the *chaebol* during the 1970s was very impressive. The fastest-growing one was Daewoo, the youngest of the ten, which recorded an astonishing 53.7 percent average annual growth rate in total assets (see Table 5.1). This was followed by Hyundai's 38 percent. What these two *chaebol* share in common was their heavy investment in state-targeted heavy and chemical industries. Their impressive growth matches the shift in the state's industrial policy toward HCI. By 1980, 51 percent of Hyundai's total assets and 38 perce Daewoo's were in heavy manufacturing (see Table 5.2).

A closer examination of the heavy and chemical firms in which Hyundai and Daewoo invested will help us see the correlations between state policy shifts and the growth of the *chaebol*. For example, Hyundai's key heavy manufacturing firms during the 1970s were automobiles and shipbuilding. The Hyundai Motor Company has been a major producer of auto-

Table 5.2
Share of Assets in Business in the Four Largest *Chaebol*, 1970–80[a]
(in percentages)

Rank[b]	*Chaebol*	Year	Light Manu.	Heavy Manu.	Const- ruction	Finances
1	Hyundai	1970	0	85	15	0
		1975	0	86	12	2
		1980	1	51	37	3
2	Samsung	1970	66	8	0	22
		1975	51	13	0	18
		1980	29	28	7	21
3	Lucky–	1970	0	84	0	0
	Gold Star	1975	0	93	2	2
		1980	1	85	3	5
4	Daewoo	1970	21	0	79	0
		1975	1	39	43	11
		1980	2	38	51	7

Notes: a. Share of total assets was calculated using 1980 constant prices.
b. Rank order is based on total assets in 1980.

mobiles in South Korea. It had technology transfers and FDI from the Ford Motor Company of the United States in the late 1960s,[12] and it is currently working with Mitsubishi Motor Company of Japan. Hyundai began to export its automobiles to Canada in 1984, and it entered the U.S. market in 1986. Hyundai Motors has been a very successful producer of passenger automobiles for both the domestic and export markets. Hyundai's Excel was the best selling import car in the subcompact category in the United States from 1987 to 1989.

Daewoo's large investment in heavy and chemical firms more closely resembles the state's six target industries destined for generous loans. Most of Daewoo's twenty-four firms at the end of the 1970s were in automobiles, heavy machinery, ship-building, electronics, and construction. Daewoo invested in heavy manufacturing with the large amount of capital it acquired from exporting textiles to the United States from the late 1960s to the early 1970s. And because of its success in exports, it also received the state's export-aid loans, which carried an interest rate roughly one-third that of loans from private banks (S. K. Kim 1987). Daewoo became a major heavy manufacturing *chaebol* by the mid-1970s, using capital earned from the lucrative export business and low-interest state loans. In the eyes of Park, Hyundai and Daewoo were obedient conformists to the state's industrial policies, and they were rewarded generously.

Another large *chaebol* with considerable investment in the heavy manufacturing sector tells a different story. Lucky–Gold Star had 84 percent of its total assets in heavy manufacturing in 1970, 93 percent in 1975, and 85 percent in 1980. In fact, except in 1970 the share of its total assets in heavy manufacturing was the highest among the four largest *chaebol*. In spite of this, its growth rate was modest among the top ten *chaebol* with an average annual growth rate of 17.2 percent in total assets.[13]

A close examination of Lucky–Gold Star's investment shows that it was almost exclusively in the electrical and electronics industry. Unfortunately, although it was designated as a state target sector for HCI, it was not targeted for extensive loan packages. Instead, it was open for FDI earlier than other sectors.

As a result, Lucky–Gold Star did not receive an infusion of loan capital and did not grow as fast as the other heavy manufacturing *chaebol*.

A look at Samsung, which was slower than Hyundai or Daewoo in diversifying into heavy manufacturing, highlights the advantages enjoyed by Hyundai and Daewoo. Samsung is an example of a *chaebol* that did not invest heavily in the state-target industries but grew quite rapidly, albeit not as fast as those that conformed to the state's drive for HCI. Samsung grew at an average annual rate of 18.4 percent during the 1970s. Although this is a growth rate twice that of the entire economy, it is modest compared to the growth rates of Hyundai or Daewoo. As a result, by the end of the 1970s, Samsung was no longer the largest *chaebol* in South Korea. That seat was then occupied by Hyundai, a HCI-*chaebol*.

Several explanations can be given to account for Samsung's relatively modest growth during the 1970s. First, it could be because Samsung was already much larger than other *chaebol* in the beginning of the 1970s—over ten times larger than Hyundai. However, this means that Samsung had a tremendous advantage over other large businesses or *chaebol* when rapid economic development began in the 1960s, and it is surprising that it was unable to hold onto its position. Another more plausible explanation is that Samsung was slow to diversify into the heavy manufacturing sector. By 1980, it had increased its share to 28 percent, but it continued to have 29 percent of its total assets in light manufacturing, which was by far the largest among the top four *chaebol*. Furthermore, even in the heavy industries, it concentrated in electrical appliances and electronics, which were not generously subsidized by the state. Samsung's reluctance to invest in the state-target industries is due in part to the souring of its relationship with the Park regime following the bitter Hanguk Fertilizer incident in 1967. (See chapter 4 for details.)

Ever since that incident, I Pyŏng Ch'ŏl has been reluctant to deal with the state, avoiding any unnecessary direct contact over and above everyday dealings. This could, in fact, have caused him to avoid the heavy manufacturing sector, where the behind-the-scene dealings with the government were necessary from time to time. Samsung turned instead to MNCs for capital and technology. In particular, Samsung turned to Japanese MNCs (partly due to I's familiarity with Japanese businesses).

A more extreme case of a *chaebol* that did not grow as fast as those that conformed to the drive for HCI is that of Kukje. Unlike Samsung, which eventually decreased its share in light manufacturing, Kukje went in the opposite direction, moving from heavy to light manufacturing. Kukje was a shoe manufacturing firm for over two decades and could not be defined as a *chaebol* until the mid-1970s, when it rapidly expanded its businesses. Its share in light manufacturing increased sharply, from none in 1975 to 11 percent in 1980. This expansion contributed to its high debt rate and finally to its bankruptcy in 1985. (See chapter 6 for details.)

Construction

The story of the *chaebol*'s growth during the 1970s does not end with a simple statement that the state's support was the sole cause of their tremendous success. The growth trajectories of the largest *chaebol* demonstrate heterogenous growth patterns. Construction is presented as an example to illustrate how a few *chaebol*'s investment in this sector, which was not a state-target sector and thus not primed for generous state support, was important in their growth nevertheless. In fact, along with heavy manufacturing, construction experienced the most rapid growth during the 1970s, compared to light manufacturing, financial services, or trade. Construction companies played an important role in meeting the increased demands in the domestic market created by rapid industrialization and in aiding the development of other heavy industries through backward linkages to heavy machinery firms, construction material firms, and engineering companies. But more importantly, successful construction companies helped the *chaebol* to accumulate foreign exchange through overseas construction projects.

In fact, Hyundai's involvement in construction proved to be decisive for its success during the 1970s. It was the first South Korean construction company to go to the Middle East.

Although Japan had already made this move a few years before, Hyundai still managed to get large construction contracts, including the $931-million Jubail Industrial Harbor Project in Saudi Arabia. With its tremendous success in the Middle East, by 1978 Hyundai became the largest *chaebol* in South Korea. Hyundai, which was not even a *chaebol* when Park came into power, became the largest *chaebol* in less than two decades.

As a result of Hyundai's success in the Middle East, other large *chaebol* quickly founded construction companies and sent them to the Middle East. By 1980, all of the ten largest *chaebol* had construction companies. However, because of the saturation of the Middle Eastern construction market, increased unrest in that region, and limited experience of some construction companies, those *chaebol* that went into construction in the late 1970s with the specific goal of entering the Middle Eastern market left with little profit or, in some cases, went bankrupt.

Samsung, which was late in investing in construction lost its position as the largest *chaebol* and became the second largest. Its more conservative business strategy led it to take a "wait and see" attitude toward risky ventures such as overseas construction. Such a conservative business strategy did not help Samsung outpace its more bold competitors.

Hyundai's success in the overseas construction business and many other *chaebol*'s failure in it provide us with important insights. First, the most successful *chaebol* during the 1970s were not complacent conformists to the state's policies. They were led by bold and shrewd entrepreneurs, who took advantage of both the domestic and international markets. Second, contrary to the myth that the South Korean state bails out *chaebol* from business failures, quite a few construction firms that belonged to the *chaebol* went bankrupt. Thus, the success and failure of the *chaebol* and firms do not depend entirely on the state.

Diversification

An important feature of the *chaebol* is their horizontal diversification into often unrelated sectors. Through diversification, the *chaebol* are able to compete effectively in the lower end of the international market and, more importantly, they are able to become less dependent on the state. The *chaebol's* growing prosperity and diversification during the 1970s allowed them to gain more leverage against the state.

During the 1970s, the largest *chaebol* experienced growing diversification, especially in unrelated sectors (see Table 5.2). In 1970, the largest ten *chaebol*, with the exception of Samsung, were involved in either light or heavy manufacturing. Samsung alone had firms in both heavy and light manufacturing. However, in 1980, nearly all of the ten largest *chaebol* were involved in both areas (the exceptions were Han Jin, which operates exclusively in passenger transportation including Korean Airlines, and Dae Lim [Tae Lim], which is exclusively in construction).

The *chaebol's* diversification into services is particularly noteworthy. They diversified into construction, financial services, and trade. By 1980, all ten *chaebol* invested in construction, and nine also invested in financial institutions and eight in trading. There is no consistent pattern of a decrease or increase in services throughout the 1970s. This contrasts with the conspicuous increase in the share of assets in the heavy manufacturing sector in almost all the largest *chaebol*.

Although there is no general pattern in the *chaebol's* involvement in services, some interesting changes occurred in the 1970s. Between 1970 and 1975, there was a decrease in the share of assets in services in seven of the largest *chaebol*. This is probably more a result of a sharp increase in heavy manufacturing in response to the state's HCI. However, during the latter half of the 1970s, seven of the ten largest *chaebol* experienced increases in services.

The increases in construction and financial institutions are particularly noteworthy. As discussed earlier, increase in construction is due to rising domestic demands with infrastructure projects and industrialization as well as growing demands in the overseas construction business. However, construction was not singled out by the state as an industry in need of governmental support. The growth in this industry reflects the private sector's recognition of the growing demands in the domestic and international markets. An important difference between heavy manufacturing and construction is that while the former was clearly initiated and led by the state, the latter implies a greater degree of autonomous decision making on the part of the private sector.

The growth in financial institutions is yet another story. This is a clear case in which the *chaebol* reacted to the state's nationalization of the banks and its resultant control of the economy. The *chaebol* invested in the nonbanking financial institutions in order to become less dependent on the state for capital. As is discussed in chapter 3, nonbanking financial institutions, such as the investment companies and insurance companies, deal with large sums of cash and are able to channel cash to member firms in need and to provide short-term loans without having to go through the complex banking system. Such speedy cash transactions allowed the *chaebol* to avoid short-term cash flow problems. As a result, it allowed the *chaebol* increasing leverage against the state-owned banks.

Multinational Corporations as a Source of Capital and Technology

Multinational corporations became an important alternate source of capital and technology for some of the *chaebol* that did not want to (or, could not, for whatever reason) conform to the state's industrial policies and receive generous loan packages from the state. The electrical and electronics industry provide an interesting story regarding MNCs and the *chaebol*. Because the state deemed this sector to be more advanced than other state-target sectors, it did not provide generous loan packages. In turn, it was open for FDI earlier than the other sectors. Interestingly, those *chaebol* that did not invest in the other more lucrative state-target sectors invested heavily in the electrical and electronics sector. Samsung and Lucky–Gold Star were the two prime examples. They sought MNCs for the needed capital and technology more often and in larger amounts than the other large *chaebol*, who relied more on the state.

Lucky–Gold Star was known as a *chaebol* built on plastics and on electrical appliances and electronics. However, it had no large firms in machinery or construction. It was very successful in attracting FDI and technology transfers from MNCs and in acquiring foreign loan capital; in fact, Lucky–Gold Star was involved in more FDI and technology transfers than any other major *chaebol* during the 1970s. The following is a list of Lucky–Gold Star's technology transfers:

- Gold Star Telecommunications Co., Ltd.: Siemens Aktien Gesellschaft (W. Germany)
- Gold Star Alps Electronics Co., Ltd.: ALPS Electric Co., Ltd. (Japan)
- Gold Star Electric Co., Ltd: Nippon Electric Co., Ltd. (Japan)
- Gold Star Instrument and Electric Co., Ltd.: Fuji Electric Co., Ltd. (Japan)
- Gold Star Semiconductor Ltd.: AT&T (U.S.)
- Shin Yeong [Shin Yŏng] Electric Corp.: Mitsubishi Electric Co. (Japan); Mitsubishi Corp. (Japan)

Of the four largest firms in Lucky–Gold Star, the three largest received FDI. These were Honam Oil Refinery Co. Ltd.: Caltex Ltd. 50 percent joint venture (U.S.); Gold Star Co., Ltd.: International Finances Corporation; and Lucky, Ltd.: National Plastic Company (Japan).

Lucky–Gold Star had a good relationship with the South Korean government in the 1960s. In the early 1960s, Lucky–Gold Star won at least three controversial deals involving foreign loan capital and local bank loans against its biggest competitor, Taihan [Taehan] Electric Wire Co., Ltd. Behind Lucky–Gold Star was Ku T'ae Hoe, a key member of the ruling party under Park. However, in the 1970s, Lucky–Gold Star did not emerge as a favorite of the Park regime. This could be because it did not follow the state's drive for the HCI. Whether the state decided not to award lucrative state-target industry loans to Lucky–Gold Star or whether Lucky–Gold Star decided not to invest in such industries, the results were the same. Lucky–Gold Star did not invest in the lucrative state-target sectors. Instead, it sought FDI and technology from MNCs and invested heavily in electronics and electrical appliances.

Like Lucky–Gold Star, Samsung had many technology transfers from MNCs, especially in electrical and electronics firms, with some in shipbuilding, textiles, and petrochemicals. Most of Samsung's FDI partners are Japanese, with a few U.S. MNCs. Of the four largest firms in Samsung, only the largest— Dong Bang Life Insurance Co., Ltd.—had FDI from both Japan and the United States: Kyoei Life Insurance and Lincoln National, respectively. The list of Samsung's technology transfers is as follows:

- Samsung Shipbuilding and Heavy Industries Co., Ltd.: Ishikawajima Heavy Industries Company (Japan).
- Sam Sung Electron Devices Co., Ltd.: Nippon Electric Co. (Japan); Joowoo Co. (Japan)
- Samsung Corning: Corning Co., Ltd. (U.S.)
- Sam Sung Electronic Parts Co., Ltd.: Sanyo (Japan)
- Cheil Synthetic Textiles Co., Ltd: Tore (Japan); Mitsui (Japan)   *Torai*
- Sam Sung Petrochemical Co., Ltd: Amoco Chemicals Co. (U.S.); Mitsui Petrochemical Co. (Japan)

As noted earlier, Samsung's relations with the Park regime spoiled after the Hanguk Fertilizer incident. And like Lucky–Gold Star, Samsung was not quick to invest in state-targeted and state-funded sectors in the 1970s.

Unlike Samsung or Lucky–Gold Star, which had a large presence of FDI from MNCs, Hyundai and Daewoo had relatively few cases of FDI. Hyundai was known to resist FDI from MNCs, except when it was accompanied with technology transfers. And even when Hyundai received FDI, it tried to retain majority ownership. For example, a deal with General Motors failed because Chŏng Chu Yŏng of Hyundai refused to accept a fifty-fifty joint venture. General Motors subsequently entered into such a venture with Daewoo Motors, while Hyundai agreed to a limited FDI with Mitsubishi Motor Company and Mitsubishi Corporation. These two Japanese corporations had 10 percent ownership when Hyundai signed the contract in October 1981. Of the four largest firms in Hyundai, the third largest, Hyundai Motor Company, is the only one with FDI. In 1985, the Mitsubishi Motor Company had 7.5 percent, and the Mitsubishi Corporation had 7.5 percent ownership in the Hyundai Motor

Company (Ministry of Finance 1990b). Thus, the Mitsubishi Motor Company and the Mitsubishi Corporation had only minority ownership in the Hyundai Motor Company, which limited the former's ability to control the management of the latter.

Daewoo was known as one of the favored *chaebol* of the Park regime. Daewoo received preferential treatment in the distribution of the takeover of insolvent enterprises by the state. Because many of the takeovers by Daewoo involved enterprises in financial difficulties, it also received low-interest-rate loans from the state. The cases of takeover by Daewoo included the following: Daewoo Heavy Industries Ltd., received in 1976 from Shinjin (and previously owned by the state); Daewoo Motor Co., Ltd., received in 1977 from Shinjin; and Daewoo Shipbuilding, received from Taihan Chosŏn Kongsa (state enterprise). On the other hand, there were not many technology transfers in Daewoo. Of the four largest firms in Daewoo, the fourth largest, Daewoo Motor Company, Ltd., was the only one with FDI. In 1982, this firm entered a fifty-fifty joint venture with General Motors.

The trend in MNC involvement among the *chaebol* shows that those that had good relationships with the state and had large investments in heavy manufacturing did not have much FDI or many technology transfers. On the other hand, those *chaebol* that were not heavily involved in the state's direct-support industries were more inclined to have FDI and technology transfers from MNCs. Samsung and Lucky–Gold Star, which did not shift their industrial production toward heavy manufacturing industries, were more dependent on MNCs for capital and technology than on the state. And although their growth rates were somewhat slower (Samsung had 18.4 and Lucky–Gold Star had 17.2 percent average annual growth rate in total assets) than that of Hyundai's or Daewoo's, their growth rates were much faster than the economy as a whole. The evidence suggests that Samsung and Lucky–Gold Star were quite successful in attracting FDI and technology transfers from MNCs. Their growth stories illustrate that the *chaebol* have more independence than assumed in the state-centered studies of South Korean development.

Concluding Remarks

The 1970s was a decade of growing symbiosis between the state and the *chaebol*. The state was much more in need of the *chaebol*'s support in the 1970s compared to the 1960s. The drive for HCI required the financial capabilities of the large businesses, which could afford the capital- and technology-intensive heavy and chemical industries. On the other hand, although reluctant at first, the *chaebol* saw a real opportunity to prosper with the state's generous subsidies and protection.

The tight alliance between the state and the largest *chaebol* helped consolidate a conservative coalition, solidifying the support of the *chaebol* for the state. The heavy and chemical industrialization and the president's Emergency Decree show the changing nature of the state-business relationship: the alliance was no longer between the state and large businesses, but more specifically between the state and a few *chaebol* chosen by Park. There was growing interdependence and symbiosis between the two, since the cooperation from the *chaebol* had become important in the face of political uncertainty.

The 1970s was a period of growth for both the state and the *chaebol*. The comprehensive developmental state restructured to become even more interventionist in the economy. The EPB and the Ministry of Trade and Industry, in particular, strengthened those departments and bureaus whose main task was to promote HCI. The newly strengthened economic ministries vigorously pursued HCI under the leadership of the Blue House.

The *chaebol*, at first, were not enthusiastic about HCI. Having had less than a decade of growth based on light industries did not prepare the *chaebol* to plunge into an unpredictable future in heavy and chemical industries. However, with the state's promise for generous support, several *chaebol*—most notably, Hyundai, which was already in heavy industries, and Daewoo, and Ssangyong—joined hands with the state for HCI. The success of these *chaebol*, however, cannot be attributed solely to the comprehensive developmental state's support. Hyundai, for example, went to the Middle East with its construction company, and, at the end, it was the success in construction that helped Hyundai become the largest *chaebol* by the end of the 1970s. Thus, the arguments made by state-centered studies, which tend to equate *chaebol* success with state intervention, are exaggerated and somewhat misguided. State support is important, but that is not the whole story. The favorable international economy and, more importantly, the *chaebol*'s entrepreneurship were vital for the success of the *chaebol* in the 1970s.

The growth of the other *chaebol*, especially Samsung and Lucky–Gold Star, also shows that state support is not the only ingredient for *chaebol* success. These *chaebol* were not selected by the state as partners for HCI, and/or the *chaebol* themselves decided not to pursue a tight collusive alliance with the state. Reasons may vary, but the results were similar. These *chaebol* invested in industrial sectors, in which state control and supervision was less pronounced, and reached out to MNCs for capital and technology. The success of these *chaebol* in the 1970s is affirmation that the *chaebol* can grow even when they do not adhere closely to the state's initiatives.

The 1970s also witnessed a growing diversification in *chaebol*'s businesses, especially in the nonbanking financial services. This implies the growing independence of the *chaebol* from the state. In the next chapter, we examine how the autonomy of the *chaebol vis à vis* the state continued to grow in the 1980s.

6

The Decline of the Developmental State and the Rise of the Chaebol (1980s)

The 1980s were a time of great social, economic, and political upheaval in South Korea. The Chun Doo Hwan regime (1980–88) faced pressures from the large *chaebol* and labor to restructure the comprehensive developmental state. The South Korean formula for economic growth—i.e., a strong, comprehensive developmental state, a tight alliance between the state and the *chaebol*, and exclusion and repression of labor—had worked well during the 1960s and 1970s but came under fire as the *chaebol* and labor grew. The *chaebol* in particular flourished during the 1980s in spite of reduced state support. By the end of the 1980s, South Korean media and publications referred to the increasing dominance of the *chaebol* in the nation's political, social, and economic arenas as the *"Chaebol* Republic"[1] (*Wŏlgan Chosŏn* 1989; Yu 1991). Labor, which had hitherto been relatively obsequious, exploded with discontent toward the end of the 1980s. Despite one of the most repressive regimes with regard to labor, South Korea had developed one of the most militant labor movements in Asia's history (Deyo 1987b). In response to these pressures, the comprehensive developmental state was restructured to become a limited developmental state.

On the political front, a more dramatic change occurred. The Chun regime faced increasingly violent demonstrations for democracy in 1986 and 1987. As a result, the authoritarian state broke down and democratic consolidation began. In December 1987, a direct presidential election was held for the first time in almost two decades. The newly elected President Roh Tae Woo (1988–92) and his regime continued the restructuring of the comprehensive developmental state, amid some confusion as democratization presented added challenges to the process of state restructuring.

Changes in the world and in South Korea also made the latter more connected to the changes abroad compared to the earlier two decades of growth. First, the world in general had become much more tightly knit with improved communication and technology. This is a phenomenon that had affected all nations in the world. This, coupled with the fact that many families in South Korea could afford television sets compared to the 1960s, when there were fewer than one television set per ten households, made the impact of the shrinking world quite palpable to the South Koreans. Second, South Korea became more intricately integrated in the world economy with exports, MNC investments in South Korea, and South Korea's investments overseas. Perhaps more so than other developing nations, which pursued inward-looking industrialization strategies, South Korea had become quickly and inexorably linked to the world economy. And finally, South Korea's remarkable economic success made it a target of the U.S. trade war. Unlike before, South Korea's increased visibility in the international economy prompted a closer scrutiny by its trading partners. The United States increased its pressure toward Japan and other NICs in East Asia, prompted primarily by the continued trade deficit with Japan. One of the United States's demands toward South Korea was that it open the economy to U.S. investments, products, and services. Although the United States did not pressure South Korea to restructure its economy, as it did Japan, the pressure to open the South Korean economy had indirectly implied that the South Korean state should reduce the protection of domestic businesses.

These changes were felt and crystallized within the state. The comprehensive developmental state was forced to reevaluate its *raison d'être*: since the main goal of the state—i.e., economic development—was attained, the rationale for the comprehensive developmental state no longer existed. In particular, the EPB and the Ministry of Trade and Industry faced the greatest challenges to reestablish their institutional goals and functions.

Despite these major international and domestic political, economic, and social changes, the South Korean economy continued to outperform its counterparts in the developing world. The average annual growth rate of GNP per capita was 13.8 percent during the 1980s, with the figure rising from $1,734 to $5,569 by the end of the decade (National Statistical Office 1991). For the GDP, the average annual growth rate during this decade was 9.7 percent, making the economy's rate of growth the second fastest in the world (Ibid.). South Korea's remarkable economic recovery after a negative growth in 1980 (–5.2 percent) following the domestic social and political unrest of the 1979 assassination of President Park, and the second oil crisis in the same year, belied the image of a developing nation that could attain only short-term growth (Ibid.).

The economic structure continued to mature. The percentage of workers employed in agriculture, forestry, fishing, and mining decreased from 35.1 percent in 1981 to 18.3 percent in 1990, while the percentage in manufacturing rose from 20.4 percent to 26.9 percent and those in services from 44.5 percent to 54.4 percent (Ibid.). Exports remained vital for development and grew rapidly during the 1980s. Throughout the 1980s, exports accounted for more than 35 percent of South Korea's GNP with an average annual growth rate of 12.8 percent; in 1990, South Korea was the tenth-largest exporter in the world, with an export figure of $65 billion (World Bank 1992). South Korean–made products were no longer found only in huge piles of reduced-price goods at discount stores. While the country's export products had once been primarily stuffed toys, wigs, sneakers, and cheap clothing, they now included electrical and electronic appliances, computers, and automobiles. And many existing products moved out of the market's low end into the middle and upper ranges.

This chapter addresses the following questions: How was South Korea able to grow at a rapid pace in spite of major changes in the South Korean formula for economic development? What domestic and international political and economic factors contributed to the transition of the developmental state? What was entailed in the process of transition, and what became of the developmental state? How did the *chaebol* and labor change in the process? How did democratization impact upon economic restructuring? And, is the 1980s formula for growth in South Korea qualitatively different from that of the 1960s and 1970s?

The Transition of a Comprehensive Developmental State to a Limited Developmental State

A developmental state changes over time. If the developmental state fails to deliver its primary objective—i.e., economic growth—, those in charge of development policies will not be reelected or will be forced to resign, and the economic policies and the way in which they are implemented will have to change. Unless the political system is completely closed, it is reasonable to expect such outcomes. The irony of the South Korean case lies in the fact that the state was forced to reevaluate its *raison d'être* upon its success in attaining economic growth. After nearly two decades of phenomenal economic development, the South Korean state, which had been largely responsible for that development, had to loosen its tight control of the economy. Moon (1988) argues that the neoconservative economic reforms undertaken by the Chun government resulted in the demise of the developmental state in South Korea. This is different from the argument that I am making here, which is that economic reforms are the likely outcome of the success of a developmental state. These reforms are not arbitrary political choices but are attempts to deal with the fundamental contradictions and inherent limits of a developmental state. They are, therefore, not the *cause* of the decline of a developmental state, but rather *symptoms* of a declining developmental state.

Several domestic and international conditions came together during the late 1970s and early 1980s and prompted the state to restructure. The formula based on a comprehensive developmental state, a tight alliance between the state and the *chaebol*, and repressive state policies toward labor, which brought two decades of phenomenal economic growth, came under fire. In particular, the state's HCI strategy of the 1970s helped produce a small group of super-wealthy *chaebol*. They became an important voice demanding that the state reduce its control in the economy, in spite of the fact that they owed much of their earlier prosperity to the state's subsidies and protection.

Labor, on the other hand, was repressed during the 1960s and 1970s. However, labor mobilized, first underground and later legally with changes in the labor law. Ironically, the HCI of the 1970s brought relatively well-educated workers into large factories, providing fertile ground for labor union mobilization. Unlike labor unions in other nations, South Korean labor unions clearly saw that both the state and capitalists were culprits in keeping wages low and working conditions poor in the preceding decades. Thus, labor's two enemies became the state and the capitalists. And as soon as the labor union law was changed in 1987, labor unrest skyrocketed. In 1987, after years of repressive labor policies and relatively dormant labor activities, the number of labor strikes reached a record high of more than 3,600 cases.

Although the demands of capitalists and labor differed significantly, they both wanted the state to alter its old method of managing and controlling the economy. The capitalists wanted the state to become a *protectionist government*: one that continued to provide protection to, but ceases the heavy-handed control of, the private sector. Selective control, especially control of the labor movement and of wages, continued to be favored by the large capitalists, as they lamented that labor uprising since the mid-1980s had caused decreased production. On the other hand, labor pressed the state to become a *welfare state*: one that would protect the rights of workers and provide social services to citizens. Labor also wanted the state to control and limit the increasing power of the *chaebol*. The state was obligated to listen to the demands of both groups, since the political environment was one of democracy and not of autocracy by the end of the 1980s.

Incentives to change the economic policies were also based on the political climate of the early 1980s. When Chun came into power in August 1980 without a popular democratic election, he adopted an economic policy distinct from his predecessor, Park, with whom he was closely identified. This was to dispel the popular belief that Chun would be another strong military-based authoritarian leader. It had now become a legacy for the South Korean presidents without legitimacy to try to obtain public support through economic delivery. In his effort to make a clear departure from Park's legacy, Chun studiously followed the advice of key economic advisors such as Kim Chae Ik and Kang Kyŏng Shik, who promoted the ideas of "free market" (Amsden 1994a; Moon 1988).[2] This "free market" team, which was composed of Kim Chae Ik, Kang Kyŏng Shik, and Kŭm Chin Ho, blamed the previous regime's overinvestment in the heavy industries for the negative growth of 1980. Although the negative growth was largely a result of the second oil crisis (a crisis that affected the entire world economy), and domestic turmoil following President Park's assassination in 1979, the "free market" team made Park's HCI a sacrificial lamb.

It is an irony that although Park was largely known as the proponent of growth-oriented economic development strategies, it was Park who first announced plans to liberalize the economy. On April 17, 1979, six months before his assassination, Park announced the Economic Stabilization Measures. These measures had two major objectives: price stabilization and the establishment of a competitive market system through economic liberalization (C. W. Kim 1981; Moon 1988). The measures were not pushed vigorously by the Park regime, and they suffered a major setback following the assassination of President Park on October 26, 1979. This case is analogous to the Charges on Illicit Accumulation of Wealth, which were initially devised by the Chang regime but were not forcefully implemented until the Park regime came into power in 1961 and were used as a tool to sever ties with the past and demonstrate the power of the new regime.

The push to restructure the economy also came from abroad. The growing trade deficit between the United States and several East Asian nations, including Japan, South Korea, and Taiwan, became an important impetus for change. The Reagan administration pressured these nations to open their markets to U.S. goods and financial institutions to redress the trade deficit. Although the pressure was greatest for Japan, which had the largest trade surplus with the United States among the East Asian nations, South Korea was also visited by the Commerce secretary, Carla Hills, who demanded that the country implement a series of economic liberalization and internationalization measures.

These pressures point to the increasing contradictions associated with a comprehensive developmental state, which I outline in chapter 2. First, economic development as a national priority was no longer warranted due to over two decades of phenomenal economic growth. Hence, there was a growing need for the comprehensive developmental state to reassess its goals and functions. Second, the comprehensive developmental state was increasingly perceived as performing roles that the private sector was willing and capable to provide. And finally, the autonomy of the state also began to erode, as the capitalist class grew in size and influence and as the number of marriages between the offspring of the state officials and business leaders increased leading to blurred class distinction between the two groups.

South Korea's popular monthly magazines and books have dealt with the growing complex web of marriages within the capitalist class and between the capitalist class and the political elites (Seoul Kyŏngje Shinmun 1991). Even the *Wall Street Journal* devoted almost a quarter of a page to this phenomenon with a diagram of family ties. The article by Damon Darlin was titled, "South Korea Contract Award Spotlights Marriage of the Nation's Political and Business Families" (*Wall Street Journal* August 21, 1992:A4). It focused on the speculation that large *chaebol* were yielding considerable influence in the political arena through such family ties. For example, the article questioned the cause-and-effect link between the fact that President Roh's daughter was married to the son of the chair of the Sunkyong *chaebol* and that Sunkyong just won the lucrative rights to start South Korea's second mobile telephone company (Ibid.).

The contradictions in terms of the institution and autonomy intensified with successful economic development. These inherent contradictions of the comprehensive developmental state, and other pressures discussed earlier, forced the Chun regime to restructure the state. Thus, President Chun promoted "Economic Stabilization and Economic Liberalization" as his main economic policy. The following changes occurred in the comprehensive developmental state: *reprioritizing of industrial policies, economic liberalization,* and *internationalization.* These three processes signify a transition of the developmental state from comprehensive to limited. First, active state intervention that was developmental decreased to a limited number of industrial sectors. Second, policies that were regulatory rather than developmental had become prominent. In other words, industrial policies that provided incentives for businesses were phased out, and policies that regulated business activities *post facto* increased. And, finally, important policy tools (e.g., state-owned domestic banks, policy loans, industrial licensing, and industrial targeting) were removed from the government. These processes irreversibly altered the way the state intervened in the economy. Since the state dispensed most of its effective tools of enforcement, it would be extremely difficult to return to a more extensive and comprehensive state intervention in the future.

In South Korea, this process of transition of the developmental state faced added challenges when democratic consolidation progressed in the late 1980s. The democratization movement escalated against the repressive Chun regime. In the spring of 1987, thousands of angry demonstrators filled the streets of Seoul and other major cities. Scenes of political unrest were broadcast daily around the world, just as South Korea was preparing to host the 1988 Summer Olympics. On June 29, 1987, Roh Tae Woo announced the Declaration for Democracy, ending nearly three decades of dictatorial military rule. In December of that year, the country held a direct presidential election for the first time in almost two decades.

However, this period of great promise for a democratic South Korea also brought confusion to the transition of the developmental state. As discussed in chapter 2, democratization entailed a broader set of changes that engulfed the transition of the developmental state. The political climate of democratization prompted the state to cater to divergent demands, and its economic policies oscillated between probusiness and prolabor policies during the late 1980s and early 1990s.

Reprioritizing of Industrial Policies

Reprioritizing of industrial policies was carried out in the 1980s to find new institutional goals of the state, since economic development could no longer be the sole primary policy objective. Welfare and foreign policy were introduced as new objectives. Although foreign policy was important during previous administrations, it never received the attention and material support as economic development did. Welfare, on the other hand, was seen by past presidents as something South Korea could not afford. "Economic growth first and distribution (and provision of welfare services) later" was South Korea's implicit goal during the Park regime. Thus, the introduction of welfare and foreign policy as the foremost priorities of the state was a new development in the 1980s.

Provision of welfare services became a focal point in the 1980s, and the economic development plan was renamed to add "social" to its title, becoming the Fifth Five-Year Economic and Social Development Plan (1982–86). The promotion of national welfare and the equitable distribution of income became the heart of the social development programs. Specific goals included: increasing employment opportunities, increasing opportunities for education, providing health care and improving living conditions for the low-income class, implementing the national pension system, extending national medical insurance, and enhancing cooperative labor-management relations (EPB 1983, 1986). As a result, the proportion of the population covered by medical insurance increased dramatically, from a mere 0.06 percent in 1970 (18,713 of 32.24 million people) to 92 percent in 1989 (39,887,770 of 42.38 million) (EPB 1990). Government expenditure on social and welfare services rose steadily, while defense spending decreased (see Table 6.1). Social and welfare services accounted for almost 40 percent of government expenditures in 1990, up from about a quarter in 1976.

Table 6.1
Government Expenditure on Selected Items, 1976–90
(in percent)

	1976	1980	1985	1990[a]
General Administration	9.2	8.3	9.3	10.1
Defense	26.4	25.4	21.6	18.5
Social and Welfare Services	26.1	28.7	31.7	39.2
Education	14.6	14.8	16.3	15.9
Health	1.6	2.0	2.3	3.0
Social Services and Welfare	4.1	5.5	4.6	6.9
Housing	5.1	5.9	7.3	6.2
Other	0.7	0.5	1.2	0.5
Total (billion Won)	2,922.2	9,255.8	18,443.1	38,615.3

Note: a. Budget.
Source: Bank of Korea 1986, 1990, 1991.

However, by the end of the 1980s, the *chaebol* began to urge the state to return to growth-oriented policies and to abandon welfare services. Between 1989–90, President Roh announced revisions in the Sixth Five-Year Economic and Social Development Plan, which included slowing down of the provision of welfare services, and appointed economic ministers identified as supporters of growth-oriented policies.

President Roh put foreign policy as one of his regime's top priorities. The Roh regime successfully established diplomatic relations with many previously socialist Eastern and Central European nations. South Korea, along with North Korea, finally became a member of the United Nations on September 17, 1991, which was a long-held aspiration of many Koreans. The drive for reunification with North Korea became an important topic in the 1980s, although the government, and the student activists and dissidents diverged widely in the scope and in the speed of the reunification process. On December 27, 1990, Roh promoted the National Unification Board's minister to become one of the two ex-officio deputy prime ministers. Prior to this, the minister of the EPB had been the only deputy prime minister. On December

13, 1991, the two Koreas signed a Nonaggression Pact in Seoul, formally ending the Korean War, and on December 31, 1991, officials from South Korea and North Korea initialed an agreement banning nuclear weapons from the Korean peninsula. Through the latter agreement the two Koreas decided to ban the usage and manufacture of nuclear weapons, to not own plutonium refining facilities, and to sign an agreement for mutual monitoring of nuclear facilities. At the end of January 1992, North Korea finally agreed to the International Atomic Inspection Agency's (IAEA) treaty and allowed the IAEA to visit North Korea in order to inspect Yŏngbyŏn, where U.S. intelligence believed that North Korea had nuclear facilities.

Much has happened in the 1990s in South and North Korean relations. These include inspections by IAEA of North Korea's nuclear facilities. Each IAEA inspection was conducted after a great deal of intense and often fragile negotiations among the North Korean government, the IAEA, the U.S. government, and the South Korean government. On February 15, 1994, IAEA announced that North Korea had agreed to an inspection of the North Korean facilities. In response, the Clinton administration decided to postpone the "Team Spirit" joint annual military exercise between the United States and South Korean troops. On March 21, 1994, South and North Korea announced that a historic presidential talk between South Korea's President Kim Young Sam and North Korea's President Kim Il Sŏng would take place on July 25, 1994, in North Korea's capital, P'yŏngyang. This was the first time a presidential-level talk was planned between the two Koreas. However, less than three weeks before the historic talk, President Kim Il Sŏng of North Korea died suddenly on July 8, 1994, and the talk was derailed.

After much consternation, North Korea and the United States finally signed an agreement for a framework to work on the nuclear issues on October 20, 1994, in Geneva, Switzerland. In return for halting the development of nuclear weapons, which North Korea neither confirmed nor denied it had, North Korea was to receive assistance in building a light-water nuclear reactor. This facility would diminish the chance that North Korea would develop nuclear weapons using spent fuel. A consortium of advanced industrialized nations and South Korea is currently working on this proposal, with a large part of the funds to be provided by the South Korean government. The agreement in Geneva was seen as a step toward a full normalization of relations between North Korea and the United States. The South Korean government announced that South Korean businesses could resume their business ventures in North Korea after the Geneva agreement, since the agreement met the condition put in place by the South Korean government for allowing South Korean businesses to invest in North Korea. South Korean businesses have since then established joint ventures and are in the process of establishing joint ventures and investing in the Rajin-Sŏnbong Special Economic Zone (Namkoong 1995:54–55). However, there are still many obstacles to overcome for South Korean businesses to invest in North Korea on a larger scale. Perhaps the most important issue is that the North Korean government is concerned that even a partial opening of its economy could lead to a ground swell of demands for political change from its citizens (Ibid.). Such concerns have made the North Korean government reluctant to fully open its market and let market reforms take place, despite its need for an infusion of foreign capital and technology in order to sustain its fragile economy. North Korea has also been pursuing normalization with Japan by initiating a government-level contact with Japan in August 23, 1994 (Yoo 1995: 24).[3]

Economic Liberalization

Economic liberalization involved the restructuring of industrial policies so that they would become more limited in scope and would change from being developmental to being regulatory. Each of the three economic ministries undertook measures toward this end but not without any problems.

The EPB significantly reduced policy loans to the private sector, which had been used as effective tools of state intervention: that is, loans with substantially lowered interest rates were provided as inducement for private enterprises to invest in strategic industries, and loans were withheld to punish private enterprises that did not comply with government policies. Policy loans were abundant, accounting for 63 percent of total bank loans in 1979 (S. K. Kim 1987:181). Between 1977 and 1979, 80 percent of total investment in manufacturing went to the heavy industry in the form of policy loans (Moon 1988:69). The *chaebol* had a strong presence in this industry and so were the largest beneficiaries of the loans. However, these loans were gradually abandoned with the drive for economic liberalization and the fiscal tightening of the 1980s (Ibid.).

The policies of the EPB also changed to become more regulatory than developmental. Instead of having policy loans to proactively encourage private enterprises to enter certain industries (i.e., developmental policy), the government announced the Monopoly Regulation and Fair Trade Law on December 31, 1980, which became effective on April 1 of the following year. This is a prime case of a regulatory policy that received much attention from the government (EPB 1982). Under this law, the Fair Trade Commission and the Office of Fair Trade were established within the EPB in 1981 (EPB 1989). With these changes the EPB lost much of its luster of the 1960s and 1970s when it was the mastermind of the five-year economic development plans. One important role it retained through the restructuring process is the compiling of the national budget.

In 1981, the Ministry of Finance began to privatize domestic banks that had been owned by the government for the past two decades. However, in the privatization process, the *chaebol* were specifically prohibited from acquiring these banks. The *chaebol* were prevented from owning more than 8 percent of any one bank's stocks. This was to prevent the *chaebol* from ever becoming as formidable as the pre–World War II *zaibatsu* of Japan, which owned both financial institutions and industrial enterprises. The privatization was completed by 1983 (FKI 1987). The Bank of Korea, which is the central bank, still remains under the control of the Ministry of Finance. A tug of war continues between the Ministry of Finance and the Bank of Korea, as each try to be in charge of the central bank in the financial liberalization process. The Ministry of Finance would like to retain its ability to control the Bank of Korea, while the latter would like to become an independent organization.

The Ministry of Trade and Industry, which was on the front line dealing with individual private enterprises, underwent the most drastic changes in the 1980s. The following is based on interviews with the director of the Division of Transportation Equipment at the Ministry of Trade and Industry, Mr. Han Tŏk Su, in the summer of 1988. Han was a central figure in streamlining the industrial targeting laws and in promoting the new Law on Industrial Development, promulgated in July 1986. The streamlining met with criticisms within the ministry, since it significantly reduced employee work loads, thus threatening employee cutbacks during a time of economic hardship. However, it was ultimately implemented with the backing of the president, who was by then a staunch believer of economic liberalization.

The two most significant achievements of this legislature were the removal of entry barriers to most industries and the introduction of a finite time limit for the state's protection and support of industries. First, by the mid-1980s, industrial targeting changed from the selection of sectors that promised the most growth in the future to the selection of sectors in greatest need for the state's financial assistance and protection. Those included a select number of both infant and declining industries. The amount and scope of subsidies were also cut during this restructuring. In comparison, during the 1970s, six heavy and chemical industries were selected as state target sectors and received low-interest-rate loans (with the exception of electrical and electronic firms), tax breaks, and tariff exemptions. In July 1986, the Law on Industrial Development was put in practice. This law replaced seven industry-specific promotion laws for development (the industries were iron and steel, petrochemicals, nonferrous metal, textiles, machinery, electronics, and shipbuilding). The new law was promulgated in line with the general goal of economic liberalization and internationalization.

Targeting was given a finite limit of three years, so that private enterprises could no longer depend on government subsidies indefinitely. Han argued that the time limit provided the protected industry to grow in order to withstand market competition, and, more importantly, the finite time limit disciplined the private sector from becoming a rent-seeker. Lastly, licensing was simplified, and in most cases it no longer required advance government approval. As a result, the hallways of the Ministry of Trade and Industry were no longer flooded with managers from private enterprises trying to obtain industrial licensing or other subsidies. For the author, it was an unexpected benefit, since bureaucrats were eager to talk for one to two hours, because their work load had been cut relative to the previous decades.

Internationalization

Internationalization included decreases in regulations for foreign direct investment and imports and the opening up of the financial system. The pressure from the Reagan administration was important in this process. During President Reagan's second term in office (1984–88), several high-level trade dialogues were convened between the United States and Japan and the United States and other East Asian NICs. The mounting trade deficit between the United States and South Korea in the early to mid-1980s prompted the United States to urge South Korea to open its domestic market to foreign goods and foreign investors.

In response to these pressures, in 1987 the Foreign Investment Law was changed to remove most of the restrictions regarding which sectors would be closed to foreign direct investment, as well as the amount of investment allowed. As a result, the share of manufacturing industries open to foreign direct investment increased to 92.5 percent (EPB 1986b). During the Fifth Five-Year Economic and Social Development Plan (1982–86), import liberalization and the reduction of tariff rates were instituted (EPB 1988). Foreign banks' share in the lending market increased from 4 percent in 1975 to 12.9 percent in 1984, after the South Korean government promulgated a policy to gradually open its capital market to foreigners in 1981 (FKI 1987:39–40).

The Growth of the *Chaebol*   181 – 200

The *chaebol* continued to expand and dominate the South Korean economy, even after state subsidies were drastically cut in the early 1980s. The *chaebol*'s growth can be explained by the following reasons. First, the *chaebol* were in a vantage point relative to other domestic and foreign capitalists due to two decades of state support in terms of low-interest-rate loans and other protective measures. Second, the "Three Low Period" between 1986 and 1988 could not have happened at a more fortuitous time for the *chaebol*. This export boom, which was created largely by Japan's rising yen, allowed the *chaebol* (who were the largest exporters in South Korea) to profit handsomely.

The economic climate of the 1980s, in which the *chaebol* continued to prosper despite the reduction of state subsidies provided room for the *chaebol* to gain political leverage *vis-à-vis* the state. The *chaebol* were able to show that they could function and prosper without state support. Although even the weakened South Korean developmental state was still more influential than comparable states in East Asia, the developmental state's relations to the *chaebol* had changed: the developmental state was no longer the omnipotent power holder relative to the powerless capitalists, who relied on the state for vital resources. The 1980s, thus, represented a period of negotiation of power between the two actors. The *chaebol* were becoming more visible and influential in economic policy-making and were increasingly voicing their collective demands to the state. Reports of collusive deals between politicians and the large *chaebol* further fueled the public belief that the *chaebol* had become a powerful group that was capable of manipulating the state.

As the *chaebol* gained prosperity and some independence from the state, its relationship with the state became more interdependent and, in some cases, conflictual. In contrast to its former dominant role, the state now had a lot to lose if it did not have the support of the *chaebol*, which had become a major source of political funding. More importantly, the nation's economy had become so dependent on the *chaebol* that their collapse would jeopardize the entire economy, at least in the short run.

In the political arena, the *chaebol*'s owners and upper-level managers began to enter politics. Although the number was still very small, they symbolized the growing political influence of this group. This section examines the economic growth of the large *chaebol* and the various ways in which the *chaebol*'s growing political influence were manifested.

The Growing Prosperity of the Chaebol

Two decades of sheltered growth produced a handful of very large conglomerates in South Korea. Economic liberalization measures that were promoted since the early 1980s did not seem to affect the growth rate or the rate of concentration of wealth in the largest *chaebol*. By 1987, the share of sales from the five largest *chaebol* comprised 75.2 percent of manufacturing GDP (Table 6.2).

Table 6.2
Share of Big Business Groups in Selected Nations

Nation	Year	Number of Groups	Share in the Economy
S. Korea[a]	1971	5	22.3% in total sales in GDP in manufacturing
	1987	5	75.2% in total sales in GDP in manufacturing
Pakistan[b]	1968	10	33% of all assets in private, Pakistani-controlled firms in manufacturing
		30	52% (same as above)
Japan[c]	1942	4[d]	50% of paid-in capital in financial sectors 32% of paid-in capital in heavy industry
	1974	6[e]	23–28% of the assets of all incorporated Japanese firms

Sources: a. E.M. Kim (1987) and Management Efficiency Research Institute (1988) for business groups statistics; and Economic Planning Board (1990) for GDP statistics.
b. White (1974) as presented in S.K. Kim (1987:7).
c. Goto (1982) as presented in S.K. Kim (1987:7).
Notes: d. Pre–World War II *zaibatsu*.
e. Keiretsu: Post–World War II form of business groups.

As noted earlier, the favorable international market in the mid- to late 1980s played an important role in the *chaebol*'s growth in the 1980s. The Three Low Period lasted roughly from 1986 through 1988, and the three lows refer to the relatively low price of crude oil, the relatively low value of the U.S. dollar compared to the Japanese yen, and the low interest rate. This period began after the United States and Japan agreed to increase the value of the Japanese yen against the U.S. dollar and other currencies in the world in September 1985. This was known as the Plaza Accord, since the meeting was held at the Plaza Hotel in New York City. The purpose of the accord was to redress the trade deficit between the United States and several nations by reducing imports into the United States by raising the price of foreign goods and promoting exports of U.S.-made goods by cutting their prices. The rising value of the yen made Japanese products very expensive for consumers overseas. Therefore, many buyers turned to South Korea for cheaper, albeit somewhat lower quality, goods. As a result, from 1986 to 1987, South Korean exports grew by 36.2 percent, rising from $34.7 billion to $47.3 billion. In 1988, the figure rose to $60.7 billion (National Statistical Office 1991). This unexpected export boom boosted the economy tremendously; the average annual growth rates of GNP per capita for the three years from 1986 to 1988 were 12.9 percent, 13.0 percent, and 12.4 percent, respectively.

The *chaebol* benefited the most during this boom, since they were the largest exporters (a situation different from that in Japan and Taiwan, where medium- and small-sized enterprises take the lion's share of exports). The *chaebol* not only survived the diminished state subsidies, but flourished. It is not clear how the *chaebol* would have fared without the favorable international market during this critical period of decreasing state subsidies.

The pattern of *chaebol* growth in the 1980s presents an interesting comparison to that of the 1970s, when the fastest-growing *chaebol* were those that conformed to the state's drive for HCI. The distribution of total assets in 1988 does not show any conspicuous pattern of distribution between the light and heavy industries, compared to the 1970s (see Table 6.4 for 1988 figures and Table 5.2 for the 1970s figures). In the absence of loan packages to entice the *chaebol* to invest in state-target sectors, the growth of the *chaebol* appears to be more responsive to the changing domestic and international markets and, therefore, more heterogeneous.

The ten largest *chaebol* continued to grow rapidly during the 1980s. The fastest-growing *chaebol* was Kia, with a 30.5 percent average annual growth rate and the second fastest-growing was Samsung with a 25 percent growth rate (see Table 6.3). Kia's tremendous growth was the result of its being allowed to reenter the passenger automobile business in 1987. In August 1980 when the plans for the Reorganization of the Heavy and Chemical Industries was announced, the state prohibited Kia from producing passenger automobiles until 1987. Unlike a few larger *chaebol*, which could defy state orders, Kia had to comply with this policy. Kia specialized in buses and other transportation equipment during this period.

Among the four largest *chaebol* (each of which had total assets of more than 11 trillion Won, or $16 billion), the fastest-growing ones were Samsung and Lucky–Gold Star. In the 1970s, the two fastest-growing ones were Hyundai and Daewoo, who benefited greatly from the state's support. The rapid growth of Samsung and Lucky–Gold Star in the 1980s, on the other hand, had to do with their ability to take advantage of the export boom in the mid-1980s. In particular, the brand-name electrical and electronic appliances manufactured by these two *chaebol*, which were familiar to consumers world-wide, played a critical role during the export boom. As shown in Table 6.4, more than 21 percent of Samsung's total assets and more than 30 percent of Lucky–Gold Star's were in electronics.

Attesting to the significance of the export boom for the *chaebol*, trading was one of the largest contributors to total sales in all of the four largest *chaebol* (see Table 6.5). Trading includes sales from General Trading Companies. Individual member companies can also engage in direct exports without going through the GTC, and in such cases sales will not be calculated as part of the trading figures. In 1987, sales from trading comprised a large share of the total sales—54.3 percent for Daewoo, 44.6 percent for Samsung, 35.2 percent for Hyundai, and 20.9 percent for Lucky–Gold Star.

Table 6.3
Basic Indicators of the Ten Largest *Chaebol*, 1981–88

Rank[a]	*Chaebol*	Number of Firms 1981	Number of Firms 1988	Total Assets[b] (in million Won) 1981	Total Assets[b] (in million Won) 1988	Average Annual Growth Rate of Total Assets 1981–88 (in percent)
1	Daewoo	21	33	4,017,518	13,385,536	18.8
2	Samsung	22	41	2,754,350	13,119,875	25.0
3	Hyundai	24	33	4,714,695	12,752,262	15.3
4	Lucky–Gold Star	20	54	2,999,768	11,583,584	21.3
5	Ssangyong	11	21	1,997,913	5,500,089	15.6
6	Han Jin	12	16	1,737,506	4,962,023	16.2
7	Korea Explosives	15	26	935,861	3,951,553	22.9
8	Sunkyong	9	19	2,189,136	2,947,560	4.3
9	Dong Ah	12	16	1,331,328[c]	2,419,521	10.5
10	Kia	6	10	402,054[c]	1,988,642	30.5

Notes: a. Rank order based on total assets in 1988.
　　　　 b. Total assets in 1985 constant Korean million Won.
　　　　 c. Figures are for 1982. Average annual growth rates are for 1982–88.

Source: Bankers Trust Securities Research 1989.

Table 6.4

Distribution of Total Assets in the Four Largest *Chaebol*, 1988

Chaebol	Light	Heavy	[Electrical[a]	Other Heavy]	Services	[Nonfinancial	Financial]
Daewoo	0.3%	37.5%	[11.3%	26.2%]	62.3%	[23.6%	38.7%]
Samsung	33.6%	33.6%	[21.4%	12.2%]	56.7%	[11.8%	44.9%]
Hyundai	0.9%	43.0%	[5.5%	37.5%]	56.0%	[31.2%	24.8%]
Lucky–Gold Star	0.2%	52.1%	[30.3%	21.8%]	47.7%	[11.6%	36.1%]

Note: a. Electrical and electronic appliances.
Source: Bankers Trust Securities Research 1989.

The Three Larg[...] [s]ors to Total Sales
in the Fo[ur] [chae]bol, 1987

Chaebol	Sector	A. Sales (in million Won)	A/Total Sales
Daewoo	1. Trading	4,453,250	54.3%
	2. Metal products; machinery; and equipment[a]	2,867,359	35.0%
	3. Transportation and storage	513,858	6.3%
Samsung	1. Trading	5,669,803	44.6%
	2. Metal products; machinery; and equipment	4,586,960	36.0%
	3. Food and beverages	602,158	4.7%
Hyundai	1. Metal products; machinery; and equipment	5,440,379	36.5%
	2. Trading	5,253,780	35.2%
	3. Construction	1,858,567	12.5%
Lucky–Gold Star	1. Metal products; machinery; and equipment	3,649,211	34.6%
	2. Chemicals; petroleum; coal; rubber products[b]	3,011,076	28.6%
	3. Trading	2,201,962	20.9%

Notes: a. This category includes the following: fabricated metal products; machinery except electrical; electrical and electronic machinery; transport equipment; and scientific measuring and controlling instrument.
b. This category includes the following: industrial chemicals; other chemical products; petroleum refineries; coal products; rubber products; and other plastic products.

Source: Management Efficiency Research Institute 1988.

The most marked trend among the largest four *chaebol* was the sharp growth in financial services. In Daewoo's case, it jumped from 7 percent of total assets in 1980 to 38.7 percent in 1988. Even Samsung, which already had a large share of total assets in this sector in 1980, more than doubled its share from 21 percent to 44.9 percent in 1988. This growth in financial services is largely due to the *chaebol*'s investment in non-banking financial institutions. By the mid-1980s, eight of the ten largest *chaebol* owned at least one nonbanking financial institution—e.g., insurance, securities, and short-term finance companies (Management Efficiency Research Institute 1988).

Nonbanking financial institutions were not only very lucrative businesses but were also critical for the *chaebol* in their efforts to become less dependent on the domestic banks and the state. These institutions, developed specifically to get around the nationalized banking system, allowed the *chaebol* flexibility with day-to-day cash-flow problems and with lending within the *chaebol*. Such growth was contrary to the state's directive to prohibit ownership of private banks, which was intended to keep the *chaebol* from becoming too powerful by owning both industrial manufacturing and the banking sectors. This example shows that the *chaebol* are not complacent followers of state policy but are ingenuous entrepreneurs.

The *chaebol*'s investment in financial services also highlights a direct competition occurring between the state and the *chaebol* for the provision of such services. Although direct competition in banking is avoided due to the state's prohibition of *chaebol* ownership of banks, it still leads us to a basic question of whether a comprehensive developmental state is necessary when the private sector is mature enough to provide certain services such as banking.

In addition, the rapid growth of the large business groups led them to provide other services previously furnished by the state—e.g., research and development, and marketing—much sooner in South Korea than in countries such as Taiwan. Several large *chaebol* and the FKI established their own research facilities. The rapid growth of the large *chaebol* hastened the time in which they could start competing with the state for the provision of key services. In other NICs, the state did not promote, or actively discouraged, the growth of business groups. In such cases, the private sector could take much longer or may never reach the point in which they could compete with the state in the provision of key services.

The continued growth of large *chaebol* in the 1980s revealed several aspects of South Korean development. First, the South Korean *chaebol* do not rely solely on state support for their growth. Furthermore, the growth trajectories of the *chaebol* indicate that the *chaebol* are not monolithic. In fact, the *chaebol* do not pursue similar investment strategies, even when they are presented with the state's array of positive incentives and negative sanctions. Moreover, the *chaebol*'s increased investment in nonbanking financial institutions implies that the *chaebol* are attempting to (and, succeeding at) become more independent from the state. Second, the favorable international market in spite of reduced state subsidies helped the *chaebol* to prosper. However, two decades of protected growth meant that the Park and Chun eras' heavy industry *chaebol* would continue to be important players. This is in contrast to the transition between the Rhee and Park periods, when there was a gradual redistribution of wealth once a new set of rules were in place. These images of the 1980s imply a more mature South Korean economy compared to the earlier periods.

The Growing Political Influence of the Chaebol

As the *chaebol* gained prominence in the economy, they began to vie for more political influence. At first, there were rumors of deals behind closed doors between the state and *chaebol*. Later, as it became evident that many policies simply could not be developed and implemented without cooperation from the *chaebol*, the state invited leading *chaebol* owners to solicit their input on important policies. Despite these gestures by the state, several large *chaebol* openly defied state policies. Furthermore, instead of assuming a reactive position to the state's policies, the *chaebol* as a group began to proactively demand important policy changes and reforms. Although we are still reminded of the state's power (as aptly demonstrated by the 1985 bankruptcy of the Kukje *chaebol*), it is clear that the state now exerts much less influence over the economy than it formerly did, and that the political influence of the *chaebol* has increased.

Shady Deals

There has been widespread speculation that some *chaebol* influenced politicians and government bureaucrats with bribes and through personal and familial relationships. Although many such speculations cannot be substantiated unequivocally, they do imply the perception that the *chaebol*'s influence is growing. The following cases involve incidents where there was at least some evidence to indicate wrongdoing.

The Chun regime became the target of speculation about collusive relationships with leading *chaebol*. Rumors said that substantial financial contributions were made by leading *chaebol* and that, in turn, these *chaebol* received favored treatment from the state. It was also known in South Korea that when Chun had formal dinner parties with *chaebol* leaders, the seating arrangement was done based on the amount of contributions.[4] These rumors were substantiated during the 1989 Hearings for the Fifth Republic at the National Assembly.[5] Many of the largest *chaebol*, including Hyundai, were accused of bribery and political kickbacks. Their testimonies were broadcast daily on South Korean television and radio, providing powerful images of the corrupt *chaebol* and government that were to cast doubts about the integrity of both institutions.

Speculation about the increasing influence of the *chaebol* over government officials arose over the issue of real estate investment. During the 1980s, real estate prices skyrocketed, making it very difficult for average middle-class families to own houses. Behind these rising real estate prices were the *chaebol*, who were using their capital to buy land as speculative investment. In 1989, the National Assembly conducted an audit of government affairs, the second year after sixteen years of hiatus (*Wŏlgan Chosŏn* 1989). Among the five issues outlined by the National Assembly for the audit, concentration of wealth in the *chaebol* received special attention.[6] During the audit, the *chaebol*'s control of the nation's real estate became a big issue, befitting the popular name, "*Chaebol* Republic." According to the audit, the thirty largest *chaebol*, whose owners and families comprise 6.1 percent of the nation's population, owned 77 percent of all private land in South Korea. Moreover, these *chaebol* almost exclusively reported their real estate holdings as a business operation, thus avoiding heavy taxes imposed on idle land. However, many in the assembly speculated that a large share of land reported for business operation was in fact idle land (Ibid.).

Other cases imply that the *chaebol* may have had improper access to privileged information and/or unfair influence on government officials for preferential treatment. In one case, the public was outraged by reports that the *chaebol* were making huge profits by buying up idle land, which was immediately rezoned for industrial or commercial use. Samsung Life Insurance Company of the Samsung *chaebol*, bought land in Sŏch'odong in Seoul between 1987 and the fall of 1989. While the land was initially designated as a site for a public bus terminal, that plan was abandoned, and in December 1989 the lot was rezoned for commercial use. As a result, the property value jumped, and Samsung made a handsome profit (Y. C. Ham 1990).

Another incident was reported to the National Assembly sessions on April 16 and 17, 1990, by I Hae Ch'an of P'yŏng Min Tang (Party for Peace and Democracy). Hyundai, Samsung, and Kŭkdong Oil had purchased large pieces of land in the Ch'ungnam province. The property, which was a marsh and unfit for building residences or factories, was purchased at a very low price before the land was approved for a landfill. After the property was bought by these *chaebol*, the government announced that the land was now approved for a landfill. And, the price of the land skyrocketed from $1.8–2.2 to $118–221 per *p'yŏng*.[7] The three *chaebol*, thus made enormous profits. While no conclusive evidence was presented to prove that these *chaebol* had access to inside information or had influenced the government bureaucrats to rezone, there was also no evidence presented to dispel doubts about wrongdoing (Ibid.).

There are three possible explanations for these real estate purchases. The first one, which is the most implausible, is that these *chaebol* were very lucky. However, when not just one but many large *chaebol* became involved in these sorts of deals, the public began to suspect that there was a massive cover-up. The second explanation is that these *chaebol* received information of the rezoning prior to the announcement. The third scenario is that they purchased the land and effectively lobbied the government for rezoning. In the public's eyes, the last two scenarios appeared to be much more plausible than the first.

Chaebol Involvement in Policy Decision Making

During the 1980s, as the *chaebol* became increasingly indispensable for the South Korean economy, the state actively sought the advice of *chaebol* leaders. More than ever, the state needed the consent and cooperation of the *chaebol* to implement its policies. Such active consultation was unheard of during the 1960s and 1970s, when policies were simply decided by the state and delivered to the *chaebol*.

Soon after President Chun came to power in May 1980, the National Security Council's head of the Trade and Industry Division, Kŭm Chin Ho, and about ten others from the business sector gathered to discuss the reorganization of the heavy and chemical industries. Several *chaebol* owners were invited to attend the August 19, 1980, meeting: Hyundai's chair, Chŏng Chu Yŏng; Hyundai International Company's chair, Chŏng In Yŏng; and Daewoo's chair, Kim Wu Chung. The president of the Korea Development Bank, Pak Chun, was also present at the meeting. The next day, Kŭm announced plans for reorganizing the electrical generator and automobile firms. Daewoo was to produce electrical generators; Hyundai Motor Company was to merge with Saehan (which later became Daewoo Motor Company) and produce passenger automobiles; and Kia Motors was to specialize in larger vehicles (buses and trucks).

However, the first attempt at reorganization of the electrical generator industry failed. Daewoo's Kim Wu Chung sent a proposal for reorganizing and stabilizing the industry, which required massive amounts of capital investment that far exceeded the capacity of Daewoo. In essence, Daewoo was asking the state to provide the necessary funds to Daewoo. Without such financial support, Daewoo indicated that it would not be able to comply with the state's plan to reorganize the electricity generator industry. After some deliberation, on October 21, 1980, the state announced a new plan to establish a state enterprise.

The state's adoption of a new plan to reorganize the electrical generator industry shows the changes in the state-*chaebol* relations. First, the state invited major *chaebol* to participate in its initial decision making process. A major economic policy to consolidate the *chaebol* was made with the *chaebol* deeply involved in the decision-making process, which indicates that the state was keenly aware of the power and influence of the *chaebol*. The state recognized that it could not implement such a policy without the support of the *chaebol*. Second, when Daewoo's proposal made clear the need for massive state funding, the state reversed its initial plan. This was due to mounting pressure from other *chaebol* that the state was favoring Daewoo. The state could not jeopardize its relations with the other *chaebol* and thus reversed its decision.

The establishment of a state enterprise was a compromise solution. For one thing, the state was concerned with the animosity it would create by favoring Daewoo. Indeed, the pressure put on the state by the other *chaebol* had never been so conspicuous in all of South Korea's previous economic history. The creation of a state enterprise was a solution designed to appease the *chaebol*, and it implied the inability of the state to control the *chaebol*. In addition, when one considers that the South Korean state has maintained that it wants to develop the private sector, and to gradually privatize its public sector, this was an especially meek compromise—a direct result of the state's inability to face the challenge of the *chaebol*. Although there is no direct evidence that the state is subordinate to the interests of the *chaebol*, the fact that the state cannot or does not formulate policies without recognizing the *chaebol* is a strong indication of a change in their relations.

The Chaebol's Open Defiance of the State

The *chaebol* have openly defied important policies of the state. The Fair Trade and Anti-Monopoly Act of April 1, 1981, was an antitrust act aimed at the already huge *chaebol*. It reflected a major policy change by the South Korean state, which in the past had promoted almost exclusive support of the *chaebol* and allowed them to have monopoly or oligopoly in certain domestic markets. The Fair Trade and Anti-Monopoly Act was to regulate the unfair business activities of the *chaebol* and to control (or, more accurately, to limit) their growth. This is based on my interviews with government officials at the EPB, the Ministry of Trade and Industry, and the Ministry of Finance in the summers of 1988 and 1989.[8]

In a way, the act was similar to the Illicit Accumulation of Wealth Charges that were made against leading businesses when Park came to power in 1961. Chun, who was not a popularly elected president and thus lacked political legitimacy, went after the *chaebol* to prove to the public that he was the man of change and possessed the power to punish the *chaebol*.

However, unlike the Illicit Charges, the act did not bring compliance from the *chaebol*. According to a November 15, 1983, article in a leading daily newspaper, *Dong-A Ilbo*, there were 487 cases of new business being founded or created from the merging of firms in the two-and-a-half-year period since the announcement of the act in April 1981. Of these cases, 258 were the direct result of the large *chaebol*'s efforts to increase their horizontal integration by acquiring firms in areas in which they had no previous experience.

The growing influence of the *chaebol* was apparent in the Reorganization of the Heavy and Chemical Industries, which was first announced on May 25, 1979, followed by a series of announcements during the early 1980s (U. K. Kim 1980). One of the targets for reorganization was the electrical generator industry, which had been excessively invested in by four firms. In the reorganization, the Hyundai *chaebol* was ordered to merge with Hyundai International Company to form one company, and Daewoo and Samsung were ordered to consolidate and form the second company. This plan encountered many objections, not only because it was difficult to force two rival *chaebol*—Daewoo and Samsung—to join forces but also because the takeover of Hyundai International by the Hyundai *chaebol* presented many difficulties.[9] After almost a year of negotiations, Hyundai International's president sent a proposal to nullify the plan in May 1980. This proposal was considered rebellious and unusual by the EPB and the Ministry of Trade and Industry. The government reviewed the proposal, but still ordered the *chaebol* to continue their efforts to reorganize the industry. The plan went through a few more revisions, but it finally fell through.

In another case of open defiance, Daewoo's chair, Kim Wu Chung, showed his political capability by forcing the government to provide emergency financing at the brink of a bankruptcy of Daewoo Shipbuilding in 1988 (Yu 1989). Daewoo Shipbuilding had been experiencing financial difficulty for some time due to worldwide recession, in particular in the shipbuilding industry. Finally, in the fall of 1988, Daewoo Shipbuilding came very close to bankruptcy. In an effort to save the company, in mid-September Kim Wu Chung began to meet with high-ranking government officials, including Deputy Prime Minister (and the minister of the EPB) Na Wung Pae, Minister of Finance Sakong Il, Minister of Trade and Industry An Pyŏng Hwa, and the Secretary for Economic Affairs at the Blue House Pak Sŭng (Ibid.:435). The officials were initially opposed to helping Daewoo, for they were concerned that the government might be perceived as providing preferential treatment to Daewoo, when other firms in financial trouble were not aided. The National Assembly was in the midst of a heated debate about whether to reduce the farmers' debt, and the government's lenient treatment of Daewoo would be perceived badly by the public.

After several failed attempts to persuade the government, Kim made a public announcement at the end of October. He stated that "Daewoo Shipbuilding's insolvency is not just a responsibility of Daewoo. I urge the Korea Development Bank to refinance Daewoo Shipbuilding. Otherwise, Daewoo Shipbuilding may have to close down due to bankruptcy" (Ibid.). He also hinted that he would leave the business world if there is no active government intervention, which could lead to massive chain reactions throughout the domestic market since Daewoo was one of the four largest *chaebol*.

This was considered a brazen act. Nevertheless, after his announcement was widely publicized in the media, the chairs of the policy committees of the four political parties in the National Assembly sent an investigation team to Daewoo Shipbuilding. A few days later, President Roh ordered his economic ministers to prepare plans to resolve Daewoo's financial problem. As a result, on December 16, 1988, the National Assembly passed a legislature to revise the law on the Korea Development Bank, which was the second-largest shareholder of Daewoo Shipbuilding. This revision allowed the authorized capital of the Korea Development Bank to be raised from 1 trillion Won to 1.5 trillion Won. This increased capital could then be used to refinance Daewoo's debt, which reached 1 trillion and 80 billion Won (Ibid.).

This brazen act by Kim Wu Chung and his success in manipulating the government and the National Assembly to refinance his ailing company in a very public way clearly show that the olden days when the government could control the *chaebol* are gone. The super-large *chaebol*, which rank in the top five or so, control a growing share of the nation's manufacturing production and employ a large share of the labor force. They are not a force to be easily dealt with, even by a relatively strong state. The ripple effect of a failure of a major *chaebol* is not something that the government or the National Assembly could easily afford.

The *chaebol*, especially the largest ones, were able to openly defy state policies. The state was simply no longer in a position to force the *chaebol* to conform to all its policies. However, for smaller *chaebol* or non-*chaebol* independent firms, the story was different. Kia's vice president of business operations said the following, in an interview with me in 1992, about the 1980–81 Reorganization of the Heavy and Chemical Industries:[10]

> The government ordered Hyundai Motor Company and Daewoo Motor Company to merge and form one company. However, these two powerful *chaebol* were able to resist this order, and they became the only two passenger automobile producers in South Korea until 1987. On the other hand, Kia was unable to defy state orders to merge with another small automobile producer, Tong-a. Kia was politically powerless and had no choice but to follow the state's orders.

The smaller *chaebol*, which had relatively little political influence, could not resist the state's policies. Thus, open defiance of state policies is not an option available to all businesses but to a select group of large *chaebol*.

The Chaebol *as a Voice for Change*

During the 1980s, the *chaebol* also became much more outspoken about their position in the economy and about what they expected from the state. They became an important voice in demanding the reduction of state intervention in the economy, despite the fact that they owed much of their prosperity and wealth to the state. The 1981 annual report of the Federation of Korean Industries (FKI)[11] included "Recommendations on the Basic Directions of Management and Control of the Economy in the 1980s," which contained a succinct statement of the FKI's position on state intervention, as follows:

[1] The Establishment of Civilian-led Management and Control of the Economy
We must quickly establish a civilian-led economic management and control system which will enable us to utilize the rules of the market economy most efficiently. . . . We must actively seek and adopt the opinions and expertise coming from various corners of our society, and in particular from the *business elites*. . . . Thus, we will be able to improve the total efficiency of our economic and social activities (FKI 1981:79–80).

It was clear that the large capitalists wanted to be in charge of their individual businesses as well as of the entire economy. They were opposed to a state-led economy, with long-term goals and development plans supplied by the state.

At the 1988 New Year's press conference, the FKI's new president, Ku Cha Kyŏng (the chair of the Lucky–Gold Star *chaebol* at that time) declared that the free market was the only way South Korea could become a developed nation. He also stated that a progressive social environment, which honored the creative entrepreneurial spirit, must be established. This was considered a "bombshell announcement" by the media since Ku's predecessors used the New Year press conference to ceremonially announce the federation's support of state policies (K. M. Kim 1988). Instead, Ku was perceived to have expressed the growing sentiment among large *chaebol* that the state must refrain from intervening in the economy. On another occasion, Ku stated that, "From now on, the private sector will no longer agree with every state policy. We will voice our objections loudly and clearly when we do not agree with the policies" (Ibid.:385). Businesses, in particular the large *chaebol*, were becoming more and more open about their displeasure with the heavy-handed control of the market by the state.

An even more revealing statement was made during my interview with Chŏng Mong Jun in 1992. He is a son of Hyundai's founder, and he was the chair of the Hyundai Heavy Industries, Co., Ltd. from 1987 to 1990 and was the company's advisor at the time of the interview. When I met with him in April 1992, he had just been reelected into the National Assembly. Obviously flanked by the support he enjoyed from his constituents, about state intervention in the economy, he said,

> I think the [South] Korean government should not interfere in the market. The private sector is much more capable of taking care of the economy than the government. In fact, if the government did not intervene so much in the market, we [Hyundai] would have done far better than where we are today.

It is hard to believe that the *chaebol*, in particular, Hyundai would have been able to prosper had there been no leadership and support from the state during their infancy. What was clear, however, was that extensive state intervention was no longer seen as a critical element by the *chaebol* for their growth, but rather as a hindrance to more rapid growth. The 1980s proved to them that they could prosper without direct state support and control.

Chaebol *Involvement in Politics*

Several *chaebol* owners and high-ranking managers have run for National Assembly seats. Most prominent of these is the second-term member of the National Assembly, Chŏng Mong Jun. Family members of Hanjin's Cho Chung Hun have also run for National Assembly seats. Chŏng Chu Yŏng, founder of Hyundai *chaebol*, established a new political party in early 1992. His party, T'ongil Kungmin Tang (Reunification People's Party), won 25 percent of the National Assembly seats in the March 1992 election. This remarkable achievement came only a few months after the founding of the party. Chŏng himself ran unsuccessfully as a presidential candidate in the 1992 election.

In another case of a major *chaebol*'s involvement in politics, Daewoo's chair Kim Wu Chung announced that he would run for president in the 1992 election and then soon declared that he would not run. This aborted attempt was perceived by the public and the media as a sign of the growing rift and competition between the state and the *chaebol*. Kim Wu Chung's attempt was particularly noteworthy since he was widely believed to have had a tight collusive relation with the Chun and Roh regimes. Chŏng's and Kim's political aspirations show a trend that is unmistakably changing the state-business relations in South Korea (C. C. I 1993).

See also Fields

Still the Strong State? The Case of Kukje Bankruptcy in 1985

The public's perception of the growing influence of the *chaebol* in the 1980s is evidenced in the name, "*Chaebol* Republic." On the other hand, there is still the nagging impression that the South Korean state is capable of controlling the life and death of a *chaebol* as illustrated in the Kukje bankruptcy.

On February 13, 1985, the president of the Cheil Bank, I P'il Sŏn, announced that the seventh-largest *chaebol*, Kukje, was bankrupt and that it will be managed by a consortium of four banks—Cheil Bank, Korea Development Bank, Chohŭng Bank, and the Bank of Seoul and Trust Company (Y. H. Kim 1989). This did not make much of a headline in local news, as the banks often took over companies in financial trouble and since it came after months of speculation that the Kukje *chaebol* was suffering from insolvent operation and imminent takeover by the banks.

However, this rather insignificant announcement grew to a major headline story on February 21, 1985. Eight days after the first announcement, Mr. I announced that Kukje will be disbanded for reasons including "reckless management," "exceedingly high rates of debt," and "nepotic management by the sons-in-law of the founder" (Ibid.). This announcement, unlike the first one, sent shockwaves to the domestic and international economies. In South Korea, other businesses worried that this may mark the beginning of disbandment of other *chaebol*, and the public wondered about the arbitrariness of the state's actions. Overseas, it renewed doubts about the stability of the South Korean economy and of the state's economic policies.

The announcement on February 21 was particularly troublesome for the citizens of Pusan, which is the second-largest city in South Korea and home to many of Kukje's factories employing nearly 6 percent of Pusan's labor force. The February 12 election results of the National Assembly showed that the president's incumbent party candidate lost all seats in Pusan. Rumors abounded that the government's disbandment of Kukje was a retaliation toward Kukje as much as it was toward the city of Pusan.

To quell such growing speculations, on February 22, 1985, the Minister of Finance, Kim Mahn Je [Kim Man Che], called for a news conference, which was rather unusual, and thus highlighted the seriousness of this case. Kim announced that there will be no further adjustment measures, such as that of Kukje, for a while and strenuously argued that Kukje's bankruptcy was due to insolvent management and not other factors. The administration later argued that the disbandment of Kukje was inevitable to avoid massive chain reactions of bankruptcies to over 6,500 companies and layoffs of over 560,000 workers (Kwon 1988:460).

The chair of the Kukje *chaebol*, Yang Chŏng Mo, has said in numerous interviews that Kukje was sacrificed because the top political leaders of the Chun regime, including the Blue House, the New Village Movement's headquarters, and the Ilhae Foundation, were displeased with Kukje. Yang argues that Kukje was unduly and unlawfully disbanded, citing that there were many other *chaebol* that were indebted as much as, or even more than, Kukje but were not forced to go bankrupt. Yang lists the following reasons for Kukje's bankruptcy: (1) Yang did not contribute enough money to the New Village Movement fund, which was controlled by President Chun's brother (he was later indicted for embezzlement of the fund); (2) Yang did not actively participate and finance the Ilhae Foundation, a quasi-research foundation established by President Chun, which also acted as a major depository of his political funds; (3) Yang arrived late to a state dinner at the Blue House when Kukje was under discussion of bankruptcy at the end of 1984, and Yang was not in Pusan to welcome the president during his visit to the city; and (4) Yang had uncomfortable relations with the Minister of Finance, Kim Mahn Je (C. C. I 1993; Kwon 1988).

Whether the reasons for Kukje's disbandment were political or purely financial, the evidence during this period indicates that Kukje's bankruptcy was an uncommonly harsh treatment by the state. I think what is more alarming and illustrative about the Kukje bankruptcy is not just the bankruptcy itself but how the Kukje firms were refinanced and doled out to the other *chaebol*.

Before the bankruptcy, the Kukje *chaebol* was comprised of twenty-one companies. The Council on Industrial Policies, which is a committee headed by the deputy prime minister and comprised of the ministers of economic ministries, decided the fate of these companies. The council was headed by Kim Mahn Je, who was newly appointed as the deputy prime minister (he was the Minister of Finance who held a press conference regarding the Kukje disbandment in 1985). On September 22, 1986, Kim announced the last of that year's reorganization and normalization plans for the fifty-six insolvent companies, including twenty-one that belonged to Kukje. The government provided incentives to assist the takeover of insolvent companies. Typically, the incentives included a mix of the following measures: (1) reduction of the interest rate for a significant share of the insolvent companies' debt (which was calculated at 3 trillion Won), with a maximum of thirty years for repayment including a grace period; (2) infusion of new loans of 460 billion Won, with a low-interest-rate of 10 percent with ten-year repayment and a ten-year grace period; (3) reduction of the loan by 50 percent of the amount above the assets, which will be simply reclassified as "bank loss" by the involved banks; and (4) tax breaks for companies that will take over insolvent companies

(*Dong-A Ilbo* September 22, 1986). With these favorable conditions the businesses, which were chosen by the government to take over the insolvent companies, had everything to gain and nothing to lose. One begins to wonder whether Kukje might have had a second chance if it was offered such generous support.

A careful examination of the recipients of Kukje firms shows that the state rewarded the *chaebol* who had contributed large sums to various funds created by President Chun and the first lady, and the president's cronies received the choice companies (Yu 1988). Hanil Synthetic Textiles *chaebol*, which took over the largest number of Kukje companies (five companies), jumped from the twenty-third- to the fourteenth-largest *chaebol* as result of the takeover (*Hanguk Ilbo* November 16, 1986; *Maeil Kyŏngje Shinmun* December 23, 1986). Incidentally, Hanil was the second-largest contributor of political financing to President Chun's party. Between 1982 and 1988 it contributed nearly 13 billion Won to Chun's party (C. Y. Pak 1989). Considering that Hanil was ranked the twenty-third-largest *chaebol*, its large contribution to Chun's party is remarkable. Apparently, it paid off. Hanil's total assets prior to taking over Kukje firms was 676 million Won. They more than doubled to 1.49 billion Won after the takeover (based on 1985 figures) (*Hanguk Ilbo* November 16, 1986). Other *chaebol* also jumped in their ranking after taking over insolvent companies.

The story of Kukje's bankruptcy is not simply a case of the state's continued power. This case also points out that the state was influenced by other large *chaebol*, who were important political financiers. I am not suggesting that these large contributors manipulated the state to force Kukje's bankruptcy. Rather, I am suggesting that the takeover of Kukje companies illustrates that the state can be influenced to make favorable decisions for a few chosen *chaebol*. Top government officials are no longer the insulated elites, who appeared to make decisions without being influenced by business leaders.

The Growth of Labor and Labor Movements

The South Korean state's labor policies sought to eliminate any possibility that labor would become an active force. In 1953, the first labor law was promulgated, guaranteeing three basic rights for labor: (1) the freedom of association, (2) collective bargaining, and (3) collective action (Choi 1989:85). Although the law was explicit in its guarantee for labor rights, it had little effect on the actual labor practices of the time (S. Kim 1989:8). In 1963, the Park regime announced amendments to the 1953 labor law, providing more room for state intervention and more stringent restrictions on union membership and action.

The Emergency Decree on National Security was promulgated on December 27, 1971, as a prelude to the draconian Yushin system of October 1972. According to this law, labor affairs became an important target of government control as a means of assuring national security. Violations were treated as criminal offenses, punishable with measures according to the criminal law, which tends to be more severe than the civil law. Collective bargaining and collective action were, in effect, banned, with only freedom of association left intact. However, with labor disputes subject to government arbitration (with the decision final and legally binding), collective bargaining was effectively suspended until the mid-1980s (Choi 1989:88–89; S. Kim 1989:8–9).

In 1981, the Emergency Decree of National Security was lifted, but the government's interference with labor disputes continued until the mid-1980s (S. Kim 1989:9). In 1986, the Ministry of Labor announced that it would no longer intervene in labor disputes. And in 1987, after the June 29 Declaration for Democracy by Roh Tae Woo, the government announced that it would not intervene in labor-management disputes (Ibid.).

Along with repressive labor policies toward labor unions and their activities, the state kept wages low to keep South Korean products competitive in the world market (Deyo 1987b, 1989; S. Kim 1989; Bello & Rosenfeld 1990). Despite rising productivity, real wages did not rise. Real wages actually decreased during the 1960s, and in the 1970s, real wages increased but often at a pace behind the growth rates of productivity (Choi 1989). Choi argues that the combination of large business groups and a government policy to control the rise of consumer prices resulted in wages being kept at an artificially low rate, with profits going to the big businesses rather than to wages (Ibid.:299–300). South Korea's real wages became more comparable to other NICs in Asia by the 1980s as shown in Table 6.6. And in 1990, South Korea's real wage in manufacturing was higher than Hong Kong's for the first time.

Although wages in 1990 were more comparable to those in other nations, South Korean workers still had the longest work week of any nation—49.8 hours (see Table 6.7). They put in nine hours more per week than their counterparts in the United States and almost six hours more than those in Hong Kong.

Responding to years of low wages, poor working conditions, and repressive labor laws, the labor movement took off dramatically in the mid-1980s. The number of strikes and lockouts skyrocketed, going from 276 cases in 1986 to 3,617 cases in 1987 (see Table 6.8)—an increase of more than 1,200 percent in just one year. Nearly 7 million work days were lost in 1987, compared to 72,000 in the previous year. This eruption of labor activity had serious implications for industrial productivity.

Table 6.6

Increase in Real Wages, Productivity, and Labor Costs in Manufacturing, 1962–79 (%)[a]

Year	Real Wages[b]	Productivity[c]	Labor Costs in real terms[d]
1962–66	–0.8	8.5	
1967–71	11.2	17.3	–5.8
1972–76	8.7	9.6	–3.4
1977–79	15.9	12.7	

Note: The calculation of the rate of increase in real wages is based on the consumer price index with the base year of 1970.

Sources: a. Reconstructed from a table presented in Choi (1989: 299).

b. The Economic Planning Board (various years).

c. For the figures 1971–79, the Economic Planning Board. For the figures 1962–70, the Administration of Labor Affairs (1972).

d. The Federation of Korean Trade Unions.

Table 6.7
Working Conditions and Wages in Manufacturing in
Selected Nations, 1960–90

Nation	Hours of work per week			
	1960	1970	1980	1990
Developing Nations				
South Korea	50.3(1963)	52.3	53.1	49.8
Hong Kong	—	—	49.1	44.0
Mexico	46.3	44.9	47.7	44.5
Singapore	46.4	48.7	48.6	48.5
Thailand	50.6(1961)	45.7(1965)	—	45.3
Advanced Industrial Nations				
United States	39.7	39.8	39.7	40.8
Japan	47.8	43.3	41.2	40.8

Nation	Wages per month (US $)/Ratio to US wages (in percent)			
	1960	1970	1980	1990
Developing Nations				
South Korea	35.85/ 9	45.16/ 8	222.23/18	579.64/30
Hong Kong	—	—	226.8ᵃ/18	575.3ᵃ/30
Mexico	67.92/18	136.24/24	365.9 /29	177.08/ 9
Singapore	—	—	—	546.78/29
Thailand	—	—	61.73/ 5	94.02/ 5
Advanced Industrial Nations				
United States	385.80	573.32	1253.43	1916.51
Japan	63.17/16	199.77/35	1078.64/86	3355.77/175

Note: a. Figures for wage per day were presented. They were multiplied by 25. Years in parenthesis are different from column headings.

Sources: International Labour Office 1970, 1980, 1990, 1991; International Monetary Fund 1980, 1990, 1991.

Labor had been building strength and becoming very militant during the 1970s and 1980s; as soon as some political space was allowed, the labor movement exploded in full force, like a pressure-cooker that had been building up steam. The labor movement in South Korea is the most militant of those

Table 6.8

Strikes and Lockouts in South Korea, 1960–90

	1960	1970	1980	1981	1982	1983	1984	1985	1986	1987	1988	1989	1990
D/C	256	4	206	186	88	98	114	265	276	3617	1873	1616	322
W/T	64.3	0.5	49.0	34.6	9.0	11.1	16.4	28.7	46.9	934.9	293.6	409.1	133.9
D/J	—	—	61.3	31.0	11.5	8.7	19.9	64.3	72.0	6946.9	5400.8	6351.4	1836.3

Notes: D/C Number of strikes and lockouts.
         W/T Workers involved (thousands).
         D/J Work days not worked (thousands).

Sources: International Labour Office 1970, 1980, 1990, 1991.

among the Gang of Four in East Asia (Deyo 1989:67). Labor volatility is a critical outcome of South Korean development, and labor movement grew in spite of repressive labor policies and lack of artisan culture. Koo (1990) discusses why South Korea lacked an organized labor movement in the 1960s and 1970s. Lack of artisan culture and of working-class organization and a strong, repressive labor regime are examined as important reasons for this. Although Koo's (Ibid.) study does not cover the 1980s when the labor movement took off, he points out that the rapidity and intensity of proletarianization process was an important reason for the rise of labor movement in the 1980s.

Several factors contributed to the rapid growth of labor movement in the 1970s and 1980s. First, the state's drive for HCI in the 1970s produced companies that were much larger in size relative to the 1960s when light manufacturing was promoted. The HCI also required a more highly educated labor force. As a result, for example, the share of employees with high school and more advanced education among the skilled and semiskilled workers in the machinery sector rose from 17.6 percent in 1967 to 59.3 percent in 1984 (Bello & Rosenfeld 1990:41). A better educated labor force in a large factory setting produced fertile conditions for labor unions to grow and to organize labor movements. Thus, growth in union membership was highest in companies with over 1,000 employees—it grew from 48.2 percent of employees in 1973 to 58.7 percent in 1979 (Choi 1989:37).

Second, the role of students and church organizations was critical. Several church-based groups, such as the Urban Industrial Mission and the Young Catholic Workers, played key roles in organizing labor unions and labor movements since the late 1960s (Bello & Rosenfeld 1990:36–37; Ogle 1990). More student activists were arrested, sentenced to jail terms, and expelled from colleges and universities during eight years under Chun Doo Hwan, compared to the previous eighteen years during the Park regime. And many of these students became disguised factory workers. An unofficial estimate shows that over 3,000 students became blue-collar workers in the 1980s, concealing their college education so that they can be hired in jobs that specifically required less than a high school education

(Ogle 1990:99). They played a critical role in organizing unions and in generating militant labor movements, utilizing organizational skills they acquired from student movements. Between 1985 and 1986 alone, the police reported that 671 such "agitators" were arrested (Ibid.).

The number of labor disputes has been decreasing since its peak in 1987, but it is considerably higher than the numbers in the 1960s, 1970s, and early 1980s (see Table 6.8). However, the work days lost are still much higher than the numbers prior to 1987 and indicate that each dispute is lasting much longer. South Korea's strike and lockout figures are still among the highest in the world (see Table 6.9).

Labor movements targeted both the state and the capitalists. To the state, labor demanded that it become a welfare state, which guarantees the rights of labor and provides basic welfare services. It wanted the state to stop the following practices: suppress wages below the minimum standard of living; enforce repressive labor policies regarding freedom of association, collective bargaining, and collective action; and provide exclu-

Table 6.9
Strikes in Selected Nations, 1960–90

Nations	1960	1970	1980	1985	1989	1990
Developing Nations						
South Korea	256	4	206	265	1616	322
Hong Kong	—	47	37	3	7	15
Mexico	—	206	1339	159	118	149
Brazil	—	—	81	843	4189	—
Thailand	2	17	18	4	10(1987)	9
Taiwan[a]	52	15	700	1622	1458(1986)	—
Advanced Industrial Nations						
United States	3333	4	187	54	51	44
Japan	1063	1542	1133	627	362	—

Notes: Years in parenthesis are different from column headings.
          a. Figures for 1980–89 are from Bello and Rosenfeld (1990: 224). Definition used was total number of disputes.
Sources: International Labour Office 1970, 1980, 1990, 1991.

sive support for big businesses that tend to be hostile toward labor unions and that exacerbated the skewed distribution of wealth (Bello & Rosenfeld 1990; Choi 1989; Deyo 1989; S. Kim 1989; Ogle 1990).

Concluding Remarks

The developmental state in South Korea was a powerful agent of social change. Unparalleled in its influence in society, the state carried out bold economic development plans that produced one of the most successful cases of development near the end of the twentieth century. However, the policies and plans that produced rapid growth also planted the seeds for the decline of the developmental state. The contradictions of the autonomy and of the institution appear to have been accentuated and exacerbated by two important policies adopted by the South Korean state: *industrial policies,* which supported the growth of big businesses and which provided fertile ground for labor mobilization; and *repressive labor policies.* These policies resulted in the shaping of the two powerful groups that would make the strongest demands for the reduction in the state's degree and method of economic intervention. Pressures from within the state and from the United States also prompted the comprehensive developmental state to liberalize. The state, in response, undertook various economic reform measures throughout the 1980s.

The continued growth of the *chaebol* in spite of reduced state subsidies allowed the *chaebol* to become more independent from the developmental state. Several incidents, in which the *chaebol* openly defied, or appeared to have influenced or manipulated, state policies show that the state-*chaebol* relations have changed. They have changed from state dominance to interdependence and symbiosis to competition. The *chaebol* leaders have also entered politics, a domain previously closed to them. In both the economic and political arenas, the competition and tension between the state and the *chaebol* has become more conspicuous during the 1980s.

The 1960s and 1970s formula for South Korean development changed significantly during the 1980s. The comprehensive developmental state significantly reduced its heavy-handed control of the economy. In the process, the developmental state discarded its chief "carrot"—i.e., the low-interest-rate policy loans—, making it difficult to revert back to the 1960s-style state-guided economic development.

However, the limited developmental state is far from a *laissez faire* or a protectionist state. It still is a stronger state than that in many other developing nations, as demonstrated in the 1985 bankruptcy of the Kukje *chaebol*. The limited developmental state is still a state committed to providing services to further advance economic growth and at the same time is a state trying to balance economic growth with welfare and foreign policy. The transition toward a limited developmental state became more unstable as the process was subsumed under greater political changes toward democratization. Thus, the transition of the developmental state faced even greater uncertainties than in other nations, and the state has fluctuated openly back-and-forth from the *chaebol*'s demand for a growth-oriented protectionist state to labor's welfare state.

7
Collusion and Conflict:
The State and Business in
the Development Process

South Korea's phenomenal economic development since the 1960s has brought tremendous changes to the nation. Poor farm families are no longer starving every spring while waiting for the next harvest. More people work in factories, offices, and service jobs than on farms. Compared to the early 1960s, when fewer than one out of ten households had a black-and-white television set, today almost every home has a color television set. And while the average annual income in 1961 was $82, in 1993 it was $7,660 (World Bank 1995).

After two decades of rapid growth based on exports, South Korea continued to grow at an impressive rate of 8.7 percent between 1980 and 1991 in terms of the average annual growth rate of GNP per capita (World Bank 1993). This was the fastest growth rate in the world. In comparison, middle-income economies, the category to which South Korea belongs, recorded a mere 0.3 percent in average annual growth rate of GNP per capita during the same period (Ibid.). South Korea even outperformed its rapidly growing neighbors in the Gang of Four (Hong

Kong's growth rate was 5.6 percent and Singapore's was 5.3 percent) (Ibid.).

South Korea's sustained long-term development for over three decades is not based on a static "South Korean model." What is evident from a careful examination of South Korea's development since the 1960s is that the key institutions were transformed in the process of economic development. Obstacles and challenges facing the South Korean economy changed over time, and South Korea's strategy to overcome them varied as well. Thus, the answer to South Korea's success does not lie in one industrial strategy—e.g., export-oriented industrialization—, which supposedly worked for over three decades. *As the analysis in this book showed, a large part of South Korean success has been its agility and flexibility in taking advantage of and overcoming the obstacles presented in the changing domestic and international political economy.* Without a clearer recognition of the dynamic nature of this model, an understanding of South Korea becomes impossible.

The South Korean Model of Economic Development

It is difficult to talk about a model when it is not static but dynamic, as is the case in South Korean development. Nevertheless, let me offer some insights on key attributes of South Korean development. First, the two institutions—i.e., the comprehensive developmental state and the *chaebol*—were vital in South Korea's economic development. South Korea's remarkable economic growth since the 1960s, overcoming major obstacles including a war that left the nation in near total destruction, was achieved when the two institutions were restructured and the relations between the two were transformed. On the other hand, many economic policies since 1961 were not very different from those prior to 1961. A comprehensive developmental and comprehensive authoritarian state created in 1961 formed a tight alliance with large businesses and embarked upon a major transformation of the economy: from an agrarian- to an industrial-based economy and from an inward-oriented to an export- and outward-oriented economy. In the process, labor was repressed: wages were kept low and rights of labor were severely limited, in spite of the fact that South Korea's early economic development was based on a labor-intensive, light manufacturing sector.

Second, South Korea is only one of a handful of nations in the Third World that has achieved sustained economic development since the end of the World War II in an international economy already dominated by advanced industrialized nations. One of the structural obstacles presented to developing nations such as South Korea was the very existence of advanced industrialized nations, which were often unwilling to share its capital and the most advanced technology. It made it difficult for developing nations including South Korea to manipulate or to change the international markets or the geopolitical contexts to their advantage. However, in spite of such obstacles, South Korea and a few of its neighbors took advantage of the international context and created a niche for their economies. Such ability of the Third World nations to take advantage of, and to overcome the obstacles presented by, the international political economy has been one of the important foci of the book. The differential ability of a few Third World nations to attain economic development, when many of their neighbors failed in spite of similar opportunities and obstacles presented in the international and regional political economy, is a key to understanding South Korea's phenomenal economic development.

Third, institutions of development, especially the state, changed in the course of economic development. The South Korean state was pressured to give up the very key to its success— i.e., the comprehensive developmental state—upon the attainment of its goal. The ironies are that not only did the comprehensive developmental state's weakening come as a result of its success but also that its challengers included the *chaebol*, which the state helped to create and flourish. An examination of South Korea's economic development thus focused on the changes that took place in the key institutions of the state and the *chaebol* and in the relations between them. These observations are grounded on an assumption that rapid economic development can only be achieved by institutions that are also dynamic.

Fourth, in the course of three decades of impressive economic development, the relations between the state and businesses and among the state, businesses, and labor changed. The state dominated the alliance it formed with the large businesses in the 1960s. This alliance excluded labor from neither enjoying the fruits of its work or demanding its rights. The 1960s' economic growth led to reshuffling among the *chaebol*, and a handful of Park-era *chaebol* emerged by the end of the decade. This latter group's success led them to become indispensable for the Park regime in the 1970s, when regional security threats increased and domestic political uncertainty for the Park regime grew. The push for heavy and chemical industrialization (HCI) came about in this domestic political and international geopolitical context when there was no strong foundation based on market signals. The alliance between the state and the Park-era *chaebol* was solidified with HCI. The relatively looser alliance formed with the large businesses in the 1960s was replaced by a much tighter alliance with the leading *chaebol* in the 1970s, especially those that invested in the heavy and chemical industries. The cooperation of the large *chaebol* for HCI, and the *chaebol*'s political financing, was critical for the Park regime. Thus, the 1970s witnessed a growing symbiosis and interdependence between the state and the *chaebol*. Labor continued to be repressed in the name of national security and political stability.

By the 1980s, as a result of the *chaebol*'s continued rapid growth with the state's protection and support, the *chaebol* became competitors to the state in provision of certain services, including financial services and research and development, and increasingly so in the political arena. The comprehensive development state reacted to external and internal pressures to restructure and transformed itself into a limited developmental state. By the end of the 1980s, the growing influence of the *chaebol* in South Korea won them a title from the local media, the "*Chaebol* Republic."

Fifth, the contradictions of institution and autonomy illuminate why the comprehensive developmental state is a transitory and unstable form of government. Whether the comprehensive developmental state is successful or not, it will be forced to transform itself, albeit for different reasons. In South Korea, the contradictions and irony lie in the fact that factors that cause the comprehensive developmental state to change to a limited developmental state is its tremendous success and that one of its challengers is the *chaebol*. The process is dialectic, since the seeds of the weakening of the comprehensive developmental state was sown by itself, as it promoted HCI and fostered the growth of the *chaebol* and unwittingly shepherded the growth of labor.

Finally, the social cost of South Korean economic development is its delayed democracy, which entails severe limits imposed on civil liberties and on rights accorded to the citizens, including labor. It is difficult to weigh the benefits of political freedom against those of economic well-being as has been demonstrated in the economic and political transformations that occurred since the end of the cold war in previously socialist nations. However, it is not clear whether more political freedom and democracy in the initial phase of economic development would have meant that economic growth would not have occurred or that it would have occurred at a slower pace. Without adequate empirical evidence, it cannot be argued that an authoritarian state is a sufficient and necessary condition for economic development in a Third World nation.

An important consequence of the South Korean state's repression of labor, and its political repression in general, was massive demonstrations for democracy and the explosion of labor movements during the mid- to late 1980s. Massive mobilization against the authoritarian state is the direct result of a state's ignoring the demands of the people for a more just and democratic society. At a minimum, success in attaining economic growth does not substitute for a lack of political democracy.

Comparisons with the Japanese Model of Economic Development

The Asian nations that followed Japan's success into the world economy have often been compared with Japan. South Korea and Taiwan, in particular, have been grouped together with Japan as the northeast Asian model of development (Cumings 1987). The fact that South Korea and Taiwan are former colonies of Japan helped to advance this position. Moreover, both South Korea and Taiwan have successfully entered the world economy with strategies of development based roughly on the Japanese model—i.e., export-oriented industrialization, with a comprehensive developmental state. And all three countries are more similar than they are different in social structure and culture.

Two questions will be addressed in this section. The first question is "How similar are the experiences of the three nations?" What have been the key ingredients and trajectories of their economic development? And the second question is "Can South Korea or Taiwan become the next Japan?" as Amsden's (1989) book title *Asia's Next Giant: South Korea and Late Industrialization* suggests. In other words, can South Korea or Taiwan become an advanced industrialized nation like Japan?

Japan has been the only nation since World War II to successfully transform itself from a developing nation to an advanced industrialized nation. Among the G-Seven (Group of Seven Industrialized Democracies—United States, United Kingdom, Canada, Germany, France, Italy, and Japan), Japan is the only one to have joined this rank in the years since the World War II. Japan's model of development has been significantly different from those of the other nations in this group, both because of the status of the international economy into which it interjected itself and because of the country's domestic political economy. Several parameters of Japan's development are apparent:

- It entered the world economy when there was already a fairly stable set of advanced industrialized nations.
- The state assumed a critical role in the development process, leading and supporting the private sector (Johnson 1982; Samuels 1987). While free-market principles were not abandoned, they were significantly modified to include critical aspects of planning.
- Rather than investing in research and development to invent new technology Japan modified existing technology (Amsden 1989). Amsden argues that this learner's

role provided Japan room to develop faster than its predecessors and allowed it to catch up to the advanced industrialized nations in record time (Ibid.).

- Japan's social structure and cultural traditions are qualitatively different from the shared social and cultural traditions among advanced industrial nations in North America and Western Europe. Some scholars have argued that Japan's social structure and culture have been the main reason for the country's rapid success in the world economy.

Whether one subscribes to any or all of these factors and arguments, it is fair to argue that Japan's model of development was new to the world.

Let us turn to the first question about the commonality of the experiences of economic development in South Korea, Taiwan, and Japan. First, the influence of the Japanese in South Korea and Taiwan is based more on recent experiences with FDI, joint ventures, and technology transfers rather than the Japanese colonial experiences per se. Second, the condition of the international marketplace had changed as a result of the Japanese success in penetrating it. And this in turn has made it harder for nations such as South Korea and Taiwan to emulate the Japanese success. Third, domestic institutions, which were put in place to attain economic development in South Korea were different from those in Japan. The comprehensive developmental state in South Korea was both authoritarian and developmental, and clearly led the process of industrialization with an iron fist filled with capital. Finally, South Korea and Taiwan have not provided significant new developments in technology or labor processes, unlike its predecessors. Their soon-to-happen entry to the World Bank's category of upper-income economies will be based on older formulas for economic development. The only question that remains is how long these nations can sustain their rapid economic growth without significant new developments in technology or labor processes.

For the second question, let us examine the different models of ascendance in the world economy. So far, advanced industrialized nations have provided Third World nations with two general schemes to become like them. The first one is based on technological innovations, as were the case in many advanced industrialized nations including England and the United States. The second is based on new product development and innovations in the labor process (Amsden 1989). Amsden argues that Japan's success was based on this latter scheme, which allowed it to grow faster than its predecessors (Ibid.). What scheme should South Korea adopt in its quest to become an advanced industrialized nation?

Attempting to follow the first scheme is exceedingly difficult for Third World nations such as South Korea, since huge investments in research and development must be made. The significant advancements in technology in advanced industrialized nations since World War II make it nearly impossible for Third World nations to adopt this strategy. The second scheme, which is to follow the Japanese model, has its own problems. Because the world has experienced one Japan, there will be no other Japan. In other words, the international economy has changed significantly in response to Japan; one needs only to look at the trade barriers and other protectionist policies instituted toward Japanese products in the advanced industrialized nations in Western Europe and the United States. It is thus difficult to imagine that either South Korea or Taiwan could attain the economic status of Japan. They have been successful until now, but the success could reach a plateau if the old strategies for economic development are not modified significantly.

On the other hand, it is entirely possible that these nations could become major economic powers by relying on strategies that Japan and the other advanced industrialized nations did not use. However, in neither South Korea or Taiwan have we witnessed any indications of this to date. South Korea and Taiwan are poised to soon become members of the upper-income economies (based on the criteria of the World Bank) and join the other two members of the Gang of Four if their economies continue to expand at a rate faster than the rest of the world's. This will allow them to obtain GNP per capita levels of upper-income economies without significant breakthroughs in technology, labor processes, or by any other means.

To conclude, South Korea and Taiwan have attained economic development learning from Japan's experience of economic development in the post–World War II era. It is important to note that South Korea and Taiwan had to modify the Japanese model to fit the domestic political climate of opportunities and constraints, and the status of the international economic and geopolitical contexts. The developmental state's selection of private big businesses in South Korea and the selection of state-owned enterprises in Taiwan reflect the different domestic political configurations in the respective nations. The stronger alliance formed between the developmental state and big businesses in South Korea, compared to both Taiwan and Japan, was based on extensive subsidies provided by the state to the private sector. Different ways in which the Japanese experience was utilized in each nation reflect that it is not easy to simplify the experiences of the three nations as fitting one grand model.

South Korea and Taiwan continue to be influenced by the Japanese economy. This is because Japanese investment, technology transfers, and export goods continue to successfully penetrate these markets, after a short lull when Japan's bubble economy burst in the early 1990s. Japan continues to outperform the United States in terms of investment and trade in Asia. However, because Japan exists and it has been somewhat reluctant to share its most advanced technology with its Asian neighbors and because many advanced industrialized nations have erected trade barriers partly as a result of Japan's phenomenal success in exports, it will be unlikely to see either South Korea or Taiwan emerge as the next Japan in the near future.

South Korea's Lessons for Third World Nations

What lessons can the South Korean development provide to other Third World nations that are aspiring to attain rapid economic development? Before I attempt to answer this question, let me point out that a South Korean model, which is static and is easily transferrable to other Third World nations, does not exist. In fact, the two key institutions—the authoritarian and comprehensive developmental state, and the *chaebol*—, which led the rapid growth during the early phase, changed considerably in the process.

With this caveat in mind, let me provide some policy recommendations for Third World nations aspiring to emulate the South Korean experience. This book has been devoted to uncovering key attributes of South Korean development, which could conceivably be used as guidelines for other developing nations aspiring to emulate the South Korean experience. Therefore, in this section I focus on conditions that make it *difficult* for other nations to emulate South Korea. First, South Korea's geopolitical significance to the United States made a crucial difference during the early phase of development. U.S. aid and loans were important for South Korea's economic development, albeit not sufficient in and of themselves. However, it is important to note that South Korea's strategic importance to the United States was a historical accident. It is not a situation that South Korea manipulated in order to receive foreign capital. Even if South Korea had some control over the situation of heightened security concerns/threats, it would not have opted for this since the cost was the devastating Korean War. Thus, being a strategically important nation to a Super Power is not a precondition that a small, developing nation can, or should try to, emulate. Furthermore, becoming a recipient of military assistance has become an increasingly difficult precondition in the post–cold war era, since the United States and Russia are no longer vying for the support of developing nations and wooing them with military and economic aid.

Second, the comprehensive developmental state requires, from the beginning, a state bureaucracy that will allow an efficient and effective implementation of policies. However, resources are required in order to build an efficient government bureaucracy. And, not many Third World nations have resources— this is *why* they are trying to develop. The predicament facing Third World nations aspiring to develop is that they lack the necessary resources, and relying on foreign capitalists to obtain resources presents significant constraints and dilemmas. (These have been dealt with extensively in the dependency writings about Latin America.) Most importantly, foreign capitalists may not be willing to support the build-up of a developmental state, which could introduce restrictions on foreign capitalists' access to markets. Other sources of foreign capital, such as the International Monetary Fund and the World Bank, have put many stipulations on their loans to developing nations, including economic reforms. These reforms prescribe a more liberalized economy than that of South Korea's. The IMF and the World Bank have not provided funds to develop a strong, comprehensive developmental state, which flies in the face of a liberalized market economy they would like to foster in developing nations. In fact, in former–Soviet bloc eastern and central European nations, the IMF and World Bank were explicitly attempting to create a market economy without strong developmental states similar to those in Japan and South Korea (Amsden, Kochanowicz & Taylor 1994). The dilemma for Third World nations, which may see a solution for economic development in the creation of a comprehensive developmental state, is that resources to build such an institution is not readily available from either foreign or domestic sources.

Third, the comprehensive developmental state is predicated upon a high degree of autonomy from dominant social classes and groups. This means that, among other things, the comprehensive developmental state should not rely upon the domestic capitalist class for political funds and capital resources. If the comprehensive developmental state must rely heavily on the domestic capitalist class, the former's ability to effectively intervene in the economy could be severely hampered. Thus, resources are critical for the comprehensive developmental state to have some autonomy from the domestic capitalist class. In addition, in South Korea, the comprehensive developmental state had a considerable amount of capital it could use to entice businesses to invest in state-target sectors. If the comprehensive developmental state was unable to distribute and channel domestic and foreign capital to state-target sectors, it would not have been quite so successful in intervening in the economy. For all these reasons, capital resources, which are under the control of the comprehensive developmental state, are important. And, unfortunately, resources are what many developing nations do not have.

Fourth, South Korea's comprehensive developmental state was also a very repressive authoritarian state. Amsden argues that the state's ability to discipline the private sector was important in South Korea's development, helping the alliance between the state and big businesses to be productive rather than prone to corruption (1989). Repression of labor, through the suppression of wages and the forbidding of collective action and bargaining, ensured a steady output of price-competitive products for exports.

However, the authoritarian state delayed democratization in South Korea. Repression of workers in particular and citizens in general, cost the regime dearly in the 1980s. Massive displays of frustration toward the regime and its authoritarian cast resulted in a period of social upheaval and chaos. Political repression, in the name of securing a stable economy and society for economic development and national security, simply went too far. As noted in more critical studies about South Korean development, there were numerous cases of abuse of workers and prosecution of antigovernment organizers as "communist agitators," which could result in a death sentence under the National Security Law (Bello & Rosenfeld 1990; Hart-Landsberg 1993; Ogle 1990). Delaying political democracy in the name of economic development is a critical and consequential question that requires a serious debate and deliberation by *all* citizens of a nation embarking upon a South Korean–type economic development. It is not a choice that should be made by government officials without regards to the plight, however short-term and limited, of its workers and citizens.

Finally, the success of South Korean development should also be viewed in light of the costs to millions of workers. For example, female labor was exploited in the export industries throughout much of the 1960s and 1970s. For both male and female workers, the fruits of the country's economic development were not immediately translated into higher wages and improved working conditions. Rather, the economic rewards were reaped by the *chaebol*. Suppression of wages and repression of labor rights for collective bargaining continued until the late 1980s. When the level of frustration and despair felt by millions of workers reached the boiling point, it finally spilled over.

The legacy of South Korea's phenomenal economic developments since the 1960s is a difficult one for other Third World nations to emulate. Not only are the positive international factors difficult to emulate, but the social costs are real. Nonetheless, South Korea's lessons for other Third World nations are important. The fact that a relatively small Third World nation in the midst of advanced industrialized nations and many developing nations succeeded should be a positive reminder that economic development can be attained. Second, various components of the South Korean legacy can be selectively emulated. For example, a comprehensive developmental state can be established without a concomitant repression of labor. Perhaps by dissecting the South Korean model and selecting the factors that fit a particular nation would be the only way to learn from the South Korean case. In that sense, this book provides a critical analysis of both the strengths and problems of the South Korean model of economic development.

Future Prospects of South Korea

As South Korea is at the verge of becoming an advanced industrialized nation, there are still important hurdles that it must overcome. Unlike Singapore and Hong Kong, which are now classified as "high-income economies" by the World Bank, South Korea's GNP per capita was $7,660 in 1993 (World Bank 1995).[1] As a late-latecomer, South Korea faces challenges to develop indigenous technology and/or to "create new products and [labor] processes" (Amsden 1989: 328). As a nation that developed its economy with an iron fist, the South Korean state is in the process of renegotiating its relations with the capitalists and labor as these two forces gain political influence. As a small nation surrounded by powerful neighbors, South Korea must constantly negotiate its geopolitical and economic relations with them and, in particular, with the United States and Japan. And finally, as a nation divided, South Korea also faces the possibility of the daunting task of paying for the reunification with North Korea, which, even by a conservative estimate, could easily wipe out its upper-middle-income economy.

South Korea has been engaged in democratization since the mid-1980s. As Rueschemeyer, Stephens, and Stephens (1992) noted, economic development brings pressure for democratization through changes in class configuration and class relations. In South Korea, the growth of the urban middle class and the mobilization of the working class were critical in forcing the breakdown of an authoritarian regime, which existed from the 1960s to the late 1980s. The workers, who were aided initially by student and church groups, formulated their class interests against both the capitalists and the authoritarian state. Their participation in the democracy movement was vital and enabled the democracy movement in the mid-1980s to become a broad-based coalition that included students (and intellectuals), religious leaders, workers, and the urban middle class. Democratic transition is continuing with a newly elected civilian president, Kim Young Sam (1993–98). Under Kim's leadership, South Korea has enacted various measures to consolidate democracy. This means that South Korea is likely to continue with major social and political changes in the near future, where contested groups may challenge specific measures along the way.

Less than a decade since democratic transition began in 1987, South Korea continues to face pressure to continue its economic reform, in particular to restructure the *chaebol*. However, the Kim administration, in spite of its success in initiating significant reforms in the military and in real-name banking and so on, has not been able to drastically change the private sector. This has earned the new regime an ominous label, "*Chaebol* Republic," which had been used since the late 1980s but took on a much more critical connotation with the Kim regime (see chapter 6). In the mid-1990s, this term implied the inability of the government to control and limit the influence of the *chaebol*, the same way previous regimes were unable to control and limit the influence of the military (H. Y. Cho 1993b; Nam 1995). The tremendous economic power amassed by the *chaebol* makes them almost invincible from the state's and society's will to restructure. The most pressing issues that need to be negotiated between various actors in the economy are: (1) the role of the interventionist developmental state in the economy; (2) the (unchecked) growth of the large *chaebol,* which continues to threaten the small- and medium-sized enterprises; and (3) the rights of labor.

Internationally, South Korea faces challenges due to its tremendous economic success. Its economic prowess as a major exporter, along with the other East Asian neighbors, has prompted First World nations to erect trade barriers. At the same time, there is growing pressure, in particular, from the United States to open the South Korean economy for foreign financial institutions, products, and services. It is an irony that the United States and other First World nations are enacting protectionist measures, and, at the same time, they are pressuring East Asian nations to reduce protectionist measures.

South Korea also faces pressure from the so-called "second-tier NICs" in the Third World, which include the People's Republic of China, Malaysia, Thailand, and Indonesia. These nations have successfully penetrated the international market with their cheap manufactured products and squeezed out countries like South Korea from the bottom wrung of the market. However, the transition for South Korean companies has not been easy. South Korea is increasingly becoming aware of the limitations on its ability to penetrate the middle and upper levels of the international market without a clear advantage in technology or in labor processes.

South Korea faces an even greater challenge in terms of security issues. With the cold war all but over, South Korea is scrutinized by the United States as to whether to continue a military presence in South Korea. Reunification with North Korea appears, at different times, as a distant or an imminent possibility. This potential for reunification is increasingly seen by the South Koreans as having a huge economic price tag. Germany's costly reunification process has prompted the South Koreans to become more leery about an abrupt German-type reunification. Sheer economic costs of absorbing the ailing North Korean economy and other socioeconomic problems of reunification loom large. The latter include the following issues: (1) job shortage resulting from an influx of North Koreans to the South searching for jobs and from downsizing the military in both South and North Korea; (2) housing shortages in the South; (3) renegotiation of wages and labor union rights, which were achieved after years of labor movements in the South; (4) provision of social welfare service; and (5) potential for exacerbation of class tensions and regional rivalry. However, regardless of a potentially huge price tag, the reunification remains a deeply held "yearning" for many Koreans. Thus, many Koreans see the reunification as inevitable, with only the timing and process remaining to be negotiated, no doubt daunting tasks.

In spite of such challenges that lie ahead, South Korea will plough through them as it has in the past. This is precisely because South Korea's success lies not it in a static formula for economic development but in its creativity and flexibility in overcoming structural obstacles and challenges. The institutions of the strong state and big businesses, which were formed during the past decades in an effort to attain economic development, will be forced to change and adapt to the processes of democratic consolidation and possible reunification with North Korea.

Appendix

Romanization of Korean Words

The Ministry of Education's (Republic of Korea) Romanization Rules (1984)

한글의 로마자 표기법

A. MOE System (the Ministry of Education System of Romanization)

모	ㅏ	ㅑ	ㅓ	ㅕ	ㅗ	ㅛ	ㅜ	ㅠ	ㅡ	ㅣ		ㅐ	ㅒ	ㅔ	ㅖ	ㅘ	ㅙ	ㅚ	ㅝ	ㅞ	ㅟ	ㅢ
음	a	ya	ŏ	yŏ	o	yo	u	yu	ŭ	i		ae	yae	e	ye	wa	wae	oe	wo	we	wi	ŭi

자	ㄱ	ㄴ	ㄷ	ㄹ	ㅁ	ㅂ	ㅅ	ㅇ	ㅈ	ㅊ	ㅋ	ㅌ	ㅍ	ㅎ		ㄲ	ㄸ	ㅃ	ㅆ	ㅉ		
음	k, g	n	t, d	r, l	m	p, b	s, sh	ng	ch, j	ch'	k'	t'	p'	h		kk	tt	pp	ss	tch		

Notes

Notes for Chapter One

1. Korean names are written with the family name first, followed by the given name, as is the custom in Korea. Romanization of the Korean words is based on the Republic of Korea's Ministry of Education's 1984 Romanization Rules. The Rules are attached in the Appendix. Several well-known names such as Syngman Rhee and Park Chung Hee, which do not follow the Ministry of Education's rules, are presented in the popularly known romanization. In such cases, romanization based on the Ministry of Education's rules is provided in brackets in their first occurrence. The names of authors, who have published in English, are presented in the author's own romanization.

2. Examples are when the oil-producing Middle Eastern nations raised the crude oil prices, which led to world-wide Oil Crises in 1973 and 1979.

3. This term refers to the Gang of Four, who played a central role during the Cultural Revolution in the People's Republic of China. Many studies used this term to describe the ascending economic powers in East Asia—i.e., South Korea, Taiwan, Hong Kong, and Singapore. Other similar terms include "Four Little Dragons," and "Four Little Tigers."

4. Notable exceptions to this are found in the articles included in Evans, Rueschemeyer, and Skocpol (1985). In particular, Amsden's

(1985) study on Taiwan analyzes the changes in the state as a result of successful development.

5. Lie (1990) provides a critical review of recent studies on South Korean development that tend to glorify its success while ignoring conflicts and contradictions. See Bello and Rosenfeld (1990) for a critical discussion of East Asian development focusing on the environment, political repression, and labor problems. Also see Ogle (1990) for further discussion of repressive labor laws and abuses of labor in South Korea, and Hart-Landsberg (1993).

6. The word "dialectic" is used in reference to Hegel's theory of dialectics of "thesis," "antithesis," and "synthesis," and Marx's "dialectic materialism." In the last, history is explained as a series of stages in which the seeds of destruction for a later stage is sown in the preceding stage (Hoult 1969; Marx 1992 [1967]; Merton 1967; Sorokin 1956 [1928]). In South Korea, we can examine how the seeds for the weakening of the developmental state in the 1980s were actually sown by the developmental state itself during the 1960s and 1970s through its promotion of big businesses and the drive for heavy and chemical industrialization program.

7. More interviews were conducted with state officials than with *chaebol* owners or executives. The book does contain interviews with a few prominent *chaebol* family members—e.g., Chŏng Mong Jun of Hyundai—and other anecdotes and secondary sources. The reason why this book utilizes more first-hand interviews with government officials is because such interviews have not been readily available in scholarly or popular sources, unlike interviews with the *chaebol* and their families, which have been provided in greater numbers at least in South Korean sources.

Notes for Chapter Two

1. For a more detailed comparative analysis of economic development in East Asia and Latin America, see Gereffi and Wyman (1990).

2. See Collier (1979) for debates on bureaucratic authoritarianism in Latin America, and see Im (1987) for a discussion of bureaucratic authoritarianism in South Korea. However, bureaucratic authoritarianism as a development strategy has had mixed results in Latin America, and the theoretical model itself has been heavily criticized.

3. I will use Claus Offe's definition of contradiction: "the tendency inherent within a specific mode of production to destroy those very pre-conditions on which its survival depends" (1984: 132).

4. Many studies on South Korean democratization have been published. See Cheng and Kim (1994), and Kim and Kihl (1988).

Notes for Chapter Three

1. When financial data including total assets and total sales were presented for the fifty largest business groups based on 1983 data, a natural break occurred at the largest four and the largest ten (including the top four). The analysis of the *chaebol* in this book focuses on this group of the largest ten. The 1993 figures also show a natural break at the largest ten and at the largest five.

2. The growth rate was based on total assets. The average annual growth rate was calculated using 1980 constant prices in Won.

3. The rate (7.9%) is based on the average annual growth rate of real GNP between 1971 and 1980.

4. This example is inspired by Janelli's (1993) translation of a quote from Kang, Ch'oe, and Chang (1991).

5. In most cases, terms such as "Daewoo man," "Samsung man," and "Hyundai man" refer only to the male workers. Although women work in these conglomerates (mostly as low- and semi-skilled workers and secretaries), they are not considered a part of the corporate world, to which these terms apply.

6. I Ch'ang Hŭi left Samsung to start his own business. Saehan Media Corporation, which he established in 1973, was quite successful, and became a small *chaebol*. I Ch'ang Hŭi died of leukemia in 1991.

7. A survey of South Korean businesses, which belong to the *chaebol* and other independent ones, were conducted in the spring of 1992, with funding provided by the Nihon University of Japan and the East-West Center. Six hundred firms were selected based on two-stage stratified sampling. Three hundred twenty-two firms participated in this survey. See E. M. Kim and Julle Cho (1993) for details.

8. The GTC's affiliation to the *chaebol* can be identified by the name of the company, which often includes the *chaebol*'s name.

9. Kukje *chaebol* went bankrupt in 1985. Kukje Corporation was later absorbed by Hanil Synthetic Textiles on December 30, 1986 (Maeil Kyŏngje Shinmun 1989).

10. This GTC is a member of the Lucky-Gold Star *chaebol*.

11. See Amsden (1989) and I and I (1990) for statistical analyses of the growing diversification of business investments by the largest *chaebol*.

12. This is an association of the owners, chief executive officers, and high-ranking managers of the *chaebol* and large businesses. It regularly lobbies the government and other agencies to promote the interests of large capitalists.

13. The Kangwha Treaty was an unequal trade treaty signed by the Koreans, giving Japan access to Korean ports. This treaty was followed by trade treaties with Western nations, including the United States, United Kingdom, and Russia.

14. The Japanese *zaibatsu* were disbanded after Japan's defeat in World War II. General MacArthur of the U.S. military government ordered the *zaibatsu* to disband due to their support of Japan's war efforts. Family-ownership and family-management were separated, and more importantly, financial institutions (banks) were separated from industrial manufacturing.

15. Of course, higher education in economics or business administration in the United States is not monolithic. It includes conservative as well as radical ideologies regarding capitalism and the free market. However, as Amsden notes, many South Korean students were educated in programs where the free market ideology tended to predominate (Amsden 1994a).

16. I conducted this interview with Mr. I in his office in the Hyundai Motor Company in Seoul, South Korea. The interview was conducted on June 19, 1990, and it lasted for 1 hour and 45 minutes.

17. Mr. Kim was a director of operations at the time of interview, which took place at his office in Seoul on June 25, 1990, from 11:00 A.M. to 12:30 P.M.

Notes for Chapter Four

1. This was also substantiated in a discussion with Dr. Bon Ho Koo in 1993. Dr. Koo worked closely with President Park while he was the director of the Korea Development Institute in the 1970s.

2. See, for example, Mardon (1990) and Pyŏn (1980) for details on why Gulf Oil left South Korea after eighteen years. Mardon (1990) also discusses the results of a survey of MNCs in South Korea, which show that a majority of the MNCs experienced difficulty working in South Korea.

3. For a detailed theoretical discussion of these issues, see Frieden (1981) and E. M. Kim (1989). For a detailed breakdown of different types of foreign capital entering the Korean economy, see E. M. Kim (1989), Mardon (1990), and Stallings (1991).

Notes for Chapter Five

1. The State of the Nation message is similar to the U.S. president's State of the Union message.

2. Sŏ was working in legal affairs office of the EPB at the time of the interview, which was June 16, 1988. The interview took place in his office at the EPB for about one hour.

3. At the time of the interview, Mr. Pak was deputy director of the Industrial Machinery Division, Machinery Industry Bureau of the Ministry of Trade and Industry. The interview was conducted from 3:30 to 6:00 P.M. on June 17, 1988, in Pak's office at the ministry.

4. The first reason cited by Pak was the development of heavy and chemical industries to achieve a more balanced economy between light and heavy industries, as announced in the Third Five-Year Economic Development Plan.

5. The presidential election was held on April 27, 1971. The results were announced on May 1, 1971. There was a 79.9 percent participation rate. The results show that of the 12,387,487 votes, President Park received 6,342,828 votes (51 percent) and Kim Dae Jung received 5,395,900 votes (44 percent), with the rest of votes divided among five other candidates.

6. See Im (1989) and Chŏng (1985) for details of the Yushin Reformation.

7. Mr. Kim Kwang Mo was the President of Technoservices, Co., Ltd. in Seoul when I interviewed him in 1988. The interview took place in his office in Yŏŭido in Seoul, from 3 to 5:45 P.M. on June 20, 1988.

8. This section is excerpted and revised from Eun Mee Kim, "From Dominance to Symbiosis: State and Chaebol in Korea," *Pacific Focus* III(2):105–21, 1988.

9. Thus, it is better known as "The Emergency Decree of August 3, 1972." For further details of the Decree, see Bank of Korea (1973) and S. H. I (1985). Many options were discussed before the Emergency Decree was announced. One of them was a currency reform. This was sought as an effective measure to disable the curb market and to furnish a solid economic basis for the Yushin Reformation. However, this proposal met with opposition from the International Monetary Fund and had to be dropped (S. H. I 1985).

10. Deputy prime minister is also the minister of the EPB.

11. My discussion of the largest *chaebol* often focuses on the largest four. This is because there was a natural break in terms of total assets and sales according to the 1983 figures, when I examined financial statistics of the fifty largest *chaebol*. Another break occurred at the ten largest *chaebol*, and thus some of the discussion and statistics focus on this group.

12. Hyundai no longer works with Ford.

13. To talk about these impressive growth rates as "modest" is somewhat misleading. Their growth is quite rapid when you compare it to the economy as a whole, which was growing at a rate faster than most other nations in the world. The word "modest" is used simply to highlight a relatively slower growth rate compared to its truly remarkable competitors.

Notes for Chapter Six

1. This is a term that journalists and writers in South Korea began using in the late 1980s in order to sarcastically remark on the tremendous control the *chaebol* yielded in the South Korean society. The term took on a more ominous connotation in the mid-1990s when the civilian government of Kim Young Sam abandoned much of its economic reform programs. Thus, the term "*Chaebol* Republic" was used to mock the civilian Kim regime, as the previous regimes were mocked as "Military Republics." This new usage was introduced to me by Professor Cho Hee-Yeon of Sŏng Kong Hoe University, whose works provide important criticisms to the South Korean polity and society.

2. This was also confirmed in numerous interviews I held with EPB officials and university professors who were advisors to the Chun administration.

3. For details of the South Korean and North Korean relations, see B. P. Kim (1992), I. J. Kim (1991), Y. H. Kihl (1994), Speakman and Lee (1993), and Yoo (1995).

4. This story emerged during my 1988 interviews with a secretary who worked for a chair of a *chaebol* ranked in the top twenty. It was later substantiated during the National Assembly hearings.

5. See C. K. I (1991) and Memorial Foundation for I Han Yŏl (1991) for more detailed accounts of the hearings and other incidents of collusion between the Chun regime and the *chaebol*.

6. The National Assembly identified the following issues as the areas of concern for the government audit: (1) the Fifth Republic's (the Chun regime) wrongdoing; (2) the growing human rights violation of the Sixth Republic (the Roh regime); (3) concentration of wealth; (4) social problems including crime, traffic safety, housing shortage, and pollution; and (5) responding to the concerns of the farmers and fishermen and the urban poor (*Wŏlgan Chosŏn* 1989).

7. *P'yŏng* is a unit of area, which is equivalent to 3.954 square yards.

8. See Haggard and Moon (1988) for further discussion of the economic liberalization program in South Korea.

9. The owners of the Hyundai International and Hyundai *chaebol* are brothers, but they did not belong to the same *chaebol*.

10. Mr. Han Sŭng Chun met with me from 2:30 to 4:00 P.M. in his office in the headquarters building of Kia Motors in Yŏŭido in Seoul in March 26, 1992.

11. As discussed in chapter 3, FKI is an association of owners, chief executive officers, and high-ranking managers of *chaebol* and large enterprises. Its opinions and advisory reports to the government are published as a collection in *Annual Report: The Federation of Korean Industries*.

Note for Chapter Seven

1. In 1993, Hong Kong's GNP per capita was $18,060 and Singapore's was $19,850 (World Bank 1995).

References

Annual of Korean Transportation. 1975, 1976, 1978, 1986. *Annual of Korean Transportation*. Seoul: Kyot'ong Shinbosa.

Amin, Samir. 1976. *Unequal Development: An Essay on the Social Formation of Peripheral Capitalism*. New York: Monthly Review Press.

Amsden, Alice. 1985. "The State and Taiwan's Economic Development." Pp. 78–106 in *Bringing the State Back In*, edited by Peter B. Evans, Dietrich Rueschemeyer, and Theda Skocpol. Cambridge: Cambridge University Press.

———. 1989. *Asia's Next Giant: South Korea and Late Industrialization*. London: Oxford University Press.

———. 1994a. "The Specter of Anglo-Saxonization is Haunting South Korea." Pp. 87–125 in *Korea's Political Economy: An Institutional Perspective*, edited by Lee-Jay Cho and Yoon Hyung Kim. Boulder, CO: Westview Press.

———. 1994b. "Why Isn't the Whole World Experimenting with the East Asian Model to Develop?: Review of *The East Asian Miracle*." *World Development* 22(4): 627–33.

Amsden, Alice H., Jacek Kochanowicz, and Lance Taylor. 1994. *The Market Meets Its Match: Restructuring the Economies of Eastern Europe*. Cambridge, MA: Harvard University Press.

Ban, Sung Hwan, Pal Yong Moon, and Dwight H. Perkins. 1978. *Rural Development.* Cambridge, MA: Harvard University Press.

Bank of Korea. 1960–1991. *Economic Statistics Yearbook.* Seoul: Bank of Korea.

———. 1976, 1981, 1984, 1986. *Financial Statements Analysis.* Seoul: Bank of Korea.

———. 1973. *8,3 Kingŭp Kyŏngje Choch'i Chonghap Pogosŏ* (Full Report on the President's Decree of August 3, 1972). Seoul: Bank of Korea.

———. 1980. *Report on Automobile Industry in Korea.* Seoul: Bank of Korea.

———. 1983. *Report on Korea's Iron and Steel Industry.* Seoul: Bank of Korea.

———. 1986a. "Woeguk Ch'agwan e Kwanhan T'onggye Charyo" (Statistical Information on Foreign Capital Loan). Unpublished Data. Seoul: Bank of Korea.

———. 1986b. "The Korean Economy - Performance and Prospects." Unpublished Paper. Seoul: Bank of Korea.

Bankers Trust Securities Research. 1989. *Zaebols in Korea.* Seoul: Korea Investors Service, Inc.

Barrett, Richard E., and Soomi Chin. 1987. "Export-oriented Industrializing States in the Capitalist World System: Similarities and Difference." Pp. 23–43 in *The Political Economy of the New Asian Industrialism,* edited by Frederic C. Deyo. Ithaca: Cornell University Press.

Barrett, Richard E., and Martin King Whyte. 1982. "Dependency Theory and Taiwan: Analysis of a Deviant Case." *American Journal of Sociology* 87(5): 1064–89.

Bello, Walden, and Stephanie Rosenfeld. 1990. *Dragons in Distress: Asia's Miracle Economies in Crisis.* San Francisco: The Institute for Food and Development Policy.

Block, Fred. 1987. *Revising State Theory: Essays in Politics and Postindustrialism.* Philadelphia: Temple University Press.

Cardoso, Fernando Henrique, and Enzo Faletto. 1979. *Dependency and Development in Latin America.* (Translated by Marjory Mattingly Urquidi.) Berkeley: University of California Press.

Chaebol Munje Yŏnguso. 1985. *Ttŏlŏjin* Chaebol *ŭi Pyŏldŭl (The Fallen Stars of the* Chaebol*).* Seoul: Tong Kwang.

Cheil Synthetic Textile Co. 1982. *Cheil Hapsŏm 10 Nyŏnsa (The 10 Year History of the Cheil Synthetic Textile Company).* Seoul: Cheil Synthetic Textile Co.

Cheng, Tun-jen. 1990. "Political Regimes and Development Strategies: South Korea and Taiwan." Pp. 139–78 in *Manufacturing Miracles: Paths of Industrialization in Latin America and East Asia,* edited by Gary Gereffi and Donald Wyman. Princeton: Princeton University Press.

Cheng, Tun-jen, and Eun Mee Kim. 1994. "Making Democracy: The South Korean Case." Pp. 125–47 in *The Politics of Democratization: Vicissitudes and Universals in the East Asian Experience,* edited by Edward Friedman. Boulder, CO: Westview.

Cheng, Tun-jen, and Stephan Haggard. 1987. *Newly Industrializing Asia in Transition.* Berkeley: Institute of International Studies, University of California at Berkeley.

Cho, Hee-Yeon. 1993a. *Hyŏndae Hanguk Sahoe Wundong kwa Chojik (Contemporary Korean Society's Social Movements and Organizations).* Seoul: Hanwul.

———— 1993b. "Saerowun Chŏngch'i Hyŏnshil kwa Chinbo Wundong ŭi Chinro" (New Political Realities and Prospects for Liberal Social Movements). *Kyŏngje wa Sahoe (Economy and Society)* 4: 138–68.

Cho, In Ho, and Myŏng Kyun Kim, eds. 1986. *Chŏngbu T'uja Kigwan Kyŏngyŏng T'onggye Charyojip (The Research Data Book on Economic Statistics of the State-Invested Organizations).* Seoul: Korea Development Institute.

Cho, Tong Sŏng. 1988. *Hanguk ŭi Chonghap Muyŏk Sangsa (General Trading Companies in Korea).* Seoul: Pŏbmunsa.

————. 1990. *Hanguk* Chaebol *Yŏngu (Study of the Korean* Chaebol*).* Seoul: Maeil Kyŏngje Shinmun.

Cho, Yong Bŏm, and Yun Hyŏng Chŏng et al. 1984. *Hanguk Tokjŏm Chabon kwa* Chaebol *(Korea's Monopoly Capital and* Chaebol*).* Seoul: P'ulbit.

Ch'oe, Bŏm Chong. 1973. "An Economic Study of the Free Trade Zones." Korea Development Institute Interim Report 7310.

Ch'oe, Chong Hyŏn. 1991. *Tojŏn Hanŭn Chaga Mirae rŭl Chibae Handa (Only the Challenger will Conquer the Future).* Seoul: Koryŏ Sŏjŏk.

Ch'oe, Nak Tong. 1984. "Park Chung Hee Shidae 'Kyŏngje School'" ('Economic School' During the Park Chung Hee Era). *Chŏng Kyŏng Munhwa* 1984 (4).

Choi, Jang Jip. 1989. *Labor and the Authoritarian State: Labor Unions in South Korean Manufacturing Industries, 1961–1980.* Seoul: Korea University Press.

Choi, Jang Jip, ed. 1985. *Hanguk Chabonjuŭi wa Kukka (Korean Capitalism and the State).* Seoul: Hanwul.

Chŏn, Ch'ŏl Hwan. 1984. "Kukje Kyŏngje ŭi Ch'ejil Pyŏnhwa wa Ch'ilshipnyŏndae ŭi Hanguk Kyŏngje" (Changes in the International Economy and the Korean Economy in the 1970s) in Hyŏn Ch'ae Pak et al., *Hanguk Sahoe ŭi Chaeinshik I (Re-Understanding of the Korean Society I).* Seoul: Hanwul.

Chŏng, Chu Yŏng. 1991. *Siryŏn ŭn Issŏdo Silp'ae nŭn Ŏpta (There may be Hardship, but there is no Failure).* Seoul: Chesam Kihoek.

Chŏng, Kwan Yŏng. 1985. "Kwanryojŏk Kwonwijŭŭi Taedu wa Chunghwahak Kongŏp Chŏngch'aek" (Emergence of the Bureaucratic Authoritarianism and Policies on the Heavy and Chemical Industry) in Sang Jin Han et al., *Hanguk Sahoe Pyŏndong kwa Kukka Yŏkhwal e Kwanhan Yŏngu (Studies on the Changes in the Korean Society and the Role of the State).* Seoul: Hyŏndae Sahoe Yŏnguso.

Chŏng, Mong Jun. 1990. *Kiŏp Kyŏngyŏng Inyŏm* (Ideology of Enterprise Management). Wulsan, Republic of Korea: Wulsan University Press.

Chŏng, Sŏng Chin. 1986. "Minjok Kyŏngjeron ŭi Chemunje" (Problems in Nationalist Economics) in Chin Kyun Kim et al., *Sanŏp Sahoe Yŏngu (Research on the Industrial Society).* Seoul: Hanwul.

Chŏng, T'ae Su. 1980. "Ch'ŏlgang Kongŏpkye ŭi Naemak" (The Inside Stories of the Iron and Steel Industry). *Shindonga* 1980 (9).

Chŏng, Yun Hyŏng. 1984. "Kaebang Ch'ejero ŭi Ihaeng kwa Ch'ŏnkubaekkuship nyŏndae Kyŏngje Kaebal ŭi Sŏnggyŏk" (Towards a Freer Economic System and the Nature of Economic

Development in the 1990s) in Hyŏn Ch'ae Pak et al., *Hanguk Sahoe ŭi Chaeinshik I (Re-Understanding of the Korean Society I)*. Seoul: Hanwul.

Choo, Hak Chung. 1972. "Effects of the Vietnam War and the Normalization of the Korean-Japanese Relations on the Korean Economic Development in the 1960's." KDI Working Paper 7201.

Chosŏn Ilbo. October 28, 1993.

Chu, Chong Hang. 1985. Chaebol *Kyŏngjeron (Economics of* Chaebol*)*. Seoul: Chŏngŭm Munhwasa.

Chung-Ang Daily News. 1983. Series on "New Map of Chaebol." *Chung-Ang Daily News*. May, 1983.

Chunghwahak Kongŏp Ch'ujin Wiwonhoe Kihoekdan (Committee on Development of the Heavy and Chemical Industry). 1979a. *Chunghwahak Kongŏp Chŏngch'aeksa (History of the Making of Policies on the Heavy and Chemical Industry)*. Seoul: Chunghwahak Kongŏp Ch'ujin Wiwonhoe Kihoekdan (Committee on Development of the Heavy and Chemical Industry).

———. 1979b. *Chunghwahak Kongŏp Chŏngch'aek Kwachŏng ŭi Imyŏnsa (The Inside History of the Making of Policies on the Heavy and Chemical Industry)*. Seoul: Chunghwahak Kongŏp Ch'ujin Wiwonhoe Kihoekdan (Committee on Development of the Heavy and Chemical Industry).

———. 1979c. *Chunghwahak Kongŏp Ch'ujin Shiljŏk kwa Hyogwa (The Progress and Results of the Development of the Heavy and Chemical Industry)*. Seoul: Chunghwahak Kongŏp Ch'ujin Wiwonhoe Kihoekdan (Committee on Development of the Heavy and Chemical Industry).

———. 1979d. *Chunghwahak Kongŏp Paljŏnsa (The History of the Development of the Heavy and Chemical Industry)*. Seoul: Chunghwahak Kongŏp Ch'ujin Wiwonhoe Kihoekdan (Committee on Development of the Heavy and Chemical Industry).

Cole, David C., and Princeton N. Lyman. 1971. *Korean Development*. Cambridge, MA: Harvard University Press.

Cole, David C., and Yung Chul Park. 1983. *Financial Development in Korea, 1945–1978*. Cambridge, MA: Harvard University Press.

Collier, David, ed. 1979. *The New Authoritarianism in Latin America.* Princeton: Princeton University Press.

Cumings, Bruce. 1981. *The Origins of the Korean War.* Princeton: Princeton University Press.

———. 1987. "The Origins and Development of the Northeast Asian Political Economy: Industrial Sectors, Product Cycles, and Political Consequences." Pp. 44–83 in *The Political Economy of the New Asian Industrialism,* edited by Frederic C. Deyo. Ithaca, NY: Cornell University Press.

———. 1990. *The Two Koreas: On the Road to Reunification?* New York: Foreign Policy Association.

Cutright, Philips. 1963. "National Political Development: Measurement and Analysis." *American Sociological Review* 28.

DeVos, George A., and Takao Sofue, eds. 1984. *Religion and Family in East and Southeast Asia.* Berkeley: University of California Press.

Deyo, Frederic C., ed. 1987a. *The Political Economy of the New Asian Industrialism.* Ithaca, NY: Cornell University Press.

———. 1987b. "State and Labor: Modes of Political Exclusion in East Asian Development." Pp. 182–202 in *The Political Economy of the New Asian Industrialism,* edited by Frederic C. Deyo. Ithaca, NY: Cornell University Press.

———. 1989. *Beneath the Miracle: Labor Subordination in the New Asian Industrialism.* Berkeley: University of California Press.

Diamond, Larry, Juan J. Linz, and Seymour Martin Lipset, eds. 1989. *Democracy in Developing Countries: Asia.* Boulder, CO: Lynne Rienner Publishers.

DiMaggio, Paul J., and Walter W. Powell. 1983. "The Iron Cage Revisited: Institutional Isomorphism and Collective Rationality in Organizational Fields." *American Sociological Review* 48: 147–60.

Dong-A Ilbo. 1982. "Report on Expansion of Large Firms." *Dong-A Ilbo,* October 24, 1982.

———. 1983. "Report on 19 Industrial Complexes." *Dong-A Ilbo,* December 12, 1983.

———. 1986. "Readjustment of the Insolvent Companies: Problem Lies Ahead with Normalized Management." *Dong-A Ilbo,* September 22, 1986.

Dore, Ronald. 1986. *Flexible Rigidities: Industrial Policy and Structural Adjustment in the Japanese Economy 1970–80.* Stanford, CA: Stanford University Press.

Dos Santos, Teotonio. 1970. "The Structure of Dependence." *American Economic Review* 60(5): 235–46.

Eckert, Carter J. 1991. *Offspring of Empire: The Kochang Kims and the Colonial Origins of Korean Capitalism 1876–1945.* Seattle: University of Washington Press.

Economic Planning Board. 1960–1993. *Korea Statistical Yearbook.* Seoul: Economic Planning Board.

———. 1962–1984. *Five-Year Economic Development Plans: I, II, III, IV.* Seoul: Economic Planning Board.

———. 1978–1991. *Major Statistics of the Korean Economy.* Seoul: Economic Planning Board.

———. 1982. *Kaebal Nyŏndae ŭi Kyŏngje Chŏngch'aek: Kyŏngje Kihoekwon 20 Nyŏnsa* (Economic Policies of the Development Era: The Twenty Year History of the Economic Planning Board). Seoul: Economic Planning Board.

———. 1983. *Revised Plans for the Fifth Five-Year Economic and Social Development Plan.* Seoul: Economic Planning Board.

———. 1984. *Kongjŏng Kŏrae Paeksŏ (White Book on Fair Trade).* Seoul: Economic Planning Board.

———. 1986a. *The Sixth Five-Year Economic and Social Development Plan.* Seoul: Economic Planning Board.

———. 1986b. *Analysis of Economic Policies of the 1980s.* Seoul: Economic Planning Board.

———. 1986c. *White Book on Foreign Capital Loan.* Seoul: Economic Planning Board.

———. 1989. *Monopoly Regulation and Fair Trade in Korea.* Seoul: Economic Planning Board.

Eisenstadt, S. N. 1964. "Modernization and Conditions of Sustained Growth." *World Politics* 16(4): 576–94.

Enos, John. 1984. "Government Intervention in the Transfer of Technology: The Case of South Korea." *IDS Bulletin* 15(2): 26–31.

Evans, Peter B. 1979. *Dependent Development: The Alliance of Multinational, State, and Local Capital in Brazil*. Princeton: Princeton University Press.

―――. 1987. "Class, State, and Dependence in East Asia: Lessons for Latin Americanists." Pp. 203–26 in *The Political Economy of the New Asian Industrialism*, edited by Frederic C. Deyo. Ithaca, NY: Cornell University Press.

―――. 1989. "Predatory, Developmental, and Other Apparatuses: A Comparative Political Economy Perspective on the Third World State." *Sociological Forum* 4(4): 561–87.

―――. 1995. *Embedded Autonomy: States and Industrial Transformation*. Princeton: Princeton University Press.

Evans, Peter B., Dietrich Rueschemeyer, and Theda Skocpol, eds. 1985. *Bringing the State Back In*. Cambridge: Cambridge University Press.

Evans, Peter B., and John D. Stephens. 1988. "Development and the World Economy." Pp. 739–73 in *Handbook of Sociology*, edited by Neil J. Smelser. Newbury Park, CA: Sage Publications.

Federation of Korean Industries. 1981. *1981 Annual Report: The Federation of Korean Industries*. Seoul: Federation of Korean Industries.

―――. 1986. *Hanguk Kyŏngje Chŏngch'aek 40 Nyŏnsa (The 40 Year History of the Korean Economy)*. Seoul: Federation of Korean Industries.

―――. 1987. *Korea's Economic Policies (1945–1985)*. Seoul: Federation of Korean Industries.

Frank, Andre Gunder. 1967. *Capitalism and Underdevelopment in Latin America*. New York: Monthly Review Press.

Frieden, Jeff. 1981. "Third World Indebted Industrialization: International Finance and State Capitalism in Mexico, Brazil, Argentina, and South Korea." *International Organization* 35(3): 407–31.

Gereffi, Gary. 1990. "Big Business and the State." Pp. 90–109 in *Manufacturing Miracles: Paths of Industrialization in Latin America and East Asia*, edited by Gary Gereffi and Donald Wyman. Princeton: Princeton University Press.

Gereffi, Gary, and Peter Evans. 1981. "Transnational Corporations, Dependent Development, and State Policy in the Semiperiphery: A Comparison of Brazil and Mexico." *Latin American Research Review.* 16(3): 31–64.

Gereffi, Gary, and Donald Wyman, eds. 1990. *Manufacturing Miracles: Paths of Industrialization in Latin America and East Asia.* Princeton: Princeton University Press.

Gerschenkron, Alexander. 1962. *Economic Backwardness in Historical Perspective.* Cambridge, MA: Harvard University Press.

Gold Star Co. 1985. *Kŭmsŏngsa 25 Nyŏnsa (The Twenty-Five Year History of the Gold Star Company).* Seoul: Gold Star Co.

Gold, Thomas B. 1986. *State and Society in the Taiwan Miracle.* Armonk, NY: M.E. Sharpe.

Haggard, Stephan. 1990. *Pathways from the Periphery.* Ithaca, NY: Cornell University Press.

Haggard, Stephan, and Tun-jen Cheng. 1987. "State and Foreign Capital in the East Asian NICs." Pp. 84–135 in *The Political Economy of the New Asian Industrialism,* edited by Frederic C. Deyo. Ithaca, NY: Cornell University Press.

Haggard, Stephan, and Chung-in Moon. 1990. "Institutions and Economic Policy: Theory and a Korean Case Study." *World Politics* 17(2): 210–37.

Ham, Yŏng Chin. 1990. "Speculative Real Estate Investments by the Chaebol." *Wŏlgan Chosŏn* (June 1990): 180–203.

Hamilton, Clive. 1984. "Class, State and Industrialization in South Korea." *IDS Bulletin* 15(2): 38–43.

———. 1986. *Capitalist Industrialization in Korea.* Boulder, CO: Westview.

Hamilton, Gary, ed. 1991. *Business Networks and Economic Development in East and Southeast Asia.* Hong Kong: University of Hong Kong Press.

Hamilton, Gary G., and Nicole Woolsey Biggart. 1988. "Market, Culture, and Authority: A Comparative Analysis of Management and Organization in the Far East." *American Journal of Sociology* 94(Supplement): s52–s94.

Hamilton, Nora, and Eun Mee Kim. 1993. "Economic and Political Liberalization in South Korea and Mexico." *Third World Quarterly* 14(1): 109–36.

Han, Sang Jin. 1981. "Kaebal Tosang Sahoe esŏŭi Kukka ŭi Yŏkhwal" (The Role of the State in a Developing Nation). *Hyŏndae Sahoe* 1981 (Winter).

Hanguk Ilbo. 1984. "50 Largest Chaebol in Korea." *Hanguk Ilbo,* June-December, 1984.

———. 1986. *Korea's Fifty Major Financial Groups.* Seoul: Hanguk Ilbo.

———. 1986. "*Chaebol* Kyŏngjeryŏk Chipjung man Kasokhwa: Pushil Kiŏp Chŏngli hu Chaekye P'ando Pyŏnhwa" (*Chaebol's* Concentration of Economic Power Intensified: The Changes in the Capitalists after the Reorganization of the Insolvent Companies). *Hanguk Ilbo* November 16, 1986.

———. 1991. "Hanguk Kyŏngje Panseki" (A Half Century of Korea's Economy). *Hanguk Ilbo* April 6, 1991.

Hart-Landsberg, Martin. 1993. *The Rush to Development: Economic Change and Political Struggle in South Korea.* New York: Monthly Review Press.

Hasan, Parvez. 1976. *Korea: Problems and Issues in a Rapidly Growing Economy.* Baltimore: Johns Hopkins University Press.

Hasan, Parvez, and D. C. Rao. 1979. *Korea: Policy Issues for Long-Term Development.* Baltimore: Johns Hopkins University Press.

Ho, Samuel. 1982. "Economic Development and Rural Industry in South Korea and Taiwan." *World Development* 10(11): 982–90.

Hofheinz, Roy, and Kent E. Calder. 1982. *The Eastasia Edge.* New York: Basic Books.

Hong, Mun Shin, and Chang Ho Ch'oe. 1986. *Sŏmyu Sanŏp ŭi Kujo wa Chŏngch'aek (The Textile Industry's Structure and Policies).* Seoul: Korean Institute for Economics and Technology.

Hong, Wontack, and Anne O. Krueger. 1975. *Trade and Development in Korea.* Seoul: Korea Development Institute.

Hoult, Thomas Ford. 1969. *Dictionary of Modern Sociology.* Totowa, NJ: Littlefield, Adams and Co.

Hsiao, Hsin-Huang Michael, Wei-yuan Cheng, and Hou-sheng Chan, eds. 1989. *Taiwan: A Newly Industrializing State*. Taipei: National Taiwan University.

I, Ch'ang Kyu. 1991. *Kyŏngje nŭn Tangshin i Taet'ongryŏng iya: Chun Doo Hwan Shidae ŭi Kyŏngje Pisa (For the Economy, You are the President: The Secret Economic History During the Chun Doo Hwan Regime)*. Seoul: Chung-Ang Daily News.

I, Ch'ang Mo. 1974. "Report on MAFEZ." *Ch'angjak kwa Pip'yŏng* 1974 (Winter): 1191–1259.

I, Chong Chae. 1993. Chaebol *Iryŏksŏ (The C.V. of the* Chaebol). Seoul: Hanguk Ilbo.

I, Hak Chong, and Ku Hyŏn Chŏng. 1986. *Hanguk Kiŏp ŭi Kujo wa Chŏnryak (The Structure and Strategies of Korean Enterprises)*. Seoul: Pŏbmunsa.

I, Kap Sŏp. 1973. "Sanŏp Paljŏn kwa Chunghwahak Kongŏphwa" (Industrial Development and Heavy and Chemical Industrialization). *Sahoe Kwahak* 1973 (Vol. 12).

I, Kyŏng Nam. 1985. "Kyŏngje Kwonryŏk Paehu ŭi K'ŭnsondŭl" (Big Hands Behind the Economic Powers). *Chŏng Kyŏng Munhwa* 1985 (2).

I, Kyŏng T'ae et al. 1985. *Hanguk - Taeman - Malaysia - Singapore ŭi Chŏnja Pup'um Sanŏp Pigyo Punsŏk (Comparative Studies on the Electronics Parts Industry in Korea, Taiwan, Malaysia and Singapore)*. Seoul: Korean Institute for Economics and Technology.

I, Kyu Ŏk, and Chae Hyŏng I. 1990. *Kiŏp Kyŏlhap kwa Kyŏngjeryŏk Chipchung (Business Groups and Economic Concentration)*. Seoul: Korea Development Institute.

I, Man Yŏl. 1985. *Hanguksa Nyŏnp'yo (A Chronological Table of Korea's History)*. Seoul: Yŏkminsa.

I, Sŏng Hyŏng. 1985. "Kukka, Kyegŭp mit Chabon Ch'ukchŏk: 8'3 Choch'i rŭl Chungshimŭro" (The State, Class and Capital Accumulation: The President's Decree of August 3, 1972) in Jang Jip Choi, ed., *Hanguk Chabonjuŭi wa Kukka (Korean Capitalism and the State)*. Seoul: Hanwul.

I, Sŏng T'ae. 1990. *Kamch'uŏjin Tokjŏm Chaebol ŭi Yŏksa (The Hidden History of Monopoly Chaebol)*. Seoul: Noktu.

I, T'ae Hyŏng. 1980. "Sŏmyu Sanŏpkye ŭi Naemak" (The Inside Stories of the Textile Industry). *Shindonga* 1980 (3).

I, Tae Kŭn. 1984. "Kyŏngje Kaebal kwa Kujo Pyŏndong" (Economic Development and Structural Transformation) in Hyŏn Ch'ae Pak et al., *Hanguk Sahoe ŭi Chaeinshik I (Re-Understanding of the Korean Society I)*. Seoul: Hanwul.

I, Tae Kŭn, and Wun Yŏng Chŏng. 1984a. *Hanguk Chabonjuŭiron (Korean Capitalism)*. Seoul: Kkach'i.

———. 1984b. *Segye Chabonjuŭiron (World Capitalism)*. Seoul: Kkach'i.

I, Wu Yŏng. 1982. "Socio-Economic Characteristics of Chaebol in Korea." Unpublished paper. Department of Sociology, Yonsei University, Seoul, Korea.

Im, Hyug Baeg. 1987. "The Rise of Bureaucratic Authoritarianism in South Korea." *World Politics* 39(2): 231–57.

Im, Myo Min. 1983a. "Chŏnkyŏngryŏn ŭi Naemak—Chaebol ŭi Amt'u" (The Inside Stories of the Federation of Korean Industries—Struggle Between Chaebol). *Shindonga* 1983 (3).

———. 1983b. "Chaebol kwa Kwonryŏk—Chŏnkyŏngryŏn ŭi Kaldŭng" (Chaebol and Power—The Conflict Within the Federation of Korean Industries). *Shindonga* 1983 (4).

Inkeles, Alex, and David H. Smith. 1974. *Becoming Modern*. Cambridge, MA: Harvard University Press.

International Enterprises Management Researches. 1978. *Korean Business and Industry Directory*. Seoul: Commerce and Industry Information Center.

International Labour Office. 1970, 1980, 1990, 1991. *Yearbook of Labour Statistics*. Geneva: International Labour Office.

International Monetary Fund. 1979, 1980, 1990, 1991. *International Financial Statistics*. Washington, DC: International Monetary Fund.

Jacobsson, Staffan. 1984. "Industrial Policy for the Machine Tool Industries of South Korea and Taiwan." *IDS Bulletin* 15(2): 44–49.

Janelli, Roger L. with Dawnhee Yim. 1993. *Making Capitalism: The Social and Cultural Construction of a South Korean Conglomerate*. Stanford, CA: Stanford University Press.

Jessop, Bob. 1990. *State Theory*. University Park, PA: Pennsylvania State University Press.

Jo, Sung-Hwan. 1978. "The Economic Relations Between South Korea and Japan." KDI Working Paper 7808.

Johnson, Chalmers. 1982. *MITI and the Japanese Miracle*. Stanford, CA: Stanford University Press.

————. 1987. "Political Institutions and Economic Performance: The Government-Business Relationship in Japan, South Korea, and Taiwan." Pp. 136–64 in *The Political Economy of the New Asian Industrialism*, edited by Frederic C. Deyo. Ithaca, NY: Cornell University Press.

Jones, Leroy P. 1980. "Jae-Bul and the Concentration of Economic Power in Korean Development: Issues, Evidence and Alternatives." KDI Consultant Paper Series 12.

Jones, Leroy P., and Il Sakong. 1980. *Government, Business, and Entrepreneurship in Economic Development*. Cambridge, MA: Harvard University Press.

Jun, Sang In. 1990. Unpublished Ph.D. dissertation. Providence, RI: Brown University.

Jung, Ku-Hyun. 1988. "Business-Government Relations in the Growth of Korean Business Groups." *Korean Social Science Journal* 14: 67–82.

Kang, Ch'ŏl Kyu, Ch'oe Chongp'yo, and Chang Chisang. 1991. Chaebol: *Songjang ŭi Chuyŏk inga, T'amyok ŭi Hwashin inga*. (Chaebol: *Driving Force of Growth or Incarnations of Greed?*). Seoul: P'ibong Ch'ulp'ansa.

Kang, Myŏng Han. 1986. *Pony rŭl Mandŭn Pyŏlnan Hankukindŭl (The Special Korean People Who Made the Pony)*. Seoul: Chŏngwusa.

Kang, Kyŏng Shik. 1992. *Kanan Kuje nŭn Nara ka Haeya Handa (Eliminating Poverty must be done by the State)*. Seoul: Sam kwa Kkum.

Katzenstein, Peter J. 1985. *Small States in World Markets: Industrial Policy In Europe*. Ithaca, NY: Cornell University Press.

Kiggundu, Moses N., Jan J. Jorgensen, and Taieb Hafsi. 1983. "Administrative Theory and Practice in Developing Countries: A Synthesis." *Administrative Science Quarterly* 28: 66–84.

Kihl, Young Whan, ed. 1994. *Korea and the World: Beyond the Cold War.* Boulder, CO: Westview.

Kim, Byong-Kuk. 1988. *Kim Woo-Choong: Schumpeterian Entrepreneur.* Seoul: Pŏbmunsa.

Kim, Byoung-Lo Philo Kim. 1992. *Two Koreas in Development.* New Brunswick, NJ: Transaction Publishers.

Kim, Byung Kook. 1987. "Bringing and Managing Socioeconomic Change: The State in Korea and Mexico." Unpublished Ph.D. dissertation. Cambridge, MA: Harvard University.

Kim, Chin Kyun et al. 1985. *Hanguk Sahoe ŭi Kyegŭp Yŏngu (Research on the Stratification in Korean Society).* Seoul: Hanwul.

———. 1986. *Sanŏp Sahoe Yŏngu (Research on the Industrial Society).* Seoul: Hanwul.

Kim, Chin Pae, and Ch'ang Rae Pak. 1968. "Ch'agwan" (Foreign Capital Loan). *Shindonga* 1968 (12).

Kim, Choong Soon. 1992. *The Culture of Korean Industry: An Ethnography of Poongsan Corporation.* Tucson, AZ: University of Arizona Press.

Kim, Chung Wung. 1981. *Taewae Kŏrae Chayuhwa wa Hanguk Kyŏngje* (Liberalization of Foreign Trade and the Korean Economy). Seoul: Korea Development Institute.

Kim, Eun Mee. 1987. From Dominance to Symbiosis: State and Chaebol in Korean Development, 1960–1980. Unpublished Ph.D. dissertation. Providence, RI: Brown University.

———. 1988. "From Dominance to Symbiosis: State and Chaebol in Korea." *Pacific Focus* 3 (2): 105–21.

———. 1989. "Foreign Capital in Korea's Economic Development, 1960–1985." *Studies in Comparative International Development* 24(4): 24–45.

———. 1991. "The Industrial Organization and Growth of the Korean Chaebol: Integrating Development and Organizational Theories." Pp. 272–99 in *Business Networks and Economic Development in East and Southeast Asia,* edited by Gary Hamilton. Hong Kong: University of Hong Kong Press; Hawthorne, NY: Walter de Gruyter.

————. 1993. "Contradictions and Limits of a Developmental State: With Illustrations from the South Korean Case." *Social Problems* 40(2): 228–49.

Kim, Eun Mee, and Julle Cho. 1993. "Trends of Enterprise and Business Management in South Korea." Pp. 369–436 in *Economic and Social Development in East Asia: Policies, Management and Populations*, edited by the University Research Center, Nihon University. Tokyo: Nihon University.

Kim, Ilpyong J., ed. 1991. *Korean Challenges and American Policy*. New York: Paragon House.

Kim, Ilpyong J., and Young Whan Kihl, eds. 1988. *Political Change in South Korea*. New York: Paragon House.

Kim, Ki Man. 1988. "Chaekae ŭi Ch'ungkyŏg Sŏnŏn, Tŏ Isang 'Tongne Puk' Ilsu ŏpda" (Bombshell Announcement by the Private Sector: We Can No Longer be the 'Village Drum'). *Shindonga* 1988 (11).

Kim, Ki Pae. 1991. *Nosa Kwangye wa Kiŏp Paljŏn (Labor-Management Relations and Enterprise Development)*. Seoul: Ihwa Munhwasa.

Kim, Kŭm Su. 1986. *Hanguk Nodong Munje ŭi Sanghwang kwa Inshik (The Current Status and Understanding of the Korean Labor Problems)*. Seoul: P'ulbit.

Kim, Kŭm Su, and Hyŏn Ch'ae Pak et al. 1985. *Hanguk Nodong Wundongron I (Theories on the Korean Labor Movements I)*. Seoul: Miraesa.

Kim, Kwang Suk, and Michael Roemer. 1979. *Growth and Structural Transformation*. Cambridge, MA: Harvard University Press.

Kim, Kyong-Dong. 1979. *Man and Society in Korea's Economic Growth*. Seoul: Seoul National University Press.

Kim, Pyŏng Ha. 1991. Chaebol *ŭi Hyŏngsŏng kwa Kiŏpka Hwaldong (The Genesis of the* Chaebol *and Activities of Entrepreneurs)*. Seoul: Hanguk Nŭngryul Hyŏphoe.

Kim, Seok Ki. 1987. "Business Concentration and Government Policy: A Study of the Phenomenon of Business Groups in Korea, 1945–1985." Unpublished Ph.D. dissertation. Cambridge, MA: Harvard University.

Kim, Sŏng Tu. 1968. "Hanguk Tokjŏm Chaebol Hyŏngsŏng ŭi T'ŭkisŏng" (The Distinctive Features of the Formation of Monopoly Chaebol in Korea). *Sasanggye* 1968 (9).

Kim, Sookon. 1989. "Labor-Management Relationship: Past and Present." Unpublished manuscript. Honolulu: East-West Center.

Kim, T'ae Sŏn. 1975. "Tokkwajŏm P'ummok ŭi Naeyŏk" (Content of the Monopoly and Oligopoly Products). *Shindonga* 1975 (12).

Kim, Tal Hyŏn. 1966. "Hanguk Tokjŏm Chaebol kwa Sanŏp Chabon Hyŏngsŏng" (Monopoly Chaebol in Korea and the Formation of Industrial Capital). *Chŏngkyŏng Yŏngu* 1966 (11).

Kim, Ŭi Kyun. 1980. "Chunghwahak Kongŏp T'uja Chochŏng ŭi Naemak" (The Inside Stories of the Re-Organization of the Heavy and Chemical Industry). *Shindonga* 1980 (12).

Kim, Wu Chung. 1989. *Segye nŭn Nŏlpko Halril ŭn Mant'a. (The World is Broad, and There are Many Jobs to be Done)*. Seoul: Kimyŏngsa.

Kim, Yŏng Pong. 1979a. *Sŏmyu—Chŏnja Kongŏp ŭi T'ŭksŏng kwa Sugŭp Kujo (Characteristics and Structure of Demand and Supply of the Textile and the Electronics Industries)*. Seoul: Korea Development Institute.

———. 1979b. *Hanguk Chŏnja Kongŏp ŭi Hyŏnhwang kwa Munjejŏm (The Present Status and Problems of the Korean Electronics Industry)*. Seoul: Korea Development Institute.

Kim, Yŏng Ho. 1989. *Kwangwon Kyŏngje T'ŭkhye Kyŏngje (State-led Economy, Preferential Treatment Economy)*. Seoul: Ch'ung Am.

Kim, Yun Hyŏng. 1976. *Hanguk Ch'ŏlgang Kongŏp ŭi Sŏngjang (Growth of Iron and Steel Industry in Korea)*. Seoul: Korea Development Institute.

Koo, Bohn-Young. 1984a. "Industrial Structure and Foreign Investment." KDI Working Paper 8402.

———. 1984b. "The Role of the Government in Korea's Industrial Development." KDI Working Paper 8407.

Koo, Hagen. 1987. "The Interplay of State, Social Class, and World System in East Asian Development: The Cases of South Korea and Taiwan." Pp. 165–81 in *The Political Economy of the New Asian Industrialism*, edited by Frederic C. Deyo. Ithaca, NY: Cornell University Press.

———. 1990. "From Farm to Factory: Proletarianization in Korea." *American Sociological Review* 55(5): 669–81.

Koo, Hagen, and Eun Mee Kim. 1992. "The Developmental State and Capital Accumulation in South Korea." Pp. 121–49 in *States and Development in the Asian Pacific Rim*, edited by Richard P. Appelbaum and Jeffrey Henderson. Newbury Park, CA: Sage.

Korea Development Bank. 1976, 1980, 1984. *Industry in Korea*. Seoul: Korea Development Bank.

————. 1983. *Financial Statements Analysis of Selected Industries*. Seoul: Korea Development Bank.

————. 1984. "Iron and Steel Industry in Korea." *Korea Development Bank Report* 8 (5).

Korea Productivity Center. 1973–1982. *Korean Company Handbook*. Seoul: Korea Productivity Center.

Korea Yearbook. 1961–1990. *Hanguk Yŏngam (Korea Yearbook)*. Seoul: Hanguk Yŏngamsa.

Korean Catholic Youth Organization. 1980. "Report on Closing Down of Firms in MAFEZ." *Korean Catholic Youth Organization Research Report* 80(1).

Korean Census Bureau. 1960–1982. *The Korean Census of Mining and Manufacturing*. Seoul: Korean Census Bureau.

Korean Industrial Estates Research Institute. 1982. *Korea Industrial Estates*. Seoul: Korean Industrial Estates Research Institute.

Korean Institute for Economics and Technology. 1985a. *Sanŏp Chŏngch'aek ŭi Kibon Panghyang kwa Sanŏp Chiwon Chedo Kaesŏn Pangan (Basic Directions of Industrial Policies and Proposal for Improvements of the Industrial Support System)*. Seoul: Korean Institute for Economics and Technology.

————. 1985b. *Ich'ŏnnyŏndae rŭl Hyanghan Kukka Changgi Paljŏn Kusang <Kongŏp Pumunp'yŏn> (Long Term Development Plans for National Development for 2000 <Industrial Sector>)*. Seoul: Korean Institute for Economics and Technology.

Krueger, Anne O. 1979. *The Developmental Role of the Foreign Sector and Aid*. Cambridge, MA: Harvard University Press.

Ku, Bon Ho. 1984. "Kukka nŭn Muŏt ŭl Haeyahanŭnga—Hanguk Chabonjuŭi ŭi Paljŏn kwa Chŏngbu ŭi Yŏkhwal" (What is the Role of the State—Korean Capitalist Development and the Role of the Government). *Sasang kwa Chŏngch'aek* 1984 (1).

Ku, Cha Kyŏng. 1992. *Ojik I Kil Pakae nŭn Ŏpta (This is the Only Way)*. Seoul: Haengnim.

Kuznets, Paul W. 1971. "Korea's Emerging Industrial Structure." Social Science Research Institute. University of Hawaii. Working Paper No. 6.

———. 1977. *Economic Growth and Structure in the Republic of Korea*. New Haven, CT: Yale University Press.

Kuznets, Simon. 1973. "Modern Economic Growth: Findings and Reflections." *American Economic Review* 63(3).

Kwack, Taewon. 1984. "Industrial Restructuring Experience and Policies in Korea in the 1970s." KDI Working Paper 84-08.

Kwon, Jene. 1994. "The East Asia Challenge to Neoclassical Orthodoxy." *World Development* 22(4): 635–44.

Kwon, Sun Chik. 1988. "80 Nyŏndae ŭi Pushil Kiŏp Chŏngli ŭi Pushil Naemak" (The Insolvent Inside Stories of the Reorganization of the Insolvent Companies in the 1980s). *Shindonga* May (1988):458–67.

Lall, Sanjaya. 1994. "*The East Asian Miracle*: Does the Bell Toll for Industrial Strategy?" *World Development* 22(4): 645–54.

Lee, Chul Hee. 1980. *Automobile Industry in Korea*. Seoul: Korea Development Institute.

Lee, Ki-baik. 1984. *A New History of Korea*. (Translated by Edward W. Wagner.) Cambridge, MA: Harvard University Press.

Leff, Nathaniel H. 1978. "Industrial Organization and Entrepreneurship in the Developing Countries: The Economic Groups." *Economic Development and Cultural Change* 26(4): 661–75.

Lie, John. 1990a. "South Korean Development: The Elusive Reality of Conflicts and Contradiction." *Pacific Affairs* 63(3): 367–72.

———. 1990b. "Is Korean Management Just Like Japanese Management?" *Management International Review* 30(2): 113–18.

Lim, Hyun-Chin. 1987. *Dependent Development in Korea, 1963–1979*. Seoul: Seoul National University Press.

Lim, Young-Il. 1981. *Government Policy and Private Enterprise: Korean Experience with Industrialization*. Berkeley, CA: East Asian Institute.

Lipset, Seymour Martin. 1980 [1959]. "Some Social Requisites of Democracy: Economic Development and Political Legitimacy." *American Political Science Review* 53. Reprinted in Lipset, S. M., *Political Man*. Baltimore: Johns Hopkins University Press.

Luedde-Neurath, Richard. 1984. "State Intervention and Foreign Direct Investment in South Korea." *IDS Bulletin* 15(2): 18–25.

Macdonald, Donald S. 1990. *The Koreans: Contemporary Politics and Society*. Boulder, CO: Westview.

Maeil Kyŏngje Shinmun. 1971–93. *Maekyung: Annual Corporation Reports*. Seoul: Maeil Kyŏngje Shinmun.

Management Efficiency Research Institute. 1988–1992. *Analysis of Financial Statements—Fifty Major Business Groups in Korea*. Seoul: Management Efficiency Research Institute.

Mann, Michael. 1986. *The Sources of Social Power*. Cambridge: Cambridge University Press.

Mardon, Russell. 1990. "The State and the Effective Control of Foreign Capital: The Case of South Korea." *World Politics* 43: 111–38.

Marx, Karl. 1992 [1967]. *Capital* (Edited by Frederick Engels). New York: International Publishers.

Mason, Edward S., Mahn Je Kim, Dwight H. Perkins, Kwang Suk Kim, and David C. Cole, eds. 1980. *The Economic and Social Modernization of the Republic of Korea*. Cambridge, MA: Harvard University Press.

McNamara, Dennis L. 1990. *The Colonial Origins of Korean Enterprise 1910–1945*. Cambridge: Cambridge University Press.

Memorial Foundation for I Han Yŏl, ed. 1991. *Chintan Che 6 Kong Hwa Kuk (Prognosis of the Sixth Republic)*. Seoul: Turi.

Merriam-Webster. 1988. *Webster's Ninth New Collegiate Dictionary*. Springfield, MA: Merriam-Webster Inc.

Merton, Robert K. 1967 [1949]. *On Theoretical Sociology: Five Essays, Old and New*. New York: The Free Press.

Migdal, Joel S. 1988. *Strong Societies and Weak States: State-Society Relations and State Capabilities in the Third World*. Princeton: Princeton University Press.

Mills, Edwin S., and Byung-Nak Song. 1979. *Urbanization and Urban Programs*. Cambridge, MA: Harvard University Press.

Min, Kyŏng Hwi et al. 1982. *Chadongch'a Kongŏp ŭi Munjejŏm kwa Yuksŏng Panghyang (The Automobile Industry's Problems and Ways to Develop the Industry)*. Seoul: Korean Institute for Economics and Technology.

Ministry of Finance. 1986. "Statistical Data on Foreign Direct Investment." Unpublished Data. Seoul: Ministry of Finance.

———. 1990a. *Foreign Capital Inducement Law*. Seoul: Ministry of Finance.

———. 1990b. *Guidelines for Foreign Direct Investment*. Seoul: Ministry of Finance.

Ministry of Government Administration. 1982. *Organization of the Government in Korea*. Seoul: Ministry of Government Administration.

Ministry of Public Information. 1965. Seoul: Ministry of Public Information.

Moon, Chung-in. 1988. "The Demise of a Developmentalist State? Neoconservative Reforms and Political Consequences in South Korea." *Journal of Developing Societies IV*: 67–84.

Moore, Barrington Jr. 1966. *Social Origins of Dictatorship and Democracy*. Boston: Beacon Press.

Moore, Mick. 1984. "Agriculture in Taiwan and South Korea: the Minimalist State?" *IDS Bulletin* 15(2): 57–64.

Mun, Yong Su, ed. 1985. *Kŏbudŭl ŭi Ch'ukjŏk Haengjin kwa Insaeng Panorama (Accumulation of Wealth and the Human Drama of the Super-Wealthy)*. Seoul: Tonggwang.

Nam, Chong Hyŏn. 1979. *Ch'ŏlgang Kongŏp ŭi T'ŭksŏng kwa Sugŭp Kujo (Characteristics and Structure of Demand and Supply of the Iron and Steel Industry)*. Seoul: Korea Development Institute.

Nam, Yu Ch'ŏl. 1995. "Tasi Sonjapnŭn Kwonryŏk kwa Chabon, Shiljong dwen Chaebol Chŏngch'aek" (Political Forces and the Capitalists Reunited, the Lost Policies against the *Chaebol*). *Sisa Journal (Journal of Current Affairs)* April 14, 1995: 58–60.

Namkoong, Young. 1995. "A Change in North Korean External Economic Policies and Prospects for Inter-Korean Economic Cooperation." *East Asian Review* VII(3): 43–67.

National Statistical Office. 1991–1993. *Major Statistics of Korean Economy*. Seoul: National Statistical Office.

Nelson, Joan M. ed., 1990. *Economic Crisis and Policy Choice: The Politics of Adjustment in the Third World*. Princeton: Princeton University Press.

Nettle, J. P. 1968. "The State as a Conceptual Variable." *World Politics*. 20: 559–92.

Newfarmer, Richard J. 1980. *Transnational Conglomerates and the Economics of Dependent Development*. Greenwich, CT: JAI Press.

Newfarmer, Richard J., ed. 1985. *Profits, Progress and Poverty—Case Studies of International Industries in Latin America*. Notre Dame, IN: Notre Dame University Press.

Nordlinger, Eric. 1981. *On the Autonomy of the Democratic State*. Cambridge, MA: Harvard University Press.

O, Kap Hwan. 1975. "Chaebol in Korea." *Seoul National University Thesis Publications* 20: 207–31.

O'Donnell, Guillermo. 1973. *Modernization and Bureaucratic Authoritarianism*. Berkeley: University of California Press.

———. 1977. "Corporatism and the Question of the State." Pp. 47–89 in *Authoritarianism and Corporatism in Latin America*, edited by James M. Malloy. Pittsburgh: University of Pittsburgh Press.

———. 1978. "Reflections on the Patterns of Change in the Bureaucratic Authoritarian State." *Latin American Research Review* 13(1): 3–38.

O'Donnell, Guillermo, Philippe C. Schmitter, and Laurence Whitehead, eds. 1986. *Transitions from Authoritarian Rule*. Baltimore: Johns Hopkins University Press.

Offe, Claus. 1984. *Contradictions of the Welfare State*. Edited by John Keane. Cambridge, MA: MIT Press.

Ogle, George E. 1990. *South Korea: Dissent within the Economic Miracle*. London: Zed Books.

Okimoto, Daniel I. 1989. *Between MITI and the Market: Japanese Industrial Policy for High Technology*. Stanford, CA: Stanford University Press.

Olson, Mancur. 1982. *The Rise and Decline of Nations: Economic Growth, Stagflation, and Social Rigidities.* New Haven, CT: Yale University Press.

Pae, Pyŏng Hyu. 1980. "Chŏnja Sanŏpkye ŭi Naemak" (The Inside Stories of the Electronics Industry). *Shindonga* 1980 (1).

Pae, Ŭng To. 1960. "Hanguk ŭi Chaeboldŭl" (*Chaebols* of Korea). *Sasanggye* 1960 (4).

Paek, Sŏn Ki. 1983a. "Chaebol ŭi Sawi, Sadondŭl" (The *Chaebol*'s Son-in-Laws and the In-Laws). *Shindonga* 1983 (3).

———. 1983b. "Hanguk Kyŏngje rŭl Wumjikinŭn Sajang Paekin" (100 Company Presidents Who Move the Korean Economy). *Shindonga* 1983 (4).

Pak, Chong Yŏl. 1989. "Chipchung Haepu: Okonghwakuk Chŏngch'i Chakŭm" (An In-Depth Analysis: The Fifth Republic's [the Chun regime] Political Financing). *Shindonga* January (1989): 280–300.

Pak, Hyŏn Ch'ae et al. 1985. *Hanguk Chabonjuŭi wa Nodong Munje (Korean Capitalism and Labor Problems).* Seoul: Tolbegae.

Pak, Hyŏn Ch'ae, and Hee-Yeon Cho. 1984. *Hanguk Sahoe ŭi Chaeinshik I (Re-Understanding of the Korean Society I).* Seoul: Hanwul.

———. 1991. *Hanguk Sahoe ŭi Chaeinshik III (Re-Understanding of the Korean Society III).* Seoul: Chuksan.

———. 1992. *Hanguk Sahoe ŭi Chaeinshik IV (Re-Understanding of the Korean Society IV).* Seoul: Chuksan.

Pak, Mu. 1980. "Kŭmyunggye rŭl Wumjikin Inmaek" (People Who Moved the Financial Circles). *Shindonga* 1980 (11).

———. 1981. "*Chaebol* kwa Kŭmyung" (*Chaebol* and Finances). *Shindonga* 1981 (9).

Pak, Pyŏng Yun. 1975. "Hanguk ŭi *Chaebol*—Kŭ Saengt'ae, Kŭmmaek, Inmaek" (*Chaebol* of Korea - Its Nature, Financial Connections, and Personal Connections). *Shindonga* 1975 (12).

———. 1979. "Chadongch'a Sanŏp ŭi Naemak" (The Inside Stories of the Automobile Industry). *Shindonga* 1979 (12).

———. 1980. "Chunghwahak Kongŏp ŭi Naemak" (The Inside Stories of the Heavy and Chemical Industry). *Shindonga* 1980 (5).

————. 1982. Chaebol *kwa Chŏngch'i* (Chaebol *and Politics*). Seoul: Hanguk Yangsŏ.

Pak, Sŏng T'aek et al. 1984. *Wuri Nara Computer Sanŏp ŭi Chungjanggi Paljŏn Chŏnryak (The Medium- and Long-Term Development Strategies for the Korean Computer Industry)*. Seoul: Korean Institute for Economics and Technology.

Pak, Tong Sŏn. 1983. *Chaebol*. Seoul: Hanmaek.

Park, Chung Hee. 1966. *The Road Toward Economic Self-Sufficiency and Prosperity*. Seoul: Ministry of Public Information.

————. 1971. *To Build a Nation*. Washington, DC: Acropolis Books.

Perkins, Dwight. 1994. "There are at Least Three Models of East Asian Development." *World Development* 22(4): 655–61.

Pohang Iron and Steel Company. 1975. *Pohang Chech'ŏl Ch'ilnyŏnsa (The Seven-Year History of the Pohang Iron and Steel Company)*. Pohang: Pohang Iron and Steel Company.

Powell, Walter W., and Paul J. DiMaggio, eds. 1991. *The New Institutionalism in Organizational Analysis*. Chicago: University of Chicago Press.

Przeworski, Adam. 1985. *Capitalism and Social Democracy*. Cambridge: Cambridge University Press.

————. 1986. "Some Problems in the Study of the Transition to Democracy." Pp. 47–63 in *Transitions from Authoritarian Rule*, edited by Guillermo O'Donnell, Philippe C. Schmitter, and Laurence Whitehead. Baltimore: Johns Hopkins University Press.

Pu, Wan Hyŏk. 1966. "Chaebol kwa O Kaenyŏn Kyehoek" (Chaebol and Five Year Economic Development Plans). *Sasanggye* 1966 (August): 46–57.

Pye, Lucian W. 1985. *Asian Power and Politics: The Cultural Dimensions of Authority*. Cambridge, MA: Harvard University Press.

Pyŏn, Hyŏng Yun. 1984. "Hanguk ŭi Kyŏngje Paljŏn kwa Tokjŏm Chabon" (Korea's Economic Development and Monopoly Capital) in Hyŏn Ch'ae Pak et al., *Hanguk Sahoe ŭi Chaeinshik I (Re-Understanding of the Korean Society I)*. Seoul: Hanwul.

Pyŏn, Sang Kŭn. 1980. "Gulf 18 Nyŏn ŭi Kyŏlsan" (The Closing Accounts of the 18 Years of Gulf). *Shindonga* 1980 (10).

Research Institute for Public Affairs. 1974. "Founding of MAFEZ." Research Papers for Research Institute of Public Administration, Graduate School of Public Administration, Seoul National University.

Roberts, John G. 1989. *Mitsui*. New York: Weatherhill.

Rostow, W. W. 1971. *The Stages of Economic Growth*. Cambridge: Cambridge University Press.

Rueschemeyer, Dietrich, and Peter B. Evans. 1985. "The State and Economic Transformation: Toward an Analysis of the Conditions Underlying Effective Intervention." Pp. 44–77 in *Bringing the State Back In*, edited by Peter B. Evans, Dietrich Rueschemeyer, and Theda Skocpol. Cambridge: Cambridge University Press.

Rueschemeyer, Dietrich, Evelyne Huber Stephens, and John D. Stephens. 1992. *Capitalist Development and Democracy*. Chicago: University of Chicago Press.

Ruggie, John G. ed. 1983. *The Antinomies of Interdependence: National Welfare and the International Division of Labor*. New York: Columbia University Press.

Samil Consulting Group. 1992. *Hanguk Kiŏp ŭi Sŏnggong Chogŏn (Conditions for Success of Korean Enterprises)*. Seoul: Maeil Kyŏngje Shinmun.

Samuels, Richard J. 1987. *The Business of the Japanese State: Energy Markets in Comparative and Historical Perspective*. Ithaca, NY: Cornell University Press.

Seoul Kyŏngje Shinmun. 1991. Chaebol *kwa Kabŏl (Chaebol and the Family Networks)*. Seoul: Chishik Sanŏpsa.

Shin, Pŏm Shik. 1970. Major Speeches by Korea's Park Chung Hee. Seoul: Hollim.

Shin Sanŏp Kyŏngyŏngwŏn. 1996. *Hanguk 30 Te* Chaebol *Chemu Punsŏk (Financial Management Analysis of Korea's 30 Largest* Chaebol). Seoul: Sanŏp Kyŏngyŏngwŏn.

Shin, Eui Hang, and Seung Kwon Chin. 1989. "Social Affinity Among Top Managerial Executives of Large Corporations in Korea." *Sociological Forum* 4(1): 3–26.

Skocpol, Theda. 1985. "Bringing the State Back In: Strategies of Analysis in Current Research." Pp. 3–37 in *Bringing the State Back*

In, edited by Peter B. Evans, Dietrich Rueschemeyer, and Theda Skocpol. Cambridge: Cambridge University Press.

Sŏ, Ch'ang Won et al. 1982. *Hanguk Chŏnja Pup'um Sanŏp ŭi Kujo wa Kuksanhwa Chŏnryak (The Structure and Strategies for Increasing the Korean-made Parts of the Korean Electronics Parts Industry)*. Seoul: Korean Institute for Economics and Technology.

Sŏ, Kwan Mo. 1984. *Hanguk Hyŏndae Sahoe ŭi Kyegŭp Kujo wa Kyegŭp Punyŏl (Class Composition and Class Division in Contemporary Korean Society)*. Seoul: Hanwul.

————. 1985. "Hanguk Sahoe Kyegŭp Kusŏng ŭi Sahoe T'onggyejŏk Yŏngu" (Social Statistical Analysis of the Korean Class Structure) in Chin Kyun Kim et al., *Sanŏp Sahoe Yŏngu (Research on the Industrial Society)*. Seoul: Hanwul.

Song, Byung-Nak. 1990. *The Rise of the Korean Economy*. Hong Kong: Oxford University Press.

Song, Dae Hee. 1983. "New Policy Direction of the Korean Public Enterprise Sector as a Source of Growth." KDI Working Paper 83-07.

Song, Ho Kŭn. 1991. *Hanguk ŭi Nodong Chŏngch'i wa Sijang* (Labor Politics and Market in South Korea). Seoul: Nanam.

Sorokin, Pitrim A. 1956 [1928]. *Contemporary Sociological Theories: Through the First Quarter of the Twentieth Century*. New York: Harper & Row.

Speakman, Jay, and Chae-Jin Lee, eds. 1993. *The Prospects for Korean Reunification*. Claremont Monograph Series, Number Four, The Keck Center for International and Strategic Studies. Claremont, CA: Clarement McKenna College.

Stallings, Barbara. 1990. "The Role of Foreign Capital in Economic Development." Pp. 55–89 in *Manufacturing Miracles: Paths of Industrialization in Latin America and East Asia*, edited by Gary Gereffi and Donald Wyman. Princeton: Princeton University Press.

Steers, Richard M., Yoo Keun Shin, and Gerardo R. Ungson. 1989. *The Chaebol: Korea's New Industrial Might*. New York: Harper & Row.

Stephens, John D. 1989. "Democratic Transition and Breakdown in Europe, 1870–1939: A Test of the Moore Thesis." *American Journal of Sociology* 94(5).

Suh, Sang-Chul. 1978. *Growth and Structural Changes in the Korean Economy, 1910–1940.* Cambridge, MA: Harvard University Press.

Tu, Wei-Ming. 1984. *Confucian Ethics Today—The Singapore Challenge.* Singapore: Federal Publications.

Wade, Robert. 1990. *Governing the Market: Economic Theory and the Role of Government in Taiwan's Industrialization.* Princeton: Princeton University Press.

Wallerstein, Immanuel. 1974. *The Modern World-System I: Capitalist Agriculture and The Origins of the European World-Economy in the Sixteenth Century.* London: Academic Press.

———. 1979. *The Capitalist World-Economy.* Cambridge: Cambridge University Press.

———. 1980. *The Modern World-System II: Mercantilism and the Consolidation of the European World-Economy 1600–1750.* London: Academic Press.

Weber, Max. 1964. *The Theory of Social and Economic Organization.* Translated by A. M. Henderson and Talcott Parsons. Edited with an introduction by Talcott Parsons. New York: The Free Press.

Westphal, Larry E., 1978. "The Republic of Korea's Experience with Export-Led Industrial Development." *World Development* 6: 347–82.

Wŏlgan Chosŏn, 1989. "Chwadam: Ya 3 Tang Chŏngch'aeg Ŭichang ŭi Kukchŏng P'yŏngga: "Chaebol *wihan Haengchŏng Manatta"* (Roundtable Discussion: 3 Opposition Parties' Policy Committee Chairs' Evaluation of the National Assembly's Audit of Government Affairs: "There were many policies oriented toward the *chaebol"*). *Wŏlgan Chosŏn* November (1989): 136–46.

Woo, Jung-en. 1991. *Race to the Swift: State and Finance in Korean Industrialization.* New York: Columbia University Press.

World Bank. 1981–1995. *World Development Report.* New York: Oxford University Press.

———. 1990. *Trends in Developing Economies 1990.* Washington, DC: World Bank.

———. 1993. *The East Asian Miracle: Economic Growth and Public Policy.* Oxford: Oxford University Press.

Yanagihara, Toru. 1994. "Anything New in the Miracle Report? Yes and No." *World Development* 22(4): 663–70.

Yang, Wu Chin, and Chang P'yo Hong. 1991. *Hanguk Chabon Chuŭi ŭi Punsŏk (Analysis of Korean Capitalism)*. Seoul: Ilbit.

Yoo, Young Ock. 1995. "Pyongyang's Efforts to Improve Relations with Washington and Tokyo, and Seoul's Position." *East Asian Review* VII(3): 24–42.

Yŏsŏng Chung-Ang. 1993. "Chŏng Chu Yŏng: Kananhan Taet'on-gryŏng ŭn Mot Toekaetjiman Kanahan Ch'ŏngwadae, Puja Nara Mandŭlkaetsŏyo" (Chŏng Chu Yŏng: I won't be a Poor President, but I will make a Poor Blue House and Rich Country). *Yŏsŏng Chung-Ang* January (1993): 90–92.

Yu, In Hak. 1991. *Hanguk Chaebol ŭi Haebu (Dissecting the Korean Chaebol)*. Seoul: P'ulbit.

Yu, Young ŭl. 1988. "Chun Doo Hwan Chŏngkwon ŭi Chŏngkyŏng Yuch'ak Pili" (The Illicit Activities of the Chun Regime's Political-Economic Collusion). *Shindonga* June (1988): 382–408.

———. 1989. "P'asan Chikchŏn ŭi Taewu Chosŏn ŭi Kisahoesaeng Chakchŏn Naemak" (The Inside Stories of Last Minute Resuscitation from Bankruptcy of Daewoo Shipbuilding). *Shindonga* January (1989): 434–48.

Zeitlin, Maurice. 1989. *The Large Corporation and Contemporary Classes*. New Brunswick, NJ: Rutgers University Press.

Index

Note: Page numbers in **bold type** reference non-text material